Sylvester Rosa Koehler

The United States Art Directory and Yearbook

A Guide for Artists, Art Students, Travellers, etc.

Sylvester Rosa Koehler

The United States Art Directory and Yearbook
A Guide for Artists, Art Students, Travellers, etc.

ISBN/EAN: 9783337208905

Printed in Europe, USA, Canada, Australia, Japan

Cover: Foto ©Thomas Meinert / pixelio.de

More available books at **www.hansebooks.com**

THE

UNITED STATES ART DIRECTORY

AND YEAR-BOOK.

A GUIDE FOR ARTISTS, ART STUDENTS,

TRAVELLERS, ETC.

COMPILED

BY

S. R. KOEHLER.

————— ◆ —————

CASSELL, PETTER, GALPIN & CO.

NEW YORK, LONDON, AND PARIS.

1882.

PREFACE.

THE purpose of this little book is sufficiently explained by its title. It aspires to be a guide to artists, art students, — historical, as well as technical, — and travellers of an artistic turn of mind, in matters pertaining to the *practical* side of art; that is to say, in its educational, social, and mercantile bearings. With the æsthetic side of art it has nothing to do. In its plan it is similar to, although less ambitious than, the works of a like nature which have been published in Europe for some years.

As it is the first attempt to give a bird's-eye view of the organized efforts making in the United States in behalf of art, the reader will no doubt be inclined to look charitably upon its evident shortcomings. Nor will this charitable tendency be diminished, when it is considered that, with the exception of newspapers and periodicals, and a few of the publications of the Bureau of Education, — all of the latter, however, some years old, — no aids were available. It is manifest from this that most of the facts embodied in the lists herewith submitted had to be elicited by direct application, either by letter or personally, — a laborious proceeding under all circumstances, but rendered more difficult in this case by special conditions. Most of the societies enumerated publish no printed reports, and the answers returned to written inquiries were, in many instances, quite incomplete. If to this be added the shortness of the time necessarily allowed for doing the work, and the unfavorable character of the summer season into which it had to be crowded, the obstacles in the way of the compiler will become still more apparent. The cases in which no answers at all were returned were happily few, but the lists will show that the officials of the old-fashioned kind, who look upon every one inquiring into the interests confided to them as impertinent intruders, have not yet died out entirely.

Concerning the policy followed, the reader will please notice that facts only have been given, and that in the selection of these facts no judgment has been exercised or criticism applied. In the case of the educational institutions especially, it has been the constant aim to let them speak for themselves by quoting either the printed documents issued by them, or the written reports received from persons connected with them. The facts thus obtained and the claims thus put forward are simply offered as material from which those interested can draw their own conclusions. It will be well also to state that the length of the notices has nothing whatever to do with the importance of the institutions to which they are devoted. There is apparently a curious discrepancy in this particular. But a moment's reflection will show that the well-defined activity of so prominent an association as "The Society of American Artists" is much more easily compressed into a short paragraph, than the multifarious efforts of an amateur club in some out-of-the-way village.

One glaring instance of incompleteness will be found in the list of colleges and universities included. It would have been interesting to show the extent to which the study of art, either theoretically or practically, is carried in all these institutions, but, for the present at least, this almost Herculean task could not be undertaken. Even so, however, the few statements of college courses given will convey some idea as to the place assigned to art in our higher institutions of learning, although it was impossible to give these courses with that completeness which might have been desirable. In view of the economy elsewhere practised, it may seem strange that so much space has been devoted to the purely technical course pursued in the Military Academy at West Point. But many persons will no doubt be interested to know to what extent art is made tributary to war in this celebrated national school. As an additional excuse, it may be stated that the information here given is nowhere else to be found in print.

The list of educational institutions has been furthermore limited by excluding instruction in drawing as incorporated into the public-school system on the one hand, and purely private schools on the other. The line has been drawn, rather arbitrarily perhaps, at incorporated institutions, and associations which do not look for profit.

Some persons may possibly think that the only result of the enumeration of the Archæological Collections admitted into these lists has been an unnecessary increase in the number of pages. Archæology is, however, an indispensable aid in the study of the development of art, and as the students in this department of science are fast increasing, their interests had to be considered as well as those of others. For this reason mention has also been made, although very briefly in most cases, of the small collections, so far as known, brought together by the Historical Societies. Many of these collections contain specimens illustrating the art of the aborigines, and occasionally a few good old portraits are hidden away in them, of the existence of which the lovers of art would be glad to be informed.

It goes without saying that this Guide, even in its present incomplete form, would never have seen the light, if the aid so generously extended by kind friends had been withheld. To them, as well as to the officers of the various institutions who patiently submitted to persistent questioning and letter-writing, the heartfelt thanks of the compiler are herewith extended. It seems almost unjust to mention only one name, where so many are entitled to recognition; but a special measure of thanks must, nevertheless, be accorded to Mr. J. M. Falconer, of Brooklyn, who was never appealed to in vain where his helping hand was wanted. With such support in the future, it may not be unreasonable to hope that the next year's issue of this "Directory" will come nearer to the fulfilment of the promises of the prospectus than the present volume.

THE COMPILER.

TABLE OF CONTENTS.

ACADEMIES, ART SCHOOLS, COLLECTIONS, EXHIBITIONS, DECORATIVE ART SOCIETIES, ART CLUBS, ETC., IN THE UNITED STATES.*

A. National Institutions.

AMERICAN INSTITUTE OF ARCHITECTS. — Organized and incorporated in New York, 1857. — Officers: Pres., Thos. U. Walter, 720 N. Broad St., Philadelphia; V. Ps., the Presidents of the various Chapters of the Institute; Treas., O. P. Hatfield, 31 Pine St., New York; Sec., A. J. Bloor, 335 B'way, New York; Sec. for Foreign Cor., T. M. Clark, 178 Devonshire St., Boston. — Objects: To unite in fellowship the architects of this continent, and to combine their efforts so as to promote the artistic, scientific, and practical efficiency of the profession. The means of accomplishing this end shall be : regular meetings of the members, for the discussion of subjects of professional importance ; the reading of essays; lectures upon topics of general interest ; a school for the education of architects ; exhibitions of architectural drawings ; a library ; a collection of designs and models ; and any other means calculated to promote the objects of the Institute. — Members : Fellows (limited to 70), Associates, Corresponding, and Honorary Members. Fellows must be practising architects, and are elected by the Fellows ; initiation fee, $10 ; annual dues, $10. Associates, who must also be practising artists, are elected by the Board of Trustees ; no initiation fee; annual dues, $5. Fellows and Associates who may relinquish their practice and resign their membership, also foreign architects, civil engineers, and other scientific men, may be elected Corresponding Members. Foreign architects, scientific men, and amateurs may be elected Honorary Members. Corresponding and Honorary Members have all the privileges of the Institute, except that of voting. Number of members according to last report, 262 (Fellows and Associates, 138 ; Cor. Members, 63 ; Honorary, 61). — Any association of architects in which there are three Fellows residing in the place where the association has been formed may organize themselves into a Chapter of the American Institute of Architects, provided that upon application the association is recognized by the Board of Trustees. At the date of the last report, there were nine such Chapters, as follows : *Albany Chapter* (officers not given). *Baltimore Chapter*, Sec., John Murdoch, S. E. cor. Lexington and Charles Sts. *Boston Chapter*, Pres., Edw. C. Cabot, 60 Devonshire St.; V. P., John H. Sturgis, 19 Exchange Pl.; Sec., T. M. Clark, 178 Devonshire St.; Treas., W. G. Preston, 186 Devonshire St. *Chicago Chapter*, Pres., Aug. Bauer; Sec., S. A. Treat, 80 Dearborn St. *Cincinnati Chapter*, Pres., Jas. W. McLaughlin, 46 Johnston Bldg.; V. P., F. Anderson, 132 W. 4th St.; Sec., Chas. Crapsey, 46 Wiggins Block ; Treas., Geo. W. Raff, S. E. cor. 5th and Walnut Sts. *New York Chapter*, Pres., E. T. Littell, 48 Exchange Pl.; 1st V. P., Geo. B. Post, 15 Cortlandt St.; 2d V. P., R. H. Robertson, 121 E. 23d St. ; Sec. and Treas., A. J. Bloor, 335 B'way. *Philadelphia Chapter*, Sec., Edw. Hazlehurst, 508 Walnut St. *Rhode Island Chapter*, Pres., A. C. Morse, Providence; V.P., Alfred Stone; Sec., Geo. C. Mason, Jr., 3 Catherine St., Newport; Treas., Jas. Fludder, Newport. *San Francisco Chapter*, Sec., Geo. H. Wolfe, 240 Montgomery St. Not all the members of these Chapters are necessarily also members of the Institute. The Income of

---

* Instruction in drawing as incorporated into the public-school system, and private schools, are not accounted for in the following list.

the Institute is confined to initiation fees and membership dues. Its collections and library, which are mostly housed with the New York Chapter, receive occasional accessions from donations. — The Institute holds Annual Conventions at which, besides the usual routine business, papers of general and special interest to architects are read. The fifteenth of these Conventions was held at Washington, Nov. 16 and 17, 1881. The activity of the association, and the results so far attained by it, are thus summarized in a circular issued last year : " The Board of Trustees assume that architects old enough to remember the former drawbacks to practice recognize the fact that it is chiefly the Institute which has been instrumental in raising the profession so far towards its natural influential position. The schedule of charges recommended by it is now generally acknowledged in the Courts, by corporations, and by private individuals ; and it was mainly through the exertions of its Committee on Publications that the establishment was secured of a proper organ of communication between the profession and the public, viz., ' The American Architect and Building News.' The Institute publishes every year a pamphlet of the proceedings of its successive Annual Conventions, as well as other matter of technical and general interest to practitioners. These are but the beginnings of what may be secured by intelligent interchange and concerted action among the members of the profession, through the medium of its recognized society." — The Institute, when asked to do so, decides questions at issue between members of the profession, and its opinions are occasionally sought by the public authorities. The Committee on Examinations of the New York Chapter has for many years acted under the law, in various needful capacities, with the Building Authorities of the city named. Official letters of introduction are furnished to members travelling abroad, and these letters are particularly valuable to the younger associates, to whom they serve as passports to the professional circles of Europe.

ARCHÆOLOGICAL INSTITUTE OF AMERICA. — Organized in Boston, May 17, 1879. — Officers : Pres., Charles Eliot Norton, Shady Hill, Cambridge, Mass ; V. P., Martin Brimmer, 47 Beacon St. ; Treas., Henry L. Higginson, 191 Commonwealth Ave. ; Sec., E. H. Greenleaf, Museum of Fine Arts, Boston. — Objects : The Archæological Institute of America is formed for the purpose of promoting and directing archæological investigation and research, — by the sending out of expeditions for special investigation, by aiding the efforts of independent explorers, by publication of reports of the results of the expeditions which the Institute may undertake or promote, and by any other means which may from time to time appear desirable. Members (both sexes): Life, contributors of not less than $100 ; Annual, contributors of not less than $10 ; Corresponding ; Honorary. Number of members at date of last report, 255 : 69 life ; 186 annual. At the meeting at which the Institute was organized it was voted that, after the number of members shall have increased to 350, no more shall be admitted, except when elected by the Executive Committee. The association has already members in thirty-nine cities, scattered all over the U. S., from New England to North Carolina, New Mexico, Arizona, and California. — The work of the Institute is divisible into two departments, American and Foreign. " The vast work of American archæology," says the last (third) Report, " is only begun. The time is not ripe for safe and sure deduction. Our present business is to gather facts while to do so is yet possible. Other nations, with more or less success, are trying to do our work on our soil. It is time that Americans bestir themselves in earnest upon a field which it would be a shame to abandon to the foreigner." The Institute has made an arrangement with Mr. A. Bandelier, a well-known student in American archæology, which has enabled him to carry on investigations among the Pueblo Indians of New Mexico. The same scholar also went to Mexico in the interest of the Institute, in connection with the Lorillard Expedition, where he made a thorough examination of Cholula and its so-called pyramid, and visited Mitla and other places. Explorations are likewise being carried on in Yucatan by Mr. Louis H. Aymé, U. S. Consul at Merida, who has a commission as agent of the Institute. The results of these various investigations, which it is proposed to continue as vigorously as the funds will allow, have already been of great interest, archæologically as well as artistically, especially in relation to the architecture of the aborigines of America. The work already accomplished in the Old World is also of great archæological interest and importance, and has served substantially to increase the knowledge of Greek art and antiquity. The expedition to Assos, in charge of Messrs. Joseph Thacher Clarke and F. H. Bacon, has been singularly fortunate. The complete recovery and exact delineation of the plan, elevation, and adornment of the ancient and famous temple of Assos, which has so long offered problems of special interest to the students of Greek architecture and sculpture, takes a prominent rank among the many remarkable archæological discoveries of the present generation. The investigation of the other structures of the city, although still imperfect, and requiring to be completed by the labors of the present year, justify the belief that the remains at Assos present the most perfect idea of a Greek city that is anywhere to be obtained. Besides the architectural and sculptured fragments of the temple and other buildings, numerous sarcophagi, vessels of earthenware and of glass, etc., have also been discovered. — In addition to its Annual Reports, the Institute has published the following papers: "A Study of the Houses of the American Aborigines," by Lewis H. Morgan; "Ancient Walls on Monte Leone," by W. J. Stillman; "Archæological Notes on Greek Shores," by Jos. Thacher Clarke (the foregoing three papers in one vol., together with the First Annual Report); "Papers of the Archæological Institute of America. — Classical Series I. Report on the Investigations at Assos, 1881, by Jos. Thacher Clarke. With an Appendix, containing Inscriptions from Assos and Lesbos, and Papers by W. C. Lawton and J. S. Diller" (1 vol.), and "American Series. I. 1. Historical Introduction to Studies among the Sedentary Indians of New Mexico. 2. Report on the Ruins of the Pueblo of Pecos, by A. F. Bandelier" (1 vol.). — The Institute is dependent for its income upon membership dues and donations, under which latter heading about $6,000 were received last year. The results so far achieved have been due in great measure to the self-sacrificing spirit of the agents of the Institute. To enable it to continue its work donations will again have to be solicited. It is upon the increase in the number of members that the continued efficiency of the Institute must depend.

AMERICAN SCHOOL OF CLASSICAL STUDIES AT ATHENS (Greece). — Opened Oct. 2, 1882. — Officers of Comm. in Charge: Chairm., Prof. John Williams White, Harvard University, Cambridge, Mass.; Sec., Thomas W. Ludlow, 244 E. 13th St., New York; Treas., Frederic J. de Peyster, New York. — The object of this School will be to furnish to graduates of American Colleges an opportunity to study Classical Literature, Art, and Antiquities in Athens, under suitable direction; to prosecute and to aid original research in these subjects; and to co-operate with the Archæological Institute of America, as far as it may be able, in conducting the exploration and excavation of Classic sites. — The Archæological Institute of America was the prime mover in the establishment of this School, which is, for the present, to be maintained by the united efforts of the following colleges: Harvard, Yale, Brown, Amherst, Johns Hopkins, College of the City of New York, Columbia, College of New Jersey, and Wesleyan. The plan of the School is in the main identical with that of the French and German schools already established at Athens. The directorship for the first year has been intrusted to Prof. W. W. Goodwin, of Harvard. Graduates of the co-operating Colleges will be admitted upon presenting a certificate of competency. All other persons must make application to the Committee. Members will be required to prosecute their studies during the school year, from Oct. 1 to June 1, in Greece, under the superintendence of the Director. No fees are to be paid to the School. On the other hand, no scholarships can be offered, as there is, as yet, no endowment fund.

UNITED STATES NATIONAL MUSEUM, at Washington, UNITED STATES MILITARY ACADEMY, at West Point, and UNITED STATES NAVAL ACADEMY, at Annapolis, *see* under the respective places.

B. Local Institutions.

ARRANGED ALPHABETICALLY ACCORDING TO CITIES.

Albany, N. Y. — ALBANY ART LEAGUE. 57 State St. Organized Feb., 1882. — Officers: Pres., Theod. C. Hailes, 78 Dove St.; Treas., R. Prescott, High School; Sec, A. Fleischman, 31 N. Pearl St. — Objects: The advancement of art in Albany, and the mutual improvement of the members. — Members, male only, must be workers in or lovers of art. Present number, 39. — The League meets twice a month. A lecture is given at least once a month. It is the intention to have a public exhibition every year.

ALBANY CHAPTER OF THE AM. INST. OF ARCHITECTS. [Names of officers not given in last report of Institute. See p. 1.]

NEW YORK STATE CAPITOL. This building, of itself important as a work of architecture, contains, in the Assembly Chamber, the two mural paintings, "The Flight of Night," and "The Discoverer," executed by the late William Morris Hunt, in oil colors, directly upon the stone.

Albuquerque, New Mexico. — NEW MEXICO EXPOSITION AND DRIVING PARK ASSOCIATION. — Officers: Pres., M. W. Bremen; Treas., A. M. Codington; Sec., D. B. Emmert; Supt. of Fine Arts, Charles M. Wheelock, Las Vegas. — This association held its Second Annual Fair from Sept. 18 to 23, 1882. In Division F, Class 22, devoted to Painting, Sculpture, Drawing, Engraving, Penmanship, and Photography, twenty-two premiums were awarded (1 bullion medal, 2 silver medals, 19 diplomas).

Amherst, Mass. — AMHERST COLLEGE. — Officers: Pres. of the Corp. and of the Faculty, Rev. Julius H. Seelye, D. D., LL. D.; Sec. of the Corp., Rev. Edw. S. Dwight, D. D.; Treas., Wm. A. Dickinson; Dean of the Fac, Edw. P. Crowell, D. D. — No instruction in drawing or any other practical branch of art is provided in the college course. A course of thirty lectures upon the history of sculpture is, however, delivered before the Senior Class by Prof. Richard H. Mather, D. D., in the very attractive art-lecture room of the college. These lectures are illustrated by a collection of casts, a large number of magic-lantern views, and an extensive collection of photographs of sculpture and architecture. — *The Gallery of Art* contains a large and choice collection of casts of ancient and modern statuary, consisting in all of 141 pieces, many of these being groups and extensive reliefs, such as the "Parthenon Frieze," and a portion of Thorwaldsen's "Triumph of Alexander." The collection illustrates the art of Nineveh, Egypt, Greece (from the early period represented by the Lions of the Mycenæ Gate downward, and including some of the latest discoveries, such as the "Victory" of Paionios, and the "Hermes" of Praxiteles from Olympia), Rome, the Renaissance (works of Ghiberti, Luca della Robbia, Michelangelo, etc.), and modern times. The collection, incl. the photographs mentioned above, cost over $18,000. — Funds donated. — Open free to the public every week day from 9 A. M. to 5 P. M., in May, June, Sept., and Oct., and all other times from 10–11 A. M., and 3–4 P. M. No catalogue, as every piece is conspicuously labelled.

Annapolis. Md. — U. S. NAVAL ACADEMY. — The instruction given in drawing, etc., is entirely practical and scientific. Instructor, Chas. F. Blauvelt. The library contains some old portraits of naval officers and some naval relics, and there are several monuments in the grounds. Accessible to the public at all times.

Ann Arbor, Mich. — University of Michigan. — Officers B'd of Regents: Pres., Jas. B. Angell, LL. D.; Sec., Henry D. Bennett; Treas., Wm. A. Tolchard. Faculty: Pres., Jas. B. Angell, LL. D , S. University Ave.; Acting Pres., Henry S. Frieze, LL. D., Cornwell Pl.; Chas. S. Denison, M. S., C. E., Acting Asst. Prof. of Mech. and Free-Hand Drawing, 40 S. Ingalls St.; Joseph B. Steere, Ph. D., Curator of the Museum, S. Ypsilanti Road; Dennie J. Higley, A. M., Asst. in Museum, 18 Grove St. — The University of Michigan is a part of the public educational system of the State, governed by a Board of Regents elected by popular vote. Through the aid received from the United States and the State, it is enabled to offer its privileges, without charge for tuition, to persons of either sex qualified for admission. — Drawing (Geometrical, Mechanical, Topographical, Perspective, Free-Hand, Pen and Ink, Architect., Water-Color) is a required study in the Engineering Course only. The Classical Course includes lectures on Greek Art by Rev. Martin L. D'Ooge, Ph. D , Washtenaw Ave. — The *Museum* of the University, in a building erected in 1879–80 by means of a special legislative appropriation, besides valuable scientific collections, contains also special Departments of Archæology and Ethnology, and of Fine Arts. The Department first named consists of articles of domestic and warlike use among the North American Indians and the Islanders of the South Pacific; numerous remains of the ancient Peruvians, and many specimens of clothing, art, etc., of the Amazonian Indians, modern Peruvians, Chinese, Formosans, and natives of the East Indies and Alaska. The Fine Arts Collection was begun in 1855, and at present comprises: A gallery of casts from the antique, in full size and in reductions; over 200 reductions and models in terra-cotta, etc., of works of antique art and industry in the Museums at Naples and elsewhere; the statues of "Nydia" and "Ruth Gleaning" by Randolph Rogers; copies of statues, busts, and reliefs by Michelangelo, Canova, Thorwaldsen, etc.; a series of engravings and photographs, illustrating the architectural and sculptural remains of ancient Rome, Pompeii, Pæstum, Athens, and Corinth; a small collection of engravings of modern paintings, beginning with those prior to Raphael; the Horace White Collection of Historical Medallions (450 casts from antique gems, over 500 illustrating the mediæval period and the Renaissance; about 400 modern portrait medallions); the Governor Bagley Collection of American Historical Medallions, designed to embrace all the commemorative medals struck by order of Congress or other authorities; the Richards Collection of Coins, chiefly ancient. A catalogue has been prepared with great care by Prof. Frieze. The collections are accessible both to students and to visitors.

Austin, Tex. — Women's Exchange. — [This seems to be an association similar to the Decorative Art Societies. Information promised, but not sent.]

Baltimore, Md. — Baltimore Chapter of the Am. Inst. of Architects. — Sec., John Murdoch, S. E. cor. Lexington and Charles Sts. (See p. 1.)

Decorative Art Society. — 69 N. Charles St. Organized May, 1878. — Officers: Pres., Mrs. Wm. Reed; V. Ps, Mrs. Alan P. Smith, Mrs. D. Donohoe; Treas., Mrs. John Duer; Sec., James Carey Coale; Cor. Sec., Mrs. Henry Stockbridge. — Objects: The establishment of rooms for the exhibition and sale of decorative art-work, the promotion and diffusion of a knowledge of such work, and training in artistic industries. — The membership for the past year consisted of 128 subscribers at $5 p. a. The Society also received various liberal donations in money from wealthy patrons. Classes, limited to twenty pupils each, in Design, Crayon Drawing, Water-Colors, and China Painting. Miss Grace Carter, of South Kensington, Instructress, with assistants. Instruction is given also in Art Needle Work. — Terms, $10 per session of 24 lessons. Classes begin about the middle of September. Free pupils may be nominated by subscribers. Number of pupils during the four sessions of the past year, about 150.

Maryland Historical Society. — Athenæum Bldg., St. Paul and Saratoga

Sts. Organized 1844. — Officers: Pres., John H. B. Latrobe; V. Ps., Geo. Wm. Brown, John G. Morris, D. D., Henry Stockbridge; Cor. Sec., Mendes Cohen; Treas., Chas. L. Oudesluys; Libr. and Curator of Cabinet, John W. M. Lee. — *The Art Gallery* of the Society contains a number of casts from the antique; copies from paintings by Raphael, Correggio, Titian, Paul Veronese, Domenichino, and Cignani; a few portraits by Stuart, Polk, and other American artists; a portrait of Christopher Hughes by Sir M. A. Shee; one of Charles Carroll of Carrollton by Sir Joshua Reynolds, etc. — Open daily, the year round, except Sundays, from 9 A. M. to 4 P. M. Admission free.

MARYLAND INSTITUTE for the Promotion of the Mechanic Arts. — Organized 1848. — Officers: Pres., Saml. W. Regester; V. P., Geo. H. Rodgers; Sec., Geo. L. McCahan; Treas., Edw. W. Robinson; Comm on School of Design: Carroll Spence, Wm. H. Perkins, Geo. H. Pagels, Jos. M. Cushing, John L. Lawton, Robt. Ashcroft, Geo. L. McCahan; Actuary and Libr., Alex. F. Lusby. — Membership, per annum, $3; male life members, $25; female life members, $10. The Institute receives a yearly allowance of $3,000 from the city of Baltimore towards the support of its schools. — *The Schools of Art and Design* have a threefold object: first to diffuse a knowledge of the true principles of art more generally among the community, and especially among the working classes; secondly, to foster and direct original talent in all those branches of industry in which the raw material is worked into artistic forms; and lastly, to lay a permanent foundation for a genuine school of high art in Baltimore. — *Day School:* Director, Prof. Hugh Newell, with a competent corps of experienced assistants. Opens Oct. 2. Three sessions yearly. Elementary drawing in pencil and crayon, from the flat and objects. etc., $5 per session; Higher drawing from figures, the antique, etc., $8; Water-colors and India ink, $10; Oil painting, decorating, and painting on China, etc., $15; Annual fee for the entire course, $25. Classes for drawing and painting in oil and water-colors from life, and in sculpture and modelling in clay, etc. All the pupils of both sexes must be members of the Institute. Number of pupils, season of 1881–82, 190 (20 males, 170 females). — *Night School:* Opens Oct. 16, and continues three nights in the week, for five months. The curriculum embraces a complete course of Element ary, Artistic, Industrial, Mechanical, and Architectural Drawing. This school has been for a long time one of the most celebrated in the United States. It was thoroughly reorganized in 1879, has been placed in new and commodious rooms, and will be furnished with every appliance which modern methods of teaching demand. Pupils desiring to enter the Mechanical and Architectural classes at once, can do so without being required to go through a preliminary course of free-hand drawing. The liberality of the late Geo. Peabody enables the managers to offer premiums, amounting to $500 annually, to the highest graduates. Fee for the annual session of five months, $3. All the pupils, males only, must be members of the Institute. Number of pupils, season of 1881–82, 337.

PEABODY INSTITUTE. — Founded 1857, by the late George Peabody. — Officers B'd of Trustees: Pres., Chas. J. M. Eaton; V. P., Geo. Wm. Brown; Treas., Enoch Pratt; Sec., Geo. P. Tiffany. Officers of the Inst.: Provost, Nath'l H. Morison, LL. D.; Libr., P. R. Uhler; Asst. Libr. and Clerk, Andreas Troeger. — *The Gallery of Art* was first opened to the public on May 2, 1881. It contains an excellent collection of about 200 casts from antique and Renaissance statues, busts, and reliefs, paid for out of a fund of $15,000 donated by Mr. John W. Garrett; Rinehart's ideal statue of "Clytie," the gift of Mr. John W. McCoy; a reduced copy, in bronze, by F. Barbedienne, of Paris, of the second Ghiberti Gate, also paid for out of the Garrett fund; a marble copy of an antique Venus, and a bust, in marble, of Pocahontas, by Jos. Mozier, both presented by Mr. Geo. S. Brown, and a few paintings. The executors of Wm. H. Rinehart (b. 1825, d. 1874), " undoubtedly the most accomplished artist Maryland has produced," have also deposited in the Gallery a collection of 44 casts from the works of the sculptor named. — The Gallery is open from 11 A. M. to 4 P. M. every day, except Sundays and holidays, from Oct. 1 to June 1. Admission free. Catalogues, 10 cents. The number of visitors, during the eight months from Oct. 1, 1881, to June 1, 1882, was 10,121. — *The Library*, for reference only, open free, day and evening, except during the month of August, is well provided with books on art. — *Lectures.* Due attention is given to art in the lectures provided by the Institute during the winter season. An admission fee is charged at these lectures, 25 cents for a single ticket, $1.50 for the season.

SOCIAL ART CLUB. — Organized Sept., 1880. — Officers : Pres., Wm. T. Brigham, 128 W. Fayette St. ; Sec., Clev. P. Manning ; Treas., Edw. M. Keith. — This Club is governed without by-laws, restrictions, or fines. Any person invited by a member may join it upon contributing a piece of artistic handiwork, either the product of the candidate's own skill or otherwise, the article offered being submitted to a committee for approval.

Berkeley, Cal. — UNIVERSITY OF CALIFORNIA. — Pres., Prof. John Le Conte; Libr., Prof. J. C. Rowell. — No instruction in free-hand drawing and painting is at present given at the University ; but it is earnestly desired and confidently expected by the authorities of the University that those students who shall wish to do so, may sooner or later have the opportunity of beginning art studies in connection with their other academic employments. — *The Bacon Art Gallery of the University of California* had its origin in the gift, by Mr. Henry D. Bacon, of Oakland, Cal., of his private library, art collections, and $25,000 in money towards the erection of a suitable building, for which purpose the State also contributed $25,000, besides a later appropriation of $10,000 for furnishing. The building is mainly used for library purposes, the portion devoted to the Fine Arts being a large hall, 80 ft. in length, divided into three compartments, and averaging 32 ft. in width. Collections : — Three marble groups : " Ariadne on the Panther," a copy of Dannecker's famous work ; " Genius of America, or the Abolition of Slavery," by Johann Halbig, of Munich, originally designed as a gift to President Lincoln ; " Bathing Nymphs," by the same artist. Bronzes : Five busts by Barbedienne, of Solon, Socrates, Hippocrates, Homer, Franklin. Paintings : About 70, including Leutze's " Washington at Monmouth " ; Bierstadt's " Yosemite Winter Scene"; Gebhard's " Koenig See, Bavaria "; Jacobs's " Susannah at the Bath "; and many fine copies of the works of old and modern masters, such as Cimabue, Correggio, Albani, Stella, Guido, Claude, N. Poussin, Dürer, Rembrandt, Paul Bril, Teniers, Rubens, Picornet, Le Sueur, Besson, Grosclaude, Horace Vernet, Murillo, Rugendas, Manulich, Piloty, and others. Thus a fair beginning of a collection illustrating the history of the art of painting has been made. The Gallery was opened for the first time May 31, 1882, and a very large number of visitors (about 2,500 during the first two and a half months) have examined its contents. Admission free. A catalogue is in preparation. — *The Library* contains a large number of choice engravings, chromolithographs, and illustrated books on art, also a collection of coins, and fine specimens of the printer's and binder's art.

Boston, Mass. — ARCHITECTURAL ASSOCIATION OF BOSTON. — Museum of Fine Arts. Originally organized in 1879 as the Arch. Assoc. of the Mass. Inst. of Techn.; reorganized 1882. — Officers : Pres., Arthur Rotch, 85 Devonshire St. ; V. P., Wm. C. Richardson, 18 P. O. Sq ; Sec., F. E. Alden, care H. H. Richardson, Brookline, Mass.; Libr., H. Langford Warren, Hillside, Roxbury, Mass.; Treas., E. G. Hartwell, care Hook & Hastings. — Objects : To afford facilities for the study of architecture, to increase the knowledge and appreciation of art, to advance the interests of the profession, and to promote friendly and intellectual intercourse among the members. — Any gentleman interested in architecture may be admitted to mem-

bership. Present number of members about 65, principally young architects and
architectural draughtsmen. — The Sketch Club of the Association meets every third
Friday. Two classes are to be established this winter, one in Construction, and one
in Drawing from the Life. Arrangements are also being made for a series of lectures by prominent members of the profession and others.

BOSTON ART CLUB. — Cor. Dartmouth and Newbury Sts. Organized Jan.,
1855; incorp. Mch. 3, 1871. — Officers: Pres., Geo. P. Denny, 132 Federal St.;
V. Ps., Thos. O. Richardson, 188 Congress St., and Ernest W. Longfellow, Cambridge, Mass.; Treas., Chas. E. Stratton, 68 Devonshire St.; Sec., Wm. F. Matchett, 68 Devonshire St.; Libr., Chas. W. Scudder, 4 P. O. Square. — Objects:
To advance the knowledge and love of art, through the exhibition of works of art,
the acquisition of books and papers for the purpose of forming an art library,
lectures upon subjects pertaining to art, and by other kindred means, and to promote
social intercourse among its members. — The membership of the Club is limited to
750 members (males only), exclusive of such members as may be professional artists
resident in Massachusetts. Entrance fee, $20, which professional artists may pay
in works of art. Assessments not over $20 p. a. Present number of members,
864. — The government consists of the officers and an Executive Committee of
twelve members, four of whom at least must be professional artists. — The new Club
House, inaugurated Mch. 4, 1882, was built from plans by Mr. Wm. R. Emerson, at
a cost of about $85,000, including the ground. The necessary funds were secured
by the issue of bonds, taken by members. It contains, besides library, reading-room,
parlors, billiard-room, etc., a spacious gallery, in which the exhibitions of the Club,
two or more yearly, are held. These exhibitions have been for a number of years,
and still are, the most important general exhibitions held in Boston. Admission to
them is practically free, as tickets can be obtained from any member of the Club.
The Twenty-sixth Exhibition, devoted to Water Colors, and Works in Black and
White, opened Apr. 28, and closed May 27, 1882.

BOSTON ART STUDENTS' ASSOCIATION. — Museum of Fine Arts. Organized
1879. — Officers: Pres., W. H. Bicknell; V. P., Stacy Tolman; Treas., Miss Alice
S. Tinkham; Asst. Treas., Miss S. E. Homans; Sec., Mrs. C. M. Crocker; Asst.
Sec., Miss Edith Howes. — Objects: To hold semi-annual exhibitions of the work of
its members, and to promote the establishment of scholarships in the School of Drawing and Painting at the Museum. — Members (both sexes) must be, or must have
been, students in the School at the Museum. Initiation fee, $1; annual member-
ship, $5; life membership, $25. Present number of members, 156. The committee
in charge of the School and its instructors are honorary members, to which grade
other persons may also be elected — The Association has paid $100 to the School
towards the foundation of a scholarship, and has held several exhibitions at the
rooms of the Art Club. Visitors are admitted to these exhibitions to a limited
extent on tickets issued by the members.

BOSTON ATHENÆUM. — 10½ Beacon St. Incorporated 1807. — Officers: Libr.,
Chas. A. Cutter; Sec., Chas. H. Williams; Treas., Chas. P. Bowditch. — The Athenæum is a private association, controlled by shareholders. Its library of about
125,000 vols., which is very rich in works on art, is, however, easily accessible to students who do not belong to the association. In former years the upper floor of the
building was devoted to an art gallery, for a long time the only permanent exhibition of
the kind in Boston. In this gallery the collections of the present Museum of Fine
Arts were first displayed, and upon the completion of the Museum's building, the
Athenæum deposited most of its own art treasures with the new institution. Of the
pictures and sculptures which it retained, the casts of Ball Hughes's statue of Dr.
Bowditch, and of Houdon's Washington, Greenough's " Boy with Eagle," in bronze,
and some casts from the antique, are placed in the vestibule. On the walls of the

staircase are hung, Leslie's portrait of Benj. West, after Lawrence; Harding's Daniel Webster and Chief Justice Marshall; Cole's immense "Angel appearing to the Shepherds"; Sully's portrait of Col. T. H. Perkins; Neagle's "Patrick Lyon at the Forge"; R. W. Weir's "Indian Captive"; a landscape by Allston; several copies from old masters, etc. Paintings by Allston, Stuart, Inman, Waldo, Sully, etc., and sculptures by Dexter, Gould, Powers, Crawford, Ball Hughes, Frazee, Greenough, Clevenger, etc., are in the Reading Room, and the various other rooms. — Open from 9 A. M. to 6 P. M. in summer, till sunset in winter. The paintings, etc., in the vestibule and on the staircase can be examined by all orderly visitors. Permission to see those in the rooms must be asked of the Librarian at the desk in the Reading Room, up-stairs. There is no catalogue, but printed lists are posted on the staircase, etc.

BOSTON CHAPTER OF AM. INST. OF ARCHITECTS. — Sec., T. M. Clark, 178 Devonshire St. (See p. 1.)

BOSTON ETCHING CLUB. — 429 Washington St. Organized Feb., 1880. — Officers: Pres., W. F. Halsall, 154 Tremont St.; Treas., C. F. Pearce, 10 West St.; Sec., H. R. Burdick, 616 Washington St. — Objects: To encourage the practice of etching among its members, and to increase facilities for such practice. — The condition of membership is the prompt payment of all assessments (initiation fee $10, annual dues $6), and the production of at least two etchings p. a. Any failure forfeits membership. Present number of members, 15.

BOSTON MEMORIAL ASSOCIATION. — Established 1880. — Officers: Pres., M. P. Kennard, U. S. Treas., P. O. Bldg.; Sec., Prentiss Cummings, 82 Devonshire St.; Treas., H. H. Edes, 87 Milk St. — Objects: The ornamentation of the City of Boston, the care of its Memorials, the preservation and improvement of its Public Grounds, and the erection of Works of Art within the limits of the city. Membership limited to 150, exclusive of life members. Life membership, $50; annual membership, $5.

BOSTON MUSEUM. — 28 Tremont St. Established 1841. — This is the oldest existing theatre in Boston. In its early days it was called "The Boston Museum and Gallery of Fine Arts," and the performances were subordinate to the exhibition of paintings, statuary, stuffed animals, wax figures, and other curiosities. At present the stage, which is favorably known to all play-goers, forms the principal attraction, but something of the old character is still retained in the large hall on Tremont St., which may be regarded as the *foyer* of the theatre. Along with the stuffed beasts and birds a number of casts, engravings, and paintings may still be seen there, including some by artists of good repute in the past periods of American art, such as Rembrandt Peale's "Roman Daughter," painted in 1820; "Gen. Washington and his Family," by E. Savage (engraved by the painter himself); "The Signers of the Declaration of Independence in Carpenter's Hall, Philadelphia," by the same artist; Chas. Wilson Peale's "Portrait of David Rittenhouse"; Winstanly's "Portrait of John Adams" when minister at the Hague, 1782-5; R. E. Pine's "Mad Woman in Chains"; Sully's "Passage of the Delaware," and portraits, etc. by Copley, West, and Stuart. There are also a few good old pictures by European artists.

BOSTON NUMISMATIC SOCIETY. — 18 Somerset St. Founded in 1860. — Officers: Pres., Jerem. Colburn, 33 E. Newton St.; Sec., Wm. S. Appleton, 39 Beacon St. — The Society has a cabinet of coins and a library, and publishes the "American Journal of Numismatics." (Quarterly, $2 p. a.)

BOSTON PUBLIC LIBRARY. — Boylston, near Tremont St. Founded 1852. — Officers: Chairm. of B'd of Trustees, Wm. W. Greenough; Libr. and Clerk of the Trustees, Mellen Chamberlain. — The Library was the recipient in 1852 of $100,000 in money and books from Mr. Joshua Bates, of London, after whom the upper or

"Bates Hall " was named. Many other liberal donations and bequests were added
to this sum, besides the yearly appropriation which the institution receives from the
city. The Library (over 400,000 vols.) is very rich in works on art and its history,
including many of the celebrated illustrated folios on antiquities, and on the galleries
and churches of Europe, the large publications on the Paris Salon, Amand-Durand's
reproductions of the old masters of engraving; Charles Blanc's Rembrandt, etc.
It is well supplied also with the best foreign art journals. — There are no funds for
the purchase of paintings, statuary, and engravings as such, but the Library has
come into possession, by gift, of quite a valuable collection of works of art, the most
prominent constituent of which is the *Tosti Collection of Engravings*, next to the
Phillips Collection in the Penn. Academy at Philadelphia, the largest public print
collection in the U. S. It consists of about 6,500 prints, and was presented by Mr.
Thos. G. Appleton, who bought it in Rome of the heirs of Cardinal Tosti. About
5,100 of the prints are in bound volumes, and several hundred in portfolios. These
can be examined on application at the desk in Bates Hall, from 9 A. M. to 12 M.
Over 600 prints are framed, and are displayed in the various parts of the Library.
The curator has in charge a catalogue of the collection, and there is also a complete
card catalogue. Lists of the framed pictures, arranged numerically, can be had for
temporary use on application. In the *Fine Arts Room*, on the lower floor, is to be
seen one of the best and largest of Copley's paintings, " Charles I. demanding the
Five Members," and a number of works in marble by Thos. Ball, R. S. Greenough,
W. W. Story, Troschel, and G. Albertini. There is also an antique marble portrait
bust, a silver vase presented to Daniel Webster in 1835, and a " View of the Old
State House," painted by Salmon in 1832. This room is open to both sexes during
the day ; after 6 P. M. to ladies only. In the *Trustees' Room* are two original por-
traits of Franklin, painted by Greuze and Duplessis respectively; and portraits of
Joshua Bates, by Eddis; Edw. Everett, by J. Harvey Young; and Charles Sumner,
by Moses Wight   Access to this room can be gained on application at the desk in
Bates Hall. A number of busts, etc., are scattered through the various rooms. —
Bates Hall is open daily, Sundays and holidays excepted, from 9 A. M. to 6 P. M. from
Oct to March, inclusive, and until 7 P. M. the rest of the year. The rooms on the
lower floor are open from 8½ A. M. to 9 P. M. The general reading-room on the
lower floor, in which many large framed engravings are hung, is open also on Sundays from 2 to 10 P. M. A " Handbook for Readers," a very convenient little guide
to the Library, was published in 1879. The edition is at present exhausted, but a
new one is in preparation. Books may be taken out under certain restrictions.

BOSTON SCHOOL OF SCULPTURE. — 394 Federal St. Opened 1879 ; incorp. 1881.
— B'd of Trustees: Mellen Chamberlain, Public Library ; J. Foxcroft Cole, 433
Washington St. ; J. Boyle O'Reilly, 597 Washington St. ; E. P. Howe, 14 Pemberton
Sq. ; Frank Hill Smith, 171½ Tremont St. ; F. P. Vinton, Park Sq. ; Wm. S. Dennett,
M. D., Hotel Pelham ; R. F. G. Candage, 13 Merch. Exch. ; Arlo Bates, 299 Washington St. ; Jas. Taylor, Thos. Robinson. Director : Truman H. Bartlett. — This school
was originally started as a private enterprise by its Director, with a view to providing
adequate tuition for talented young men and women, who want to study modelling.
Tuition, $15 per month to those who can pay ; free to those who cannot pay. The
amount of tuition fees received has been about one tenth of the expenses. A few
small donations have been made towards the maintenance of the institution, and one
talented pupil, a girl, has been enabled, by the generosity of a private individual, to
go to Paris, with the intention of fitting herself to teach on her return. Present number of pupils, 6, with almost daily applicants who cannot be accommodated. Nearly
all the work thus far executed by the pupils has been modelled in terra-cotta clay,
including vases and decorated fireplaces. The latter were made to order, and about
one third of the former were sold.

BOSTON SOCIETY OF DECORATIVE ART. — 8 Park Sq. Organized Mch., 1878. — Officers: Pres., Roland C. Lincoln, 82 Devonshire St.; V. Ps., John H. Sturgis, 19 Exchange Pl., Mrs. Chas. P. Curtis, Jr., and Mrs. Freder. L. Ames; Sec., Miss Georgina Lowell Putnam; Treas., Mrs. Geo. J. Fiske. — Objects: To raise the standard and increase the production of artistic hand-wrought decoration, to furnish a market and assist art-workers, and to promote improvement of designs in manufactures. — Any person may become a member by an annual payment of $5. Number of members, Apr. 1, 1882, 122 (30 male, 92 female). — The income of the Society is derived from membership fees, donations, tuition fees, profits on work executed in its work-room, and a commission of 10% charged on sales made for outside contributors. — The School of Art Needlework maintained by the Society is in charge of Mrs. Smith, of South Kensington. Tuition fees, 6 class lessons, $5; 12 class lessons, $8. Classes are held in the Society's rooms, as well as elsewhere in Boston and the neighboring towns. Number of pupils last season, 294. The classes in china painting and in wood carving have been given up. — This Society, like all other kindred societies, combines benevolence with art. The work-rooms and salesrooms maintained by it are carried on mainly in the artistic and financial interest of the workers and of the contributors, that is, of the needlewomen, etc., who send the produce of their skill on sale. All work so sent must pass an examination, and rejected work is criticised, if the contributor demands it. As a charity the Society is worthy of support, if not for artistic reasons. It gives work to many people needing the money, in an agreeable way, who otherwise would find it difficult, if not impossible, to earn anything. Its career has been quite successful; and its present property is valued at $7,077.16. Sales last year, $12,268.93.

BOSTON YOUNG MEN'S CHRISTIAN ASSOCIATION. — Tremont St., cor. Eliot. — Officers: Pres., A. S. Woodworth; Gen'l Sec., M. R. Deming. — This Association maintains an Evening Class in Free-Hand Drawing; Albert H. Munsell, of the State Normal Art School, instructor. Present number of pupils, both sexes, 38. The class is free to members, who pay $1 annually. Special tickets are issued to ladies at $1 for the whole course of 20 lessons.

FANEUIL HALL. — Over the platform in this "Cradle of Liberty" hangs an immense picture, measuring 16 × 30 feet, "Webster replying to Hayne in the U. S. Senate, Jan. 26 and 27, 1830," painted by Geo. P. A. Healy. A key to the picture, price 10 cents, can be bought at the Superintendent's office. Numerous portraits of celebrated Americans, especially of such as are famed in the history of Massachusetts, are hung upon the walls, and a few busts stand upon the platform. There is no list, however, of these works, the superintendent does not know anything about them, beyond the names of the subjects, which are attached to the frames, and it is impossible to examine them near by. The most interesting among the older pictures, such as Copley's John Hancock and Sam'l Adams, and Stuart's full length of Washington, have been removed to the Old State House and to the Museum of Fine Arts and replaced by copies. — Open free every day, Sundays and holidays excepted, from 10 A. M. to 5 P. M. from Apr. 1 to Oct. 1; from 10 A. M. to 4 P. M. the rest of the year.

MASSACHUSETTS ART TEACHERS' ASSOCIATION. — Organized Dec. 29, 1881. — Officers: Pres., C. M. Carter, 616 Washington St.; Sec., A. H. Munsell, State Normal Art School. — Object: To promote art education in the State, and the interchange of ideas and social intercourse among art teachers. — Present number of members, both sexes, about 60. — The plans of the Association are not yet fully matured. Its main activity will probably be concentrated upon an Art Teachers' Institute, with lectures, the reading of papers, discussions, etc., to be held once a year.

MASSACHUSETTS CHARITABLE MECHANIC ASSOCIATION. — Huntington Ave. and W. Newton St. Organized 1795; incorp. 1806. — Officers: Pres., N. J. Bradlee,

18 Pemberton Sq.; Sec., Jos. L. Bates, 13½ Bromfield St.; Treas., Freder. W. Lincoln, 126 Commercial St. — This society is one of the oldest and wealthiest of its kind in the U. S. Among its founders were a number of men whose names are well known in American history, notably Paul Revere, silversmith, engraver, and patriot, and the hero of Longfellow's celebrated poem. Although originally conceived as a protective and benevolent society, the Association early turned its attention to other means of benefiting the mechanic arts and their professors, and out of this desire grew the Industrial Exhibitions, the Fourteenth of which occurred in 1881. As a rule these " Fairs " are held triennially, and the next will therefore take place in 1884. At all of them, from the very beginning, more or less space was devoted to art, and many of the artists of renown of the present day were here early encouraged and rewarded. As an example may be cited Thos. Ball, whose model of the statue of Webster, from which he afterwards executed the statue ordered by Mr. Gordon F. Burnham for the Central Park, New York, was awarded a gold medal in 1856. The Association moreover claims that it was the first in the U. S. to add the fine arts to an Industrial Exposition as a separate and distinct department, controlled by connoisseurs and artists, and bestowing medals. This was first done at the suggestion of Mr. Chas. W. Slack, at the Twelfth Exhibition held in 1874. The experiment was repeated in 1878, and the successes of these two years established the Art Department as a permanent feature of the exhibitions of the Association. The last exhibition was held in the spacious buildings erected by the society for its purposes, at a total cost of about $500,000. These buildings contain, besides two vast halls for the industrial shows, offices, etc., two large picture galleries with skylights, and seven smaller cabinets, with excellent northern exposure, all of which are given up to the various branches of art at the exhibitions. The awards consist of medals in gold, silver, and bronze, and in diplomas.

MASSACHUSETTS HISTORICAL SOCIETY. — 30 Tremont St. Founded 1791. — Officers: Pres., Robert C. Winthrop; Treas., Chas. C. Smith; Sec., Geo. Dexter; Libr., Saml. A. Green, M. D.; Keeper of the Cabinet, F. E. Oliver, M. D. — Membership limited to 100. — The library, which contains over 25,000 books and 50,000 pamphlets, may be used for reference by any person introduced by a member. The Society possesses many valuable relics and a number of interesting portraits, among which are those of Govs. Endicott, Winslow (believed to be by Vandyke), Pownall (a copy by Henry C. Pratt from a good original by an unknown artist), Dudley, Belcher, Winthrop, Hutchinson, Strong (by Chester Harding), Gore, etc. There is also a portrait of John Adams, by Gilbert Stuart Newton; a copy of a portrait of Sir Richard Saltonstall by Rembrandt; a copy of an excellent portrait of Sebastian Cabot from an original said to be by Holbein; portraits by Stuart of Jeremiah Allen, Edward Everett (unfinished), and Lt. Gov. Cobb; and others by Henly, Osgood, Sargent, Marston, Wight, etc. A catalogue of the works of art owned by the Society is in preparation.

MASSACHUSETTS INSTITUTE OF TECHNOLOGY. — Boylston St., bet. Berkeley and Clarendon Sts. Incorporated 1861. — Officers of the Corpor.: Pres., Francis A. Walker; Sec. and Bursar, Lewis Wm. Tappan, Jr.; Treas., John Cummings. Pres. of the Fac., Francis A. Walker, Ph. D., LL. D. — Objects: Instituting and maintaining a Society of Arts, a Museum of Arts, and a School of Industrial Science, and aiding generally, by suitable means, the advancement, development, and practical application of sciences in connection with arts, agriculture, manufactures, and commerce. — The Institute receives annually from the State one third part of the interest from the fund created under the act of Congress giving public lands to the States in aid of instruction in agriculture, etc. Otherwise it is dependent for its maintenance upon tuition fees and the munificence of private patrons. — There are nine regular *Courses of Instruction*, extending over four years, but provision has also been made for those who desire to pursue special or partial courses. During the first year which is the same to all regular students, a large amount of time is devoted to practice in Free-Hand and Mechanical Drawing. In subsequent years, drawing is continued with professional studies as follows : — Civil Engineering : 2d year, Descriptive Geometry and Plans and Profiles ; 3d, Engineering Drawing ; 4th, Practice in Design. Mech. Engineering : 2d year, Machine Drawing and Descriptive Geometry ; 3d, Machine Drawing and Perspective ; 4th, Machine Drawing. Mining Engineering : Drawing in the first terms of 2d and 4th years only. Chemistry : Drawing in second term of 3d year only. Metallurgy : Drawing in first term of 3d and both terms of 4th year. Natural History : Drawing during 2d year ; Drawing with the Microscope, first term of 4th year. Physics : No Drawing. General Courses (for such as may not intend to adopt a distinctly scientific profession, yet desire to obtain an education through studies of a predominantly scientific character) : Course A, Physics predominating, no drawing ; Course B, Chemistry, Botany, and Zoölogy predominating, Drawing of Crystals, first term of 2d year ; Course C, Geology, with Botany and Zoölogy predominating, Drawing of Crystals (1st term, 2d year), Topographical Drawing (2d term, 2d year), Map Drawing (2d term, 3d year, and 2d term, 4th year), and Drawing with the Microscope (1st term, 4th year). — Course in Architecture. Instructors : Theod. M. Clark, A. B., Prof. of Architecture ; Eugene Letang, Asst. Prof. of Architecture ; Wm. P. P. Longfellow, Adj. Prof. of Architectural Design ; Henry K. Burrison, S. B., Instr. in Mechan. and Free-Hand Drawing ; Geo. L. Perry, S. B., Assist. in Drawing. Lectures on special subjects are occasionally delivered by architects not connected with the Institute. It is the object of this department to give to its students the instruction and discipline that cannot be obtained in architects' offices. The course, is however, practical as well as theoretical, and, besides the scientific study of construction and materials, it comprises the study of building processes, and of professional practice and procedure, as well as that of composition and design, and of the history of the art. The students are also given some opportunity to practise carpentry in the shops of the School of Mechanic Arts (see below), and by their studies in the modern languages, literature, and history, are provided with that general culture which is needed by every person of intelligence. Drawing, including Free-Hand, Perspective, Original Design, Sketching in Water-Color, etc., plays an important part throughout the whole of this course. Besides the regular course, designed for students who wish to pursue the study of architecture in the most thorough manner, with all the appliances which literature and science may afford, there is also a special course of two years, which embraces only the architectural, without the scientific, mathematical, mechanical, and engineering studies, for those who desire to fit themselves simply as draughtsmen, or to complement the practical education received in the office. — The conditions of admission to the regular course are, in general, the training of the high school or academy, with a good grounding in mathematics ; applicants must have attained the age of sixteen. No examination is needed for the special course, but those not proficient in free-hand drawing and practical geometry are required to make themselves so during the first half-year. — Fees, for either course, $200 a year ; two terms, beginning respectively on the last Monday in Sept., and the first Tuesday in Febr. There are three scholarships, open to students in all the courses, and the Boston Society of Architects has established two special prizes in the department of architecture, of the value of $50 each, which are given in books. — The degree of Bachelor of Science is awarded to those who pass the requisite examination at the completion of the regular course. Certificates of attainment in special subjects are also given upon examination. — Number of students, season of 1881-2 : Regular 5 ; special 27 (all males). — The Architectural Museum of the school contains several thousand photographs, prints, drawings, and casts, bought with funds specially raised for the purpose. To these have been added photographs, lithographs, original drawings, etc., presented to the Institute by French, English, and American architects and architectural societies; together with specimens of metal-work, tile-work, glasswork, wood-work, etc., partly purchased, partly deposited by manufacturers, the whole forming a museum of sanitary and building appliances. A chief part of the collection of casts has been deposited in the Museum of Fine Arts, along with the architectural collections of the Museum, access to which is free to the students. — *The Library* contains nearly 400 vols. The students are besides given every facility in the use of the Boston Public Library. — *The School of Mechanic Arts* connected with the Institute affords such students as have completed the ordinary grammar-school course an opportunity to continue elementary scientific and literary studies and drawing, while receiving instruction in the use of the typical tools for working iron and wood. The shop work is conducted on the plan of the Imperial Technical School at Moscow, Russia. — Instructors: Clarence W. Fearing, A. M.; Chas. L. Adams, Instr. in Drawing. — The full course extends over two years. In the first year Mechanical and Free-Hand Drawing is taught, in the second Mechanical Drawing only. — Tuition $150 a year; special charges for special students. The student is entitled to the products of his work. Two scholarships have been founded by the Mass. Charit. Mech. Assoc., for sons of its members. — Number of students, season of 1881–2: 39 (males). — *The Lowell School of Practical Design* was founded in 1872, by the late John Amory Lowell and other manufacturers, and is maintained by the Trustee of the Lowell Institute. Instructor: Charles Kastner. Students are taught practically, as well as theoretically, the art of making patterns for prints, ginghams, delaines, silks, laces, paper hangings, carpets, oilcloths, etc. The school is constantly provided with samples of novelties, and the weaving department connected with the school, in charge of a special assistant, is provided with six looms, 1 Jacquard, 2 for fancy cassimeres, 2 for dress goods, 1 for ginghams. There is also a camera-obscura with all the appliances necessary for transferring designs to rollers. All of these have been given by manufacturers, who also supply most of the materials used in the weaving department. During the year the pupils visit print works, carpet mills, etc. — Applicants must have some knowledge of free-hand drawing and of the use of instruments. Tuition free, but students supply their own materials, etc. Number of students, season 1881–2: 49 (21 females, 28 males). The present season there are about 74. Of the graduates of the school, according to last published report, 49 are employed in carpet mills, etc., as designers and draughtsmen Of these 36 are males and 13 females. — The school is at present temporarily housed in the building of the Mass. Charitable Mechanic Association, until the completion of the new building which the Institute is about to erect alongside of its old one. — *Free Courses of Instruction*, open to both sexes, are given in the evening in a variety of subjects, including drawing and architecture. These courses vary and are announced specially each year.

MUSEUM OF FINE ARTS. — Dartmouth St. and St. James Ave. Incorporated 1870. — Officers: Pres., Martin Brimmer, 47 Beacon St.; Treas., Henry P. Kidder, 2 Newbury St.; Honorary Director, Charles C. Perkins, 2 Walnut St.; Curator, Chas. G. Loring; Sec., Edw. H. Greenleaf. — Objects: Erecting a Museum for the preservation and exhibition of works of art, making, maintaining, and exhibiting collections of such works, and affording instruction in the fine arts. — Governed by a Board of Trustees, not to exceed thirty, consisting of the original Incorporators, three persons to be appointed annually by Harvard College, three by the Athenæum, and three by the Mass. Inst. of Technology, and, *ex officiis*, the Mayor of the City, the Pres. of Trustees of the Public Library, the Supt. of Public Schools of Boston, the Sec. of the B'd of Education, and the Trustee of the Lowell Institute. Vacancies occurring among the Trustees whose annual appointment is not provided for, are filled by the whole Board. — The income of the Museum is derived from subscriptions, legacies, and donations, from entrance fees, and from the interest on several endowment funds (Everett Fund, $7,500 ; N. C. Nash Fund, $10,000; B. P. Cheney Fund, $5,000 ; John L. Gardner Fund, $20,000). The cash receipts from subscriptions, etc., up to the date of the last report, Jan. 10, 1882, amounted to $401,188.62. The popular character of the subscriptions from which the greater part of this sum resulted, the individual amounts ranging from 35 cents to $25,000, is a special and interesting feature in the history of the institution. The Museum began its existence in the galleries of the Athenæum. The present building, erected from plans by Messrs. Sturgis & Brigham, on land given by the city, was first partially opened to the public on July 4, 1876, and represents only about one third of the structure as it is to be in future. Its cost, exclusive of interior fittings, is $320,944.11. For purchases of works of art, only $24,811.68 have thus far been expended. By far the greater part of the collections was acquired by donations and bequests, supplemented by loans and deposits. — This museum, although not the richest, may justly claim that it is the most systematic and complete in the country, and, therefore, educationally the most valuable. Its collections of Egyptian antiquities, the gift of Mr. C. Granville Way and of the Lowell family, and of casts from Assyrian, Greek, and Roman sculptures, partly deposited by the Athenæum, partly purchased with funds obtained from a bequest by Chas. Sumner, illustrate almost every phase of the rise and decline of ancient sculpture. A number of Tanagra figurines, given by Mr. Thos. G. Appleton, vessels of earthen and glass ware, presented by Mr. J. J. Dixwell, Mr. Thos. G. Appleton, Mr. Henry P. Kidder, and others, a complete set of the electrotypes from ancient coins published by the South Kensington Museum, bronzes, and other objects, serve to give a good idea of the minor arts of the ancients. The collection of architectural casts is very rich, including a full-size cast of the Portico of the Caryatides, from Athens. The sculpture of the Renaissance, and its industrial arts, and the industrial arts of the East and of mediæval Europe, in ceramics, enamels, textiles, carvings, metal work, etc., are well represented, and a small beginning has also been made towards a collection illustrating the art of the aborigines of America. The weakest part of the Museum, for the present, is in pictorial art. Most of the paintings permanently to be seen there have been deposited by the Athenæum and a few have been given, but the greater part are temporary loans. Among those which are destined to remain are excellent specimens by Copley, West, Stuart (including the famous Athenæum heads of Mr. and Mrs. Washington), Allston, Newton, Hunt, and other American artists; a few good old paintings, and several by celebrated modern European artists, especially of the French School. American sculpture is represented by the work of such artists as Crawford, Richard S. Greenough, Harriet Hosmer, Dengler, Rimmer, Aug. St. Gaudens, and Olin L. Warner. The Museum is also the depository of the *Gray Collection of Engravings*, consisting of about 5500 choice impressions, illustrating the history of the art from its very beginnings, and including some rarities, as for example a copy of the "Monte Santo di Dio." This collection was bequeathed to Harvard College by the late Francis C. Gray, who also left a fund of $15,000 for its maintenance and increase. It has been deposited only temporarily, but the Museum has already begun to form the nucleus of a print collection of its own, towards which some bequests and donations have been made, one of the most important being that of the collection of engraved portraits by the late Charles Sumner. A distinctive feature of this collection is its American department. The great interest shown by the Museum in the works of the etchers, wood engravers, etc., of the country, has induced many of them to present proofs of their works, and in this they have been followed by some of the publishers. Two of the rooms on the upper floor are devoted to an exhibition of prints, which are changed from time to time. The specimens in portfolios can only be examined upon application to the secretary of the Museum, Mr. E. H. Greenleaf, who is also the curator of the Gray Collection. — *The Library* is as yet small, but is constantly growing. It can also be consulted on application to Mr. Greenleaf. — An important feature in the management of the Museum is found in its *Special Exhibitions*, most of which have been of great interest. (Spanish pictures, loaned by the Duc de Montpensier, in 1874; Works of Wm. M. Hunt, 1879–80; Works of Gilbert Stuart, of Dr. Wm. Rimmer, of Wm. Blake, 1880; Works of Washington Allston, American Etchings, American Wood Engravings, 1881, etc.) The Exhibitions of Works by Living American Artists, of which two were held in the past, had to be suspended lately, but are to be taken up again next spring. — The great need of the Museum — besides the enlargement of the building, which is already too small for the proper display of the collections — is an adequate endowment fund. "The Museum," says one of the reports, "has the ill-deserved reputation of being a wealthy corporation." The truth is that the current receipts are considerably below the current expenses, and that for purchases, it is compelled to rely almost entirely upon the generosity of its friends. — The Museum publishes a catalogue in two parts, "Part 1, Sculpture and Antiquities," "Part 2, Paintings, Drawings, Engravings, and Decorative Art." Price, 25 cents each part. Revised editions are frequently issued. Special catalogues of the special exhibitions are also issued. — Open on Mondays from 12 M., on other week days from 9 A. M. to 5 P. M.; Sundays from 1 to 5 P. M. Admission free on Saturdays and Sundays; 25 cents on other days. From Jan. 1, 1877, to Dec. 31, 1881, the Museum was visited by 779,270 persons, of whom 89,302 paid an admission fee. The numbers given do not include the students who are entitled to the privileges of the Museum; the counting is done by means of turn-stiles. — *The School of Drawing and Painting* connected with the Museum, established Dec., 1876, is under the care of a permanent committee. Officers of Comm.: Chairm., Edw. C. Cabot, 60 Devonshire St.; Sec., Wm. P. P. Longfellow, 220 Devonshire St.; Treas., Edw. W. Hooper, 40 State St. — Instructors: Otto Grundmann, Freder. Crowninshield, and assistants. — Classes: First Drawing Class; elementary work (ornament, still-life, drapery, antique, living model; elements of shades, shadows, and perspective, architectural and decorative form), such as is needed not only by painters, but also by engravers, lithographers, designers, and teachers of drawing. Second Drawing Class (antique, still-life, life, lectures in anatomy); intended as a preparation for the painting class, and mainly for those who wish to become professional artists. Painting Class; candidates must satisfy the instructors that they have sufficiently mastered the preparatory work; the instructors visit this class only often enough to make sure that the students are working in the right direction. Lectures are given on the History of Painting, Sculpture and Architecture, Mythological, Legendary and Sacred Art, Theory and History of Ornamentation and Costume. Some of the pupils also sketch from nature, and practise composition under the direction of the instructors. The Evening Class in Elementary Drawing has been discontinued, as the City Schools amply supply this instruction; but there is an Evening Class for drawing from the nude, for advanced students, without instruction, the members of which are assessed simply for the expenses incurred. — Tuition fees: Admission fee for new students, $10; fees $90 per year; to artists already practising, $50. A small sum is also charged for some of the lectures. A number of free scholarships have been established, which are assigned, on application, and after probation, to students who have been six months in the school. — Students are required to work not less than three hours a day, for four days in a week. Three terms of twelve weeks each yearly, beginning for the present season, Oct. 3, 1882, and Jan. 2 and Apr. 3, 1883. — Number of students last year, 104 (33 men, 71 women). — The fees are not sufficient to pay expenses, and the school is therefore supported in part by voluntary contributions.

NEW ENGLAND MANUFACTURERS' AND MECHANICS' INSTITUTE. — Huntington Ave. Organized 1881. — Officers: Treas., John F. Wood, 38 Hawley St.; Clerk, F. W. Griffin. — This association proposes to hold yearly fairs, and combine with them exhibitions of works of art. The first of these Art Exhibitions opened Sept. 6, and will close some time in Nov. There are to be no juries of admission at these exhibitions.

OLD SOUTH CHURCH. —Washington St., cor. Milk. — Visitors to Boston will be attracted to this building by the historical associations' connected with it, and the interest is still further enhanced by the Museum of colonial, Revolutionary, and other relics which has been established within its walls. Students who take a special interest in the history of art in America will find a few rare specimens of the rude work of the early engravers of the country, such as Peter Pelham's Portrait of Cotton Mather, engraved by him 1727, from his own painting; the Rev. Mr. Wm. Cooper, after J. Smibert, 1743, by the same engraver; the Rev. Mr. Wm. Wellsteed, painted and engraved by Copley, 1753; John Adams, engraved by Geo. Graham; Paul Revere's "Bloody Massacre." etc. There are also a few paintings, among them a full-length of Edw. Everett, executed in 1838 by Henry C. Pratt, a little known New England artist, who died Nov. 27, 1880. Open on week days from 9 A. M. to 6 P. M. Admission 25 cents. The proceeds go to the fund for the preservation of the building.

OLD STATE HOUSE. —Washington and State Sts. — The exterior of this building, and the old Council Chamber and Representatives' Hall of the Provincial period on its upper floor, have lately been restored, by order of the city authorities, as nearly as possible to their original form, and the keeping of the halls, in which an historical Museum is to be established, has been intrusted to the Bostonian Society. Among the relics, etc., already gathered are Copley's portraits of Samuel Adams and John Hancock, formerly in Faneuil Hall; a Washington, painted by Stuart for Josiah Quincy in 1810; Josiah Quincy, Jr., painted by Stuart from an engraving and from recollections; a view of the Tremont House in 1832, by R. Salmon; a very early picture by Moses Wight, "The Laying of the Corner-Stone of Beacon Hill Reservoir, Nov. 22, 1847," and a number of other old portraits, and early views in and around Boston, all of which have at least an historical interest. Open week days, free, from 9.30 A. M. to 5 P. M.

PAINT AND CLAY CLUB. —419 Washington St. Organized June, 1880. — Officers: Chairm., W. F. Halsall, 154 Tremont St.; Sec., J. B. Millet, 4 Park St.; Treas., J. Eastm. Chase, 7 Hamilton Pl. — Objects: The production of works of art, literature, and music; and the promotion of social intercourse among its members. — No person admitted who is not a member of the professions of architecture, painting, music, engraving, or literature, or of some profession connected with the practice of art; no honorary members; membership limited to 30. Present number of members, 24. Entrance fee, $15; annual assessment, $15. Special assessments may be made by a two-thirds vote. — The Club gives musical entertainments, and holds receptions and exhibitions. The first exhibition was held in Dec., 1881; the next will open Dec. 13, 1882. Non-members are admitted to these various entertainments to a limited extent. — The members of the Club have illustrated T. B. Aldrich's poems for Messrs. Houghton, Mifflin & Co, and a similar undertaking is now under consideration.

PERMANENT EXHIBITIONS of foreign and American works of art will be found at the galleries of the dealers, of whom the following are the leading ones: *J. Eastman Chase*, 7 Hamilton Pl.; *Doll & Richards*, 2 Park St.; *J. Lowell & Co.*, 70 Kilby St.; *Noyes & Blakeslee*, 127 Tremont St.; *Williams & Everett*, 508 Washington St. As a rule these galleries are open free, but the two firms last named occasionally hold special exhibitions, at which an admission fee, usually of 25 cents, is charged.

St. Botolph Club. — 85 Boylston St. Organized Jan. 10, 1880. — Officers: Pres., Francis Parkman, 50 Chestnut St.; V. Ps., John Lowell, Samuel A. Green; Treas., Francis A. Osborn; Sec., T. R. Sullivan, 155 Federal St. — Object: The promotion of social intercourse among authors and artists, and other gentlemen connected with or interested in literature and art. — Members (males only) must be twenty-one years of age; entrance fee, $20; annual assessments, $30.   Membership limited to 350. — The Club holds two exhibitions of works by its members each year, to which non-members are admitted by tickets, limited to 100, issued by the Art and Library Committee. The sum of $250 is appropriated at each exhibition for the purchase of some work offered for sale at that price. The choice is made by a vote of the members. Exhibitions of works by non-members are also held occasionally.

State House. — Cor. Beacon and Mt. Vernon Sts. — A number of portraits of historical interest, of whose authors nothing definite is known, are hung in the Senate Chamber, including the portraits of governors John Winthrop, John Endicott, John Leverett, Simon Bradstreet, Wm. Burnet, Increase Sumner, and Wm. Eustis. In the Library is a crayon head of Gen. Thos. Gage, which is of special interest as it is supposed to be the only authentic portrait in existence, and came into the possession of the State directly from the family. In the entrance hall, known as Doric Hall, is Sir Francis Chantrey's statue of Washington and Thos. Ball's statue of Gov. Andrew; also busts of Samuel Adams, Abr. Lincoln, Chas. Sumner, and Henry Wilson. Before the State House stand the statues of Horace Mann, by Emma Stebbins, and Daniel Webster, by Hiram Powers. — The Senate Chamber is accessible during the sessions of the Senate, which begin the first Wednesday in January. The Library is open on week days from 9 A. M. to 5 P. M., except on Saturdays, when it closes at 2 P. M.

State Normal Art School of Massachusetts. — 1679 Washington St. — This School was established by the State in 1873, and is controlled by the State B'd of Education. Officers of the B'd: Sec., John W. Dickinson, A. M., State House; Asst. Sec. and Treas., C. B. Tillinghast, State House. — Objects: The School is intended as a training school, for the teachers and masters required for the industrial drawing schools of the State, who shall also be able to direct and superintend instruction in industrial drawing in the public schools. — Faculty: Otto Fuchs, Acting Principal, and Instructor in Geometry and Instrumental Drawing; Geo. H. Bartlett, Free-Hand, Light and Shade Drawing; W. F. Brackett, Architecture and Perspective; C. M. Carter, A. M., Normal Instruction; A. H. Munsell, A. M., Sculpture and advanced Perspective; Miss R. L. Hoyt, Painting in Water-Color; Miss M. A Bailey, Painting in Oil. — Course of Instruction: Industrial Drawing, including both Instrumental and Free-Hand Drawing, is taught by lectures and by individual instruction; the artistic work in the studios, comprising Free-Hand Drawing and Designing, is also under the immediate direction of the Instructors. The work of the four classes, representing a four-years' course, is arranged as follows: Class A, Elementary Drawing; Class B, Form, Color, and Industrial Design; Class C, Constructive Arts; Class D, Sculpture and Design in the Round. Students, as a rule, will not be allowed to remain in any class longer than two years. Graduates may review the course of study for one year (without fee) on condition that they will devote some time to teaching in the School. Qualified students of Classes B, C, and D may be selected to act as Assistants in Class A, and from the monthly reports on their conduct and efficiency, recommendations for appointments as teachers will be made. The School does not, however, undertake any responsibility with regard to securing appointments. Special students are also admitted. — Candidates must be above sixteen years of age. An examination in free-hand drawing of ornament from copy, and object drawing from the solid, is held at the beginning of each term for admission to the regular course. There is no examination for special students. — Tuition is free to residents of the State intending to teach drawing, but $5 per term is charged for incidentals;

to students from without the State, $50 per term. Special students from Massachusetts, $25 per term; from other States, $50 per term. Materials are furnished at cost. There are two terms, running, for the present season, from Sept. 4, 1882, to Jan. 19, 1883, and from Feb. 5 to June 29, 1883. — Certificates of four grades are given by the School : First or Primary, Second or Grammar, Third or High and Normal School grades to teachers of public schools and others who have completed the works and passed the examinations prescribed for these respective grades; and the diploma of the School to those students who have completed the subjects of study, and passed the examinations of the fourth grade in all the classes. — Number of students, June 30, 1881, the date of the last report: Day Classes, 222 (179 females, 43 males) ; Evening Classes, 72 (32 females, 40 males): total, 294. The Evening Classes have since been discontinued. Number of certificates given, examination of 1881 : 1st class, 29 (21 females, 8 males) ; 2d class, 13 (8 females, 5 males) ; 3d class, 6 (3 females, 3 males) ; 4th class, 7 (5 females, 2 males) : total, 55 (37 females, 18 males). Diplomas as art masters, 2 ; art mistresses, 3 : total, 5.

Zepho Club. — 429 Washington St. Organized Dec., 1879. — Officers: Pres., H. M. Stephenson, 10 Pemberton Sq ; Treas, J. H. White, 407 Main St. ; Sec., Chas. Copeland, 17 Pemberton Sq. — Object : To provide a place where drawing from the life can be practised. — The Club has regular nights for study and a monthly social meeting, when compositions on a given subject are presented by each member. — Present number of members, 30.

Bloomington, Ill. — Historical and Art Society. — Sec., Margaret M. Templeton. (See *Central Ill. Art Union*, Springfield, Ill.)

The Palladen. — Sec , Mrs. Gertrude Fifer. (See *Central Ill. Art Union*, Spring field, Ill.)

Brooklyn, N. Y. — Adelphi Academy. — Lafayette Ave., cor. St. James Pl. Incorporated 1869. — Officers : Pres., Chas. Pratt, 232 Clinton Ave. ; Treas., Harold Dollner, 259 Washington Ave. ; Sec., Edw. F. de Selding, 9 Lefferts Pl. ; Principal, Stephen G. Taylor, A. M., Ph. D., 316 Lafayette Ave. — Objects: To afford the very best facilities to both sexes (taught together) for a thorough and complete education. Departments : Preparatory, Academic, Collegiate (with Classical, Literary, Scientific, and Commercial Courses), and Art. — *Art Department :* Drawing, as a general study, is taught in all the classes, with the exception of those of the Classical Course. The more advanced scholars and special students of art receive instruction in the Studio, which is abundantly furnished with casts from statuary, and models from nature. Unusual facilities are offered to classes for drawing and painting in oil and water-colors from life. — Tuition fees : Drawing, $10 per session of 10 weeks, or $15 for two sessions ; Painting, $15 per session. — John B. Whittaker, 745 Lafayette Ave., Prof. of Painting and Drawing ; M. Elizabeth Greely, 39 Schermerhorn St., Free-Hand Drawing. — Special Students in Art Dept., 92 (10 male, 82 female).

Brooklyn Art Association. — Montgomery, n. Clinton St. Instituted 1861 ; incorporated June 29, 1864. — Officers : Pres., Richd. W. Hubbard ; V. P., Wm. H. Husted ; Treas , Gordon L. Ford ; Sec., Theod. E. Smith. — Objects : To promote the cultivation of Fine Arts ; to establish a Gallery, a Library, and a School of Design. — Real and personal property of the Association exempted from taxation by special act of Legislature, Apr. 23, 1867, so long as the same shall be devoted exclusively to the advancement of the Fine Arts, or be used as a free school of design. Authorized to issue certificates of stock to amount of $100,000, by special act of Legislature, Apr. 30, 1881. Besides the stockholders, there are life-members, upon payment of $100, and annual subscribers, who pay $10 annually, if laymen, or $5 if professional artists. — *The Free School of Design* was discontinued for the season of

1881–2, owing to lack of funds, but is to be reorganized the coming winter. — *Exhibitions:* The Association has thus far held forty-four exhibitions, among which the Twenty-fourth, or " Chronological Exhibition of American Art," Mch. 12 to Apr. 6, 1872, deserves special mention. It contained 120 numbers, and illustrated the history of art in America, from John Watson, the first professional artist at work here of whom there is a definite record (1715), down to our own time. — The Association owns a spacious and handsome building, specially put up for its purposes, and completed in 1872. It is connected with the adjoining Academy of Music, which is utilized at the receptions given during the winter season.

BROOKLYN ART CLUB — Organized 1879. — Officers : Pres., J. B. Stearns, N. A., 349 Fulton St. ; V. P., Geo. L. Clough ; Sec., J. H. Littlefield, Phœnix Bldg. ; Treas., Frank Squier, 310 Lafayette Ave. — Objects : To advance sociability and the interest in art among its members (active, professionals only, honorary, and associate) ; to have two exhibitions each year, spring and fall, followed by auction sales. So far only three sales have been held, the last of which took place Mch. 9, 1882, at Sherk's Gallery, 435 Fulton St., and realized $3,413, for 62 pictures. Monthly meetings are held at the studios of the members. The " Artists' Fund," virtually a life insurance, formerly connected with this Club, has been given up. — Present number of members, about 30.

BROOKLYN ART GUILD. — 201 Montgomery St. Organized Dec. 23, 1880. — Officers : Pres., Benj. Lander, 14 John St., New York ; V. P., C. E. Sickels, 142 B'way, New York ; Rec. Sec., W. H. Coughlin, 56 Cedar St., New York ; Treas., F. Sheffield, 487 Henry St., Brooklyn ; Cor. Sec., Miss M. E. Robinson, 182 Willoughby Ave., Brooklyn ; Chair. Ex. Com., Miss E. R. Coffin, 321 Clinton St., Brooklyn. — This School of Art was founded for the purpose of furnishing in Brooklyn a thorough course of instruction in Drawing, Painting, and Modelling, at the lowest rates consistent with the support of the school. — The active membership is limited to artists and art students, members of the Life and Portrait classes ; annual fee, $1. Associate members, not professional, $5 p. a. Present number of members, 105. — Life and Portrait classes in Drawing, Painting, and Modelling ; Antique class ; Sketch and Composition classes ; lectures on Anatomy, Perspective, etc. ; opportunities to work from still-life afforded to those who may desire it. Instructor, Prof. Thomas Eakins, Director of the Schools of the Penns. Academy, who visits the school twice a week. — The students are mainly those who propose making art a profession. Sexes taught together, except in Life classes. Number of pupils not stated. — Tuition fees : Life and Portrait classes, non-members, $42 per season of seven months, or $7 per month ; members, $35 and $6. Antique class, $20 per season, $3 per month. Sketch and Composition classes, free to members ; non-members, $1 per month. — Four or more receptions are given each season, at which the work of the students is exhibited, together with contributions from prominent artists. — The organization of the Guild is similar in its plan to that of the Art Students' League of New York, and the course of study about the same. The success of the school during its first two seasons proves that it meets a want felt by Brooklyn students. The increased demand for instruction has caused the classes to outgrow the capacity of the rooms in which the Guild began its work, and larger rooms have therefore been engaged for the season of 1882–3. The receipts from dues and tuition fees are amply sufficient to meet expenses. — For further information address " The Brooklyn Art Guild," 201 Montague St.

BROOKLYN INSTITUTE. — Sec., A. T. Baxter. — There is an Art School connected with this institution, Prof. Fred. T. L. Boyle, 11 E. 14th St., New York, instructor. [No reply to inquiries.]

COLLEGIATE AND POLYTECHNIC INSTITUTE. — Livingston St., betw. Court St. and Boerum Pl. Incorporated 1854. — Officers : Pres. of B'd of Trustees, Isaac

II. Frothingham, 134 Remsen St.; Sec., Benj. T. Frothingham, 45 Remsen St.; Treas., Tasker II. Marvin, 50 First Pl.; Registrar and Clerk, Wm E. Leffingwell, 341 State St. Pres. of the Fac., David II. Cochran, Ph. D., LL. D., 196 Livingston St. — Architectural, machine, landscape, figure, topographical and map drawing, and perspective (Instructor, Prof. O. Hertzberg, 140 Duffield St.) are taught in the various courses, as follows : Academic Dept.: In the third and fourth grades. Collegiate Dept.: First year, three first terms of second year, first term of fourth year. Classical Course : No drawing taught. Scientific Course : Mechanical drawing in second, third and fourth term of first year ; topographical drawing, in first term, and perspective and light and shade, in third term of second year; general, in first term of fourth year. Liberal Course: In second term of first and third term of third year. Commercial Course : In first term.

DÜRER ART CLUB. — 14 Red Hook Lane. — Officers: Pres., I. H. Platt; V. P., R. L. Dickinson ; Treas., E. O. Kindberg ; Sec., W. B. Tubby ; Curator, F. Tredwell, 9 Boerum Pl. — Objects : To publish works of art and a bulletin of art matters ; to arrange art lectures; to collect works of art and an art library. — Limited to 50 members, non-professional. — The only publication issued by the Club up to the present is a series of ten etchings by F. De B. Richards, of Philadelphia.

LONG ISLAND HISTORICAL SOCIETY. — Pierrepont St., cor. Clinton. Incorporated 1863. — Officers : Pres., Rev. Richd. S. Storrs, D. D., LL. D.; Home Cor. Sec., Rev. Chas. H. Hall, D. D.; Treas., A. W. Humphreys; Libr., George Hannah; Curator of the Museum, Elias Lewis, Jr. — One of the objects of the Society is the formation of a *Museum of Works of Art, Relics, and Curiosities*, particularly such as are of historical interest in relation to this country. The Museum, which is located on the upper floor of the building occupied and owned by the Society, contains, besides curiosities and specimens illustrative of natural history, the beginnings of an archæological collection. A small number of portraits and other paintings are hung in the Library and the rooms adjoining, among them a large landscape, "The Old Roadway," by Geo. Inness, lately presented by Mr. Geo. I. Seney, and an old portrait of Jeanne d'Arc, presented by Mr. Wm. Dodsworth. — *The Library*, for reference only, which contains over 35,000 volumes, is quite rich in costly illustrated works on art and its history, many of which have also been given by Mr. Seney, and a number of other friends of the Society. It is open to members (of whom there are at present 1,414, *i. e.*, 881 annual, at $5 p. a., and 533 life, who have paid $100) from 8.30 A. M. to 9.30 P. M. Non-residents may be introduced by members to the privileges of the Library and Reading-Rooms for the period of one month. Transient visitors from other cities admitted on application to the Librarian.

PACKER COLLEGIATE INSTITUTE. — Joralemon St., near Clinton. Incorporated 1846. — Officers : Pres. of B'd of Trustees, A. A. Low ; Treas., Richd. P. Buck ; Sec., Henry P. Morgan. Pres. of the Fac., A. Crittenden, A. M., Ph. D. — Objects : To furnish to young ladies all the advantages for thorough and complete education enjoyed in the best appointed Colleges. — Drawing, as a general study, is taught in the Preparatory Dept., and in the Second (or lower) Division of the Academic Dept. In the Collegiate Dept., architecture and perspective are taught in the third quarter of the Senior (third) year only. In a Post-Graduate Course, opportunity is offered advanced pupils to pursue the study of art. The Trustees have provided instruction of the highest order in every branch of Drawing and Painting, and have fitted up apartments expressly for the accommodation of pupils in these highly useful and beautiful arts. The students are taught to draw and paint from familiar objects, the design being to cultivate the eye as well as the hand. Lectures on the history of art were given during the past winter, by Miss M. A. Hastings, to an advanced class of ladies. They will be resumed in October, 1882, and are commended to ladies who are planning a tour in Europe, or who desire to revise and systematize their recollections of its art treasures, as well as to graduates of the institution. Peculiar facilities for the study of art are afforded by an extensive series of photographs, illustrating the various schools of architecture and of painting. Casts of antique and modern statues serve not only for the use of students of art and for models in drawing, but as a means of culture to all the pupils, who are, by the daily sight of these works of art, familiarized with the purest types of beauty in form and expression. — Pencil and crayon drawing, $15 per quarter; oil, water color, and pastel painting, painting on slate and marble, decorating china, tiles, pottery, etc., and photograph painting, each $20 per quarter. — Miss Virginia Granbery, teacher of drawing, oil painting, etc.; Miss Mary M. Platt, teacher of elementary drawing. — During the last term 68 students were engaged in the study of the higher branches of drawing and painting.

REMBRANDT CLUB. — Organized 1880. — Pres., W. W. Kenyon, 368 Union St.; V. P., J. M. Burt; Sec., L. D. Mason, M. D., 171 Joralemon St.; Treas., J. W. Stearns. — Object : The cultivation and encouragement of art. — Present membership, about 40. — Initiation fee, $5 ; annual dues, $5. Honorary members may also be elected. — The Club has no rooms. The meetings, lectures, etc., are held in the drawing-rooms and picture galleries of its members.

SCRATCHERS CLUB. — Organized Jan. 25, 1882. — Officers: Pres., G. W. H. Ritchie, 109 Liberty St., New York; V. P., Carleton Wiggins ; Sec., Benj. Lander, 1354 Bergen St., Brooklyn, or 14 John St., New York; Treas., J. C. Williamson. — Object: The practical study of the art of etching among its members. — Membership confined to professional artists. — The Club meets weekly, from first Wednesday in October to fourth Wednesday of April, inclusive.

WINTER ART ASSOCIATION. — 249 Fulton St.   Organized, 1880. — Officers : Pres., Dr. Cruikshank ; Treas., M. J. Gates. — Object : To provide practical instruction, free of charge, in drawing, perspective, anatomy, composition, etc., to young people who need such knowledge in their calling, but cannot afford to visit costly institutions.   Instructor, Prof. Peter Winter, 87 Hanson Pl., who gives his services free of charge. — Present number of members, 50.

Brunswick, Me. — BOWDOIN COLLEGE. — Officers : Pres of the B'd of Trustees and of the Fac., Joshua L. Chamberlain, LL. D.; Sec. of B'd of Tr., Franklin M. Drew, A. M.; Sec. of the Fac., Henry L. Chapman, A. M.; Treas., Stephen J. Young, A. M.; Curator of the Art Collections, Prof. Henry Johnson, A. M. — No art instruction of any kind is given in the regular college course. Drawing and the history of architecture were included in the course in Engineering, but no such course was offered for the year 1881-2 — *The Gallery of Art.* By the will of the Hon. Jas. Bowdoin, the College in 1811 came into possession of his entire collection of paintings, about 100 in number, procured by him during a residence of three years in Paris, after the closing of his services as Minister of the U. S. at the Court of Madrid in Dec., 1805. It is claimed that many of these pictures are genuine works by the old masters; and when it is remembered that the time was one of great disturbance in Europe, the possibility of obtaining such works is readily seen. For years the College had no room in which the pictures could be properly exhibited, and many of them were so dingy that it was difficult to tell what they were. At the suggestion of Hon. R. C. Winthrop and others, they were, in 1850, put into the hands of D. Chase and G. Howorth, of Boston, for restoration, and when they were replaced, the College first became aware of the value of its possession. Important paintings presented by other donors, including the entire collection of the late Col. Geo. W. Boyd, have since been added, and similar donations are continually being made. The last printed report of the College acknowledges the receipt of six paintings, and quite a number of busts, casts from the antique, etc., within the year. The Gallery of Paintings occupies the room over the Library in the east end of the Chapel, and is called the Walker Gallery, in memory of Mrs. Sophia Walker. The statuary is placed in a room in the north wing of the Chapel. The Bowdoin bequest included also 138 drawings by old masters, marked with the names of Titian, Andrea del Sarto, Correggio, Tintoretto, etc., but these had been quite forgotten, until they were rediscovered some years ago. Two friends of the college have lately given $400 to provide for the care and exhibition of these valuable works. A new and complete catalogue of the gallery has lately been prepared, and will soon be published. The present catalogue, printed in 1870, contains only a list of the Bowdoin paintings and the Boyd collection. Attached to the former (some of which were sold by the board years ago as "nudities") are such names as Raphael, Titian, N. Poussin, Berghem, Hondekoeter, Van Dyck, Rubens, Vonet, Hogarth, etc Of works by American artists there are the portraits of Madison and Jefferson by Stuart, and the full-length portraits of Gov. Bowdoin and lady (1748) by Robert Feke, one of the earliest native painters who has left any record. In the Boyd collection there are also several old masters, and a portrait of Thos. Fluker by Copley. — The Art Collections will for the present be open to visitors daily, Sundays excepted, from 1 to 3 P. M.

MAINE HISTORICAL SOCIETY. — Collection of Indian relics, etc.

Buffalo, N. Y. — BUFFALO FINE ARTS ACADEMY. — Young Men's Association Building. Instituted Nov. 11, 1862; incorporated Dec. 4, 1862; gallery opened Dec. 23, 1862. — Officers (for 1881): Pres., Thos. F. Rochester; V. Ps., Geo. L. Williams, Geo. B. Hayes, Wm. H. Gratwick; Cor. Sec., Ammi M. Farnham; Rec. Sec., Alb. T. Chester; Treas., Richd. K. Noye. — Object: To encourage and cultivate the Fine Arts, and to maintain and establish a permanent gallery in the city of Buffalo, for the exhibition of paintings, sculptures, and other works of art, and to use such other means as shall be desirable and efficient for the promotion and advancement of the same. — It appears that this association has life members only (113 according to last obtainable report, 1880), who are required to contribute not less than $100 to its funds. — The Academy owns a number of paintings by American artists (A. Bierstadt, Wm. Hart, R. Gignoux, J. A. Oertel, A. D. Shattuck, W. Whittredge, W. S. Haseltine, J. Humphrey, E. D. Howard, L. G. Sellstedt, C. C. Coleman, E. Moran, E. H. Remington, Burr H. Nicholls, Hamilton Hamilton, E. K. Baker, F. Penfold, R. Swain Gifford, Thos. Le Clear, W. H. Beard, A. W. Thompson, Jervis McEntee, E. Wood Perry), Phillipoteaux's "French Revolution of 1848," a series of copies from paintings by old masters, some casts from the antique, and a small collection of photographs. It also holds transient exhibitions. [This notice is made up from documents furnished in 1881, as later documents were not obtainable, in spite of repeated requests.]

DECORATIVE ART SOCIETY. — 51 West Genesee St. Established Jan., 1879; incorporated Nov., 1881. — Officers: Pres., Mrs. E. Carlton Sprague; V. Ps, Mrs. Thos. F. Rochester, Mrs. A. P. Nichols, Mrs. Geo. Truscott, Mrs. F. H. Rosseel, Mrs. H. M. Kent; Sec. and Treas., Mrs. E. B. Seymour; Cor. Sec., Mrs. S. F. Mixer; For. Cor. Sec., Miss M. M. Love. — Objects identical with those of similar associations. — Subscribing members, $2.00 p. a. — The Society maintains the following classes: Rudimental drawing, drawing from casts, design, sketching from life, and out-of-door sketching (Edw. L. Chichester, teacher; day classes, 25 cents, evening classes, 10 cents per lesson); Flower painting in oil and water-colors (Miss Chesnutwood, 25 cents per lesson); Tapestry painting (Miss Chesnutwood, $1 per lesson); China painting (Mrs. C. F. A. Bielby, $1 per lesson); Kensington embroidery (Mrs. F. L. Dole, $3 for 6 lessons); French white embroidery (Madame Hamerel, $1.50 for 6 lessons). There is also a Children's Class. Free classes for the benefit of those whose means are limited will be established as soon as the finances of the Society will permit.

Burlington, Vt. — University of Vermont. — An art gallery, known as *The Park Gallery of Art*, is connected with this institution. [No reply to repeated inquiries.]

Cambridge, Mass. — Harvard Art Club. — Gray's Hall. — Composed of students of Harvard College. The Club has arranged several public exhibitions of etchings and of studies, etc., belonging to the Fine Arts Department of the College. It has also published Mr. J. S. Clarke's paper on the Hypæthral Question, and a series of six mezzotints executed by Mr. Chas. H. Moore, from his own drawings ; and has shared in the cost of printing the Assos Report of the Archæological Institute.

Harvard University. — Founded 1636. — Pres., Chas. Wm. Eliot, LL. D., 17 Quincy St.; Treas., Edw. Wm. Hooper, Reservoir St.; Bursar, Allen Danforth, 7 Wadsworth House. — The University comprehends the following departments: Harvard College, the Divinity School, the Law School, the Medical School, the Dental School, the Lawrence Scientific School, the Museum of Comparative Zoölogy, the Bussey Institution (a School of Agriculture), the College Library, and the Astronomical Observatory. The Peabody Museum (see below) is a constituent part of the University ; but its relations to it are affected by peculiar provisions. — *Harvard College.* The prescribed studies in the College do not include drawing ; it may, however, be taken as an elective study, and is recommended to those students who intend to study engineering. No Honors are given for proficiency in the Fine Arts, but they are included in the subjects for Honorable Mention. The marks obtained in drawing, if taken as one of the prescribed number of elective studies, are counted the same as those for any other study, in the recommendation for a degree. Among the themes proposed by the Faculty for last year's Bowdoin Prize Dissertations, there was one taken from the history of art, viz.: " The Relation between Etruscan and Greek Art." — *Lawrence Scientific School.* In the Engineering Courses, mechanical drawing, perspective, etc., are practised throughout the four years, besides free-hand and water-color drawing, four hours a week, in the third year. The course in Chemistry includes mechanical drawing, four hours a week, in the fourth year ; the courses in Natural History, free-hand and water-color drawing, four hours a week, in the second and third years ; those in Mathematics, Physics, and Astronomy, mechanical drawing, four hours a week, in the third year. Instructors : Chas. H. Moore, 19 Follen St., Drawing and Principles of Design ; Henry L. Eustis, A. M., 29 Kirkland St., Perspective ; Francis W. Dean, S. B., 40 Matthews Hall, Mechanical Drawing. — *The Department of Fine Arts.* The studies in this department are open as electives to all regular students ; special students are also admitted. It includes the following courses : 1. Principles of Delineation, Color, and Chiaro-scuro (Ruskin, Viollet-le-Duc, Pyne's Perspective) ; 2. Principles of Design in Painting, Sculpture, and Architecture (Viollet-le-Duc's "Dictionnaire raisonné de l'architecture française," Ruskin, Sir Joshua Reynolds, Woltmann's "History of Painting ") ; 3. Ancient Art (Von Reber's " History of Ancient Art," translated by Clarke) ; 4. Art in Italy from the Conquest of Greece by the Romans to the year 1600 ; 5. Greek Art ; 6. Romanesque and Gothic Art from the year 1000 to 1350. Ability to read German is required of students taking courses 3 to 6. No preparation is required for admission. The instruction begins with elementary exercises from the flat, and progresses to working from natural objects and casts, in pencil, chalk, and water-colors. The study of the nude and of oil painting is not attempted, as, for the present at least, the school is not of the nature of a professional school. The instruction given is simply disciplinary, and an auxiliary to general culture. — Instructors : Chas. Eliot Norton, A. M., Kirkland St, Prof. of the History of Art ; Chas. H. Moore, 19 Follen St., Drawing and Principles of Design. — Mr. Moore's classes are at present attended by 30 students (27 regular, 3 special ; all males) ; Prof. Norton's lectures on the history of art are much more numerously attended, mostly by regular students. — The tuition fee for regular students is $150 p. a. Special students pay at the rate of $15 for one hour a week of instruction during the academic year, up to $150, but in no case shall the fee be less than $30 a year. — *Art Collections.* The Fine Arts Department is forming a collection to illustrate the leading characteristics of the great schools of painting, sculpture, and architecture, consisting of casts, photographs, autotypes, prints (etchings, plates from Turner's "Liber Studiorum," etc), and copies in oil and water-colors (many of the latter made by Mr. Chas. H. Moore during a visit in Europe). The collection, which grows but slowly, as the appropriation is very small, has been placed in room B, Sever Hall, and is open to the public during term time, on application by letter to Mr. Moore. — *The Library* of the College in Gore Hall contains a good proportion of books on art and its history, and is being carefully completed as rapidly as the means will permit. There is also a collection of coins in the Library. The Gray Collection of Engravings, formerly kept there, has been temporarily deposited with the Museum of Fine Arts in Boston. The privilege of borrowing books is granted, under special regulations, to persons not connected with the University. — Open free every week day, except holidays, from 9 A. M. till 5 P. M., or till sunset when that is before 5; in vacation and recess the hour of closing is 2 P. M. On Sundays, during term time, open to readers only, after 1 P. M.

MEMORIAL HALL. — Cambridge and Quincy Sts. — The Dining Hall in this building (erected in commemoration of students of Harvard University who fell in the service of their country) contains a large and valuable collection of about 80 portraits and portrait busts, mostly of persons connected with the College as officers, benefactors, etc. As a record of the history of portrait painting in the U. S., this collection is quite important. Besides a number of old pictures (most of them of indifferent quality), whose authors are not known, there are specimens of the work of the following painters: Smybert, Copley (quite a number, including the fine portrait of Mrs. Thos. Boylston), Savage (portrait of Washington), Stuart, Stuart and Sully, Frothingham, Trumbull, Newton, Alexander, Alvan Fisher, Bass Otis, Chester Harding, Page, Healey, Hunt, Hayward, Jos. Ames, Mooney, and Cobb; Sculptors: Houdon (bust of Washington), Lander, Hiram Powers, R. S. Greenough, H. Greenough, Carew, Story, Crawford, Clevenger, and Dexter. There is no catalogue, but all the pictures and busts are plainly labelled. The beautiful glass mosaic windows in the same hall are by John La Farge. — Open free to the public on week days, meal hours excepted.

PEABODY MUSEUM OF AMERICAN ARCHÆOLOGY AND ETHNOLOGY. — Divinity Ave. Founded by Geo. Peabody, Oct. 8, 1866, as a department of Harvard University. — Officers B'd of Trustees : Chairm., Robt. C. Winthrop, 90 Marlborough St., Boston ; Treas., Theod. Lyman, 191 Commonwealth Ave., Boston. Officers of the Museum : Curator, F. W. Putnam ; Asst. Curator, Lucien Carr. — Of the fund of $150,000 given by Mr. Peabody, $60,000 have been set apart for building purposes, and the balance has been invested as an endowment fund. The building at present occupied by the Museum, and opened in 1878, is only one fifth of the structure contemplated. The land was given by Harvard College. — This Museum, founded especially for the study of American Archæology and Ethnology, and for the preservation of collections relating thereto, is the only one of its character in the country. To it students may come for special investigations, with the assurance that, so far as American archæology is concerned, they have access to the most important collections that have been brought together, while the material for comparison with that of other parts of the world is not wanting. The large collections from North, Central, and South America, which are extraordinarily rich in everything pertaining to the civilization of the extinct as well as the present native races of these countries, including their architecture, pottery, sculpture, etc., and the smaller collections from

Egypt, Southern Africa, Asia, Australia, and the Pacific Islands, have already been placed on exhibition in a series of rooms, while the collections from Europe, particularly rich in objects illustrating the stone age of Denmark and Italy, and in interesting remains from the Swiss Lakes, are now in course of arrangement. The Museum also sends out exploring expeditions, and the investigations carried on during the present year in Nicaragua, among the mounds and ancient burial-places of the Ohio and Cumberland Valleys, and the shell-heaps on the coast of Maine, have been very fruitful of important results. Especial interest attaches to a number of remarkable fragments of small-sized sculptures from the Ohio Valley, which place the so-called mound-builders much higher up in the scale of civilization than previous knowledge seemed to warrant. Among the later important additions to the Museum is a collection of small sculptures in gypsum from Yucatan and Mexico, presented by Mr. Alex. Agassiz. — The Museum publishes Annual Reports which are offered for sale, and which, besides the account of the growth of the institution, contain papers of interest on subjects pertaining to American archæology, etc. During the winter months the curator delivers lectures in the Museum, which are announced in advance in the Harvard Bulletin and in the Weekly Calendar published by the University. — *The Library* of the Museum, as yet small, but constantly growing, is open to students for reference. — The endowment fund being insufficient, the Museum must depend to a great extent upon donations. Its explorations are entirely carried on by funds given by patrons for the purpose. — Open free on week days, holidays excepted, from 9 A. M. to 5 P. M.

Charleston, S. C. — CAROLINA ART ASSOCIATION. — Washington Square. Organized 1857. — Officers: Pres., Dr. G. E. Manigault ; Sec., Prof. A. Sachtleben. — Objects : The promotion of the Fine Arts, by means of public exhibitions, by opening a school and a library for art, or by any other modes that may be deemed expedient. — Membership: Life, on payment of $100; annual, $5 initiation fee, and $5 p. a. Present number of members 80. — This Association was inaugurated in the early part of the year 1857. The list of its members amounted then to over 130, at $10 p. a. each. Its first exhibition of paintings was held in the same year, and consisted of a loan collection, furnished by those residents of the city who were the owners of valuable paintings. Most of these were returned at the end of the first year, and over 300 new members having then been enrolled, the Association, with other means that were contributed, was able to order an historical painting of the artist Leutze, the subject being " Sergeant Jasper rescuing the Flag during the Attack of the British Fleet upon Sullivan's Island, June 28, 1776." Arrangements were at the same time made with a picture dealer in Germany by which paintings by German artists were sent to the Association, at their expense, for exhibition and sale. Several of these were purchased, and there seemed in 1861, at the expiration of four years, every prospect of the future of the Association being assured. The great fire of Dec., 1861, however, destroyed the gallery and all of its contents, except one painting by the late J. Beaufain Irving, the subject being the execution of Sir Thomas Moore. There being a small invested fund that was still owned by the Association, it was revived in Feb., 1879, and in June of that year it defrayed the expenses of the inaugural of the bust of Wm. Gilmore Simms. In Dec., 1880, an exhibition of paintings was held in Market Hall, which was composed of works loaned by citizens and over 50 oil paintings and water-colors sent on by New York artists, all of which were for sale. The Association purchased three of the best of these, and distributed them by lot among its members. There has been no exhibition since then, but at the anniversary meeting of 1882, it was decided to establish an Art School, the arrangements for which were intrusted to a committee with full power to act. This committee has since purchased a building, well situated on Washington Square, not far from the City Hall, and it is now being altered and improved so as to be fitted for the purposes of both an Art School and an Art Gallery. It is hoped that everything will be ready for a start by Oct. 15. The instruction to be provided during the first year will be given in two classes, one primary and the other more advanced. It will consist altogether in drawing from plaster models; but if the school meets with the favor of the public, and prospers, its scope will be gradually enlarged.

Charlestown, Mass. — PUBLIC LIBRARY. — City Hall, City Square. — Libr., Cornelius S. Cartee. — This is one of the branches of the Boston Public Library. It owns a number of portraits (Washington, by Frothingham after Stuart; Jackson, by A. C. Hoit after Vanderlyn, etc.); John Pope's " Webster delivering his Address on the Completion of Bunker Hill Monument"; and " The Landing at Plymouth Rock," an early work by S. F. B. Morse, who was a native of Charlestown.

Chicago, Ill. — BOHEMIAN CLUB. — Organized 1880. — Officers: Pres., Mrs. E. L. S. Adams, 119 Drexel Boulevard; Sec., Mrs. Theo. Shaw, 2124 Calumet Ave.; Treas., Miss C. D. Wade, Chic. Acad. of F. A.; Examining Comm., Miss Marie Koupal, 70 Reaper Block, Miss Ida Burgess, 96 State St., Miss A. D Kellogg, Chic. Acad. of F. A. — Composed of women artists, at present 25, who meet every Saturday afternoon for sketching from the costumed model, the members posing in turn, and by criticising compositions brought in for the purpose. During the summer sixteen of the members went together to a farm-house in Wisconsin, and brought home over 200 sketches as the result of two weeks' work.

CHICAGO ACADEMY OF DESIGN. — Monroe St., American Express Building, Room 10. Organized 1867; incorporated 1869. — Officers (1881): Pres., Enoch Root; Rec. Sec. and Business Manager, John F. Stafford. — Objects: The founding and maintenance of Schools of Art for the cultivation of the Arts of Drawing, Painting, Sculpture, Architecture, Engraving, and Design, and for the formation of a Gallery of objects of Art. — For the season of 1881-2 classes were announced in Landscape, Figure, Flower, and Historical Painting, Drawing, and Composition, terms $20 per month (13 lessons), J. F Gookins, Director; and in Decorative and China Painting, same terms, Mrs. L. W. Holcombe, Teacher. — Previous to the great fire of 1871 the Academy was in promising condition. It had a building of its own on Adams St. Its property was (and still is) free from taxation by special act of Legislature, and the catalogue issued in the year of the fire enumerated 38 Academicians, 33 Associates, 5 Honorary Academicians (elected upon payment of $500), and 26 Fellow Members (elected upon payment of $100). Besides these, there were also annual members at $10. The schools were reported to be prosperous and amply equipped. The fire, however, swept away every vestige of the property, and the insurance proved worthless. Quarters were indeed rented, and schools opened, but the financial panic operated against them, and they closed in debt. Renewed efforts are now being made to give efficiency to the valuable charter of the Academy, and to obtain a grant of land from Congress, on the tract known as Dearborn Park. The building to be there erected is to contain free Art Schools, a free Gallery, studios (from the rental of which part of the revenue is to be derived), and an observatory 255 feet above the street level, reached by elevator, and open to visitors on payment of a small fee. — The Academy of Design is entirely controlled by professional artists. [Mostly from documents published in 1881. No later information to be obtained.]

CHICAGO ACADEMY OF FINE ARTS. — " D " Battery, Lake Front. Organized 1879. — Officers: Pres., C. L. Hutchinson; V. P., Geo. E. Adams; Treas., L. J. Gage; Sec, N. H. Carpenter. — The active control is vested in a board of twenty-one Trustees, chosen from a body of Governing Members, who are qualified, after election, by the payment of an admission fee of $100, and $25 annually. The by-laws provide also for Honorary and Annual Members, but so far the society has remained a skeleton organization, consisting of the Trustees alone. — Objects: The founding and maintenance of Schools of Art and Design, the formation of Collections of objects of art, and the cultivation and extension of the arts of design by any appropriate means. — So far the schools only have been organized. It is the aim of these schools to provide as ample facilities for obtaining an art education as do the best schools abroad. At the same time, those who prefer to go to Europe will be given the preparation necessary to enable them to pass the entrance examinations of the European schools. The leading instructors were educated in the best schools of London, Paris, and Munich. Amateurs can obtain the best possible advantages upon the most reasonable terms. — Classes : Drawing from Flat, Cast, and Life, and Painting from Costumed Model ; teachers, H. F. Spread, Miss A. D. Kellogg, A. J. Rupert, Miss C. D. Wade. Water-Color, H. F. Spread. Painting from Still-Life, J. H. Vanderpoel. Pen and Ink, Pencil Drawing, and Etching, J. H. Vanderpoel. Landscape Painting, D. F. Bigelow. Drawing and Painting from the Nude (separate classes for the two sexes), A. J. Rupert. Composition, A. J. Rupert. Fifteen-Minute Sketching Class, under direction of students Children's Class, Miss C. D. Wade. Perspective, N. H. Carpenter. Artistic Anatomy, Dr. S V. Clevenger. Sketching tours are usually made in summer by some of the students under the guidance of a teacher. Besides the Day Classes, there are also Night Classes three times a week. — Matriculation fee, $2 ; tuition fees, $25 for term of 12 weeks, $10 per month, or $7 for 10 lessons. Fractional rates for special subjects, etc. Three terms : fall term, Oct. 2 to Dec. 23, 1882 ; winter, Jan. 8 to Mch. 31, 1883 ; spring, Apr. 9 to June 30, 1883. Students may enter at any time, paying from date of entry. — No qualifications are required for drawing from the flat, perspective, anatomy, sketch class, or children's class. For antique class three drawings from the flat, for life class three drawings from the antique, must be submitted. In other classes satisfactory evidence of proficiency must be given to instructor. In the case of amateurs, the examinations will not be so rigid as with regular students. Medals and prizes are given at the end of each school year. — Number of students, season 1881–2, 300 (88 males, 212 females). — The school is reported to be prosperous, the tuition fees alone amounting to between $6,000 and $7,000 annually, and covering all current expenses. The Academy has lately purchased a building, measuring 54 by 106 ft., cor. Michigan Ave. and Warren St., at a cost of $45,000, and another building, 54 by 74 ft., is to be erected on the adjoining ground. The main building cannot be occupied until the leases on it have expired. Meanwhile the rents go to the Academy. All communications concerning the schools must be addressed to Mr. N. H. Carpenter, Sec.

CHICAGO ARTISTS' CLUB. — Sec., A. Payne, 170 State St., 5th floor. [No reply to inquiries.]

CHICAGO ART LEAGUE. — Ashland Block, cor. Clark and Randolph Sts. Organized March, 1879. — Officers : Alex. Schilling, 81 Ashland Block ; Treas., Chas. M. Erwin, 100 Ashland Block. — Objects : The general benefit and advancement of art in Chicago. — The members are all young professional artists. Candidates must submit a sketch from nature, in black and white or in color. Initiation fee, $5 ; monthly dues, $1.25. Present number of members, 18. — Last winter the League organized a life class from the nude, and the coming winter a costume class is to be added. — The First Exhibition of the League was held at O'Brien's Gallery from Feb. 15 to 22, 1881 ; it contained 73 works, of which only a few were sold, at nominal prices. The Second Annual Exhibition, held in the same gallery, from Feb. 25 to March 10, 1882, contained 91 works, of which 28 were sold for $650. — A Black and White Exhibition is to be held in November. Only members are allowed to contribute to these exhibitions. The League has rented two large rooms, which are to be fitted up as a gallery. It has been the recipient of some donations.

CHICAGO CHAPTER OF THE AMERICAN INSTITUTE OF ARCHITECTS. Pres., Augustus Bauer ; Sec., S. A. Treat, 80 Dearborn St. (See p. l.)

CHICAGO SOCIETY OF DECORATIVE ART. — Rooms 6, 7, and 8, 170 State St. Organized May 24, 1877. — Officers: Pres., Mrs. John N. Jewett, 412 Dearborn Ave.; V. Ps., Mrs. S. M. Nickerson, Mrs. Corydon Beckwith, Mrs. W. E. Stroug, Mrs. B. F. Ayer; Rec. Sec., Miss N. B. Hibbard, 1701 Prairie Ave.; Cor. Sec., Miss Mary Park; Treas., Mrs. Chas. Henrotin. 353 La Salle Ave. — Objects: To create in Chicago a desire for artistic decoration, and for a knowledge of the best methods of ornamentation; to provide training in artistic industries, and enable decorative artists to render their labor remunerative. — Any person may become a member by an annual payment of $5. Part of the revenue of the Society is derived from a commission of 10% charged on sales, but its expenses are chiefly defrayed by the annual dues of members. Number of members (1881), 249. — Classes in Kensington embroidery, pencil and crayon drawing, painting in oil and water-color, porcelain painting, and wood carving: teacher, Mr. I. E. Scott. Most of the pupils pay for the instruction given, but there are also a number of free pupils, whose tuition fees are provided for by donations. — The Society holds Loan Exhibitions, arranges lectures and conversations on subjects connected with decorative art, and maintains a lending library for the use of members and of contributors to its salesrooms.

INTERSTATE INDUSTRIAL EXPOSITION OF CHICAGO. — Exposition Building. — Art Committee: Jas. H. Dole, Chairm.; Lawrence C. Earle, Henry F. Spread; Miss Sara T. Hallowell, Sec. — The Tenth Annual Exhibition of this association was held from Sept. 6 to Oct. 21, 1882. The Art Department connected with these exhibitions has grown in excellence and importance from year to year, and the sales are considerable. At the Exhibition of 1881, 65 works of art, valued at $30,075, were sold, out of 382 exhibited. — The Exposition Company also owns a small nucleus of a permanent collection, in the shape of a number of casts from antique statuary.

Cincinnati, O. — CINCINNATI CHAPTER OF THE AM. INST. OF ARCHITECTS. — Sec., Charles Crapsey, 46 Wiggin's Building. (See p. 1.)

CINCINNATI INDUSTRIAL EXPOSITION. — Officers B'd of Comm.: Pres., W. W. Peabody; V. Ps., Hugh McCollum, Michael Ryan, Jos. Hargrave; Sec., Wm. H. Stewart; Treas., Ben. E. Hopkins; Chairm. Art Comm., Harvey Anderson. — An exhibition of works of art is connected with the yearly expositions held by this association. At the Tenth Exposition, which took place from Sept. 6 to Oct. 7, 1882, there were sold 21 pictures, valued at $3,000, and one work of sculpture, "Psyche," by E. Keyser, of Baltimore, valued at $2,000.

CINCINNATI MUSEUM ASSOCIATION. — Incorporated Feb. 15, 1881. — Officers: Pres., Jos. Longworth; Treas., Julius Dexter; Director, A. T. Goshorn; Sec., R. H. Galbreath. — Objects: Establishing and maintaining in Cincinnati a Museum, wherein may be gathered, preserved, and exhibited valuable and interesting objects of every kind and nature, and for the further purpose of using the contents of such Museum for education, through the establishment of classes and otherwise, as may be found expedient. The formation of the Museum is to be based on the general plan of the South Kensington Museum. It will include departments in art, science, natural history, etc., and instruction in the subjects illustrated by the objects deposited in the Museum. The opportunities for art education are to be the first to be made available. — The contributions toward the general fund, begun by Mr. C. W. West with a subscription of $150,000, amounted at the date of the First Annual Report, March 6, 1882, to $316,501, contributed by 455 subscribers. Mr. C. W. West has also endowed the institution with an additional fund of $150,000, which, as at present invested, yields $10,500 annually. The city of Cincinnati has ceded to the Association a tract of 19.71 acres of land in Eden Park, which it is to occupy free of all taxes, assessments, etc., so long as it maintains thereon a building or buildings devoted to the objects stated, as nearly free from all costs and charges to the public as may be consistent with keeping it in repair, etc. The rest of the grounds, not occupied by the

30 CINCINNATI, O.

buildings, are to be maintained as a free park at the expense of the Association.
The buildings to cost not less than $50,000. — The Association consists of 148 stock-
holders, who are not allowed to hold more than one share, of $25, bearing no dividend
or interest, each. [" The plan of organization of the Cincinnati Museum Association,"
says the Report, " adopted by the subscribers to the fund, gave to each subscriber the
option of becoming a shareholder in the corporation. One hundred and forty-eight
subscribers in this manner became shareholders, and represent the entire number of
shares of the corporation." The manner of becoming a shareholder is not, however,
indicated in the Report.] No share can be transferred without the consent of the
Association, and the shares of deceased members revert to the Association. It is
provided, however, that the Association shall at all times keep placed in the owner-
ship of proper persons the full number of 148 shares, and to that end shall, within
30 days after becoming the owner of a share, dispose of it to such person as the
Trustees may elect. Any 25 resident freeholders in Cincinnati may require an investigation of the Museum management and affairs, through one or more experts. —
The Trustees, ten in number, are elected by the stockholders, two being renewed each
year. The Mayor of the city is, *ex officio*, a member of the Board, and two other
members may be appointed by the Common Council. — Mr. James W. McLaughlin
has been engaged as architect, and definite steps have been taken to procure plans for
a building. Temporary rooms in Music Hall were opened to private view on Feb. 10,
1882, and have since been open to the public, from 10 A. M. to 4 P. M. daily, Sundays
excepted. Admission, 25 cents. The Trustees have accepted as gifts valuable art
treasures from Mr. Joseph Longworth (a large number of drawings by Lessing,
etc.), the Women's Art Museum Association (an older organization, now dissolved,
which began the agitation for an art museum), Mr. George Hoadley (Turner's " Liber
Studiorum "), Mrs. Eliza Longworth Flagg, Mrs. S. N. Pike, the Ninth Cincinnati
Exposition, etc. The temporary exhibition includes part of the others, viz.,
etc., by Lessing, above alluded to ; the " Liber Studiorum " of Turner ; a ceramic display exhibiting the progress of the art in Cincinnati, from the first experiments by
Miss McLaughlin to the latest work of the Rockwood Pottery ; and a loan collection
of painting, bric-à-brac, armor, etc. The only catalogue so far issued is one of part of
the Lessing collection and of the " Liber Studiorum." Price, 25 cents.

CINCINNATI POTTERY CLUB. — Organized 1879. — Officers: Pres., Miss M. Louise
McLaughlin ; Sec., Miss Clara C. Newton, 207 Eastern Ave. ; Treas., Miss Alice B.
Holabird. — Object : Painting pottery in under-glaze, and modelling in relief upon wet
clay objects in pottery. — Number of members limited to 15 ; no vacancies. — An Annual Reception is held in May. The Club used to have rooms at the Rockwood Pottery, but at present has no room.

ETCHING CLUB. — Officers : Pres., Dr. D. S. Young ; Sec., Emery H. Barton. [This
Club used to hold regular meetings, to which invitations were issued, etched by its
members. It has, however, been dormant for some time, although it is still in
existence.]

HISTORICAL AND PHILOSOPHICAL SOCIETY. — Cabinet of Indian curiosities and
Mound Builders' relics.

OHIO MECHANICS' INSTITUTE OF THE CITY OF CINCINNATI. — Organized 1828 ;
incorporated Feb. 9, 1829. — Officers: Pres, Thomas Gilpin ; V. P., Jas. Dale ;
Rec. Sec., W. B. Bruce ; Treas., Hugh McCollum ; Clerk, John B. Heich ; Comm. of
School of Design, W. B. Bruce, Wm. H. Stewart.—*The School of Design* connected with
the Institute was established in 1856. Aim : The teaching of mechanical, architectural,
and artistic drawing for the instruction of apprentices. — Departments and Teachers :
Prin., John B. Heich ; Mechanical Dept., in charge of Ernest Lietze, Geo. Wadman, Bert L. Baldwin ; Architectural, Wm. W. Franklin, W. S. Burrows; Artistic,
W. R. McComas, Alb. J. Kaiser ; Original Designing, W. R. McComas, Alb. J.

Kaiser; Modelling in Clay, C. L. Feltweis; Geometry and Mathematics, Jas. B. Stanwood. Full course, 3 years. Sessions, Tuesday and Friday of each week, from 7 to 9 A. M. The Life Class organized four years ago, because there was no adequate opportunity for such study in the city at that time, has been discontinued as no longer necessary, and in a great measure out of the particular line of tuition applied to the industrial arts. — Tuition free; pupils must provide materials and instruments. — Pupils, males only : Mechan. Dept., 117 ; Arch., 58 ; Artistic, 78 ; Modelling, 12 ; Geom. and Math., 15 : total, 280 for the season of 1881-2. — Bronze medals are awarded the first year ; silver medals the second ; gold medals or the badge of the Institute the third. "Honorable Mentions" and Degrees of Merit" are also given. Pupils who have attended for three consecutive years receive certificates attesting their attendance. —The School of Design is eventually to be developed into a *School of Technology*, and the first move toward the realization of the plan, in conjunction with other bodies, was made in 1881.

UNIVERSITY OF CINCINNATI. — Incorporated April 16, 1870. — Officers : Chairm. of B'd of Directors, Alphonso Taft ; Clerk of the B'd, T. B. Disney, N. E. cor. 3d and Main Sts. Rector, Thomas Vickers, B. D. — Upon its organization the Board received an estate left in trust for the city by Chas. McMicken in 1858. Since then the endowments have been increased by important donations from the Cincinnati Astronomical Society, Joseph Longworth, John Kilgour, and by a bequest from the Rev. Sam'l J. Browne. The University has also received assistance from the city. — It consists of three departments : The Academic, or Dept. of Literature and Science ; the School of Design or Art Dept.; and the Observatory, or Astronomical Dept. In the first and last of these departments no drawing is taught, with the exception of what is necessary in connection with engineering. — *The Art Department* was organized in 1869, as "The McMicken School of Art and Design," with one teacher and 30 pupils. Aims : The Directors desire practical results from the Art School, so that those who pass through it shall be fitted for the active duties of life, and especially for the branch of art chosen as a profession. A thoroughly graded course has been adopted, with a view of graduating such students (with a Diploma from the University) as shall have proved themselves worthy of the honor at the end of the curriculum. — Courses of Study : Drawing, Perspective and Pictorial Design, in Black and White, extending from elementary drawing to drawing from the living model, and original pictorial composition, 5 grades; Decorative Design, 4 grades ; Pen Drawing, 4 grades ; Water-Color Painting, from the elements to compositions from life subjects, 4 grades; Sculpture, 4 grades ; Wood Carving for Decorative Purposes, 4 grades. Full course, 5 years. Day and night classes in session from beginning of September to end of May. — Teachers : Principal, Thos. S. Noble; Decor. Design and Water-Color, Wm. H. Humphreys ; Drawing and Perspec., Rebecca R. Whittemore-Gregg, Martha Jane Keller ; Sculpture, Louis Thos. Rebisso ; Carving, Benn Pitman ; Temporary Teachers of Drawing, Nettie Wilson, Geo. Edw. Hopkins. — Students, both sexes, must be not less than thirteen years old, and must satisfy the principal that they are capable of pursuing the studies of the school to advantage. Application for admission to be made to the Clerk of the B'd of Directors. Attendance during season 1881-82 : Drawing and Design, day classes, 120 female, 12 male ; night classes, 20 female, 70 male : total, 222 (140 female, 82 male). Decorative Design, 42 f., 1 m.; Pen Drawing, 27 f., 1 m.; Water-Color, 32 f., 1 m.; Sculpture, 15 f., 7 m.; Carving, 26 f., 1 m. Grand total of attendance, 383 (282 f., 101 m.). The number of individual students was, however, only 281, as in the statement of attendance those pupils who attended several classes are counted more than once. — Fees : To *bona fide* residents of Cincinnati the instruction is free. Non-residents, $60 p. a. for day classes, $30 p. a. for night classes. All pupils pay $5 p. a. in the day classes, $3 p. a. in the night classes, for the use of models, etc. Materials must be furnished by the pupils. — Collections: Plaster casts from the antique, ornaments, natural fruits and flowers, etc.; autotypes from drawings of celebrated masters; library of books of reference. — At the close of the academic year a public exhibition is held of such work of the students as may seem meritorious to the Faculty. The work done in the various grades is classified into three orders of merit, and the diplomas given at the end of the fifth year are graded accordingly. Students who have completed three years with credit are entitled to a certificate stating their qualifications. [It is reported that Mr. Jos. Longworth has offered to endow the School of Design with $100,000, on condition of its being separated from the University.]

Cleveland, O. — CLEVELAND ACADEMY OF ART. — Incorp. Dec. 15, 1881. — Officers: Pres., J. H. Wade; V. Ps., Hon. G. M. Barber, W. J. Gordon; Sec. and Treas., W. H. Eckman. — Objects: To establish and maintain a School of Art, to afford facilities for the acquirement of a practical knowledge of the arts, and to procure, for the use and benefit of members and others, such appliances and material as may be necessary to further this purpose; to create and maintain a Gallery of Art. — The members of the corporation consist of the original incorporators (of whom there were 34), and of the following: 1. Members: initiation fee, $100; annual dues, $5; entitled, with the actual members of their families, to admission to the Gallery and to all exhibitions. 2. Individual members: initiation fee, $25; annual dues, $2; entitled to same privileges for themselves only. 3. Life Members, contributing $500; entitled with their families to all the privileges of the corporation during life excepting instruction. 4. Honorary Life Members, contributing $1000; entitled with their families to all the privileges of the corporation during life. Artists, in lieu of the membership fee, may present a work of art, subject to acceptance, of a value not less than $100, and shall not be subject to annual assessments. — A committee of five, known as Curators, three of whom must be artists, appointed by the Trustees, is charged with the management of all exhibitions, and everything pertaining to them. The Committee on Instruction, five in number, also appointed by the Board, must consist entirely of artists. It is placed, however, under the supervision of the Board, and the rules and regulations made by it for the use of the property of the Academy must be approved by the Board before they can be enforced. The president is *ex officio* a member of all committees, with a right to vote. — Nothing has as yet been done in the way of organizing classes; but the plans are being prepared for a building, and the collection of funds has begun.

WESTERN RESERVE AND NORTHERN OHIO HISTORICAL SOCIETY. — Museum of antiquities, principally relating to the West, including a fine collection of curiosities taken from the mounds on the Mississippi River, near Memphis; Babylonian and other Oriental antiquities. [No reply to inquiries.]

Columbia, Mo. — MISSOURI STATE UNIVERSITY. — Founded 1820; organized 1840. — Officers of the B'd of Curators: Pres., Hon. Jas S. Rollins, LL. D.; V. P., Jerre C. Cravens; Sec., Robt. L. Todd; Treas., Robt. Beverly Price. Officers of the Faculty: Pres., Sam'l Spahr Laws, A. M., M. D., LL. D.; Sec., Thos. Jefferson Lowry, S. M., C. E.; Libr. and Proctor, J. H. Drummond, A. B. — The departments of instruction are: 1. The Academic Schools of Language and Science. 2. The Professional Schools of Agriculture, Pedagogics, Engineering, Ar*, Law, Medicine, Mining and Metallurgy. Girls are admitted to the University in a special Ladies' Department, Mrs. O. A. Carr, Prin. — The University forms part of the State system of public instruction; but its only income, aside from tuition fees ($20 to $70 p a.), is from lands granted by the U. S. — In the four Academic Courses (Course in Arts, in Science, in Letters, and Girls' Course in Fine and Domestic Arts), the study of art is made a condition of graduation, the University of Missouri being the only institution in the U. S. in which this is the case. In the Girls' Course the study of drawing has to be taken completely. The work of this department is not confined to the art phase, but comprehends the study of form in general, i. e., the elements of scientific and pictorial representation. In a college course the educational feature of the work must receive more prominence than mere manual training, hence the latter is limited on the one hand to drill in the use of the compass and the straightedge, and exercises in the tracing of curves through fixed points ; on the other to surface representation, i. e., gradating of light and dark. Students are also encouraged to carve suitable examples out of soft substances. No copies are used ; all the exercises are conducted by dictation on the blackboard. The lessons thus learned must be put into practice by the students by drawing from objects at home, the work to be submitted when completed. It is stated that this system has given very good results. The subjects taught include descriptive geometry, shades and shadows, perspective, ornament, the laws of decoration and design, the forms of architecture, the laws of the beautiful, the theory of color, and object drawing practised at home, as already explained. Lead pencil and water-colors are the only media used. Professor of Art Dept , Conrad Diehl. The average annual attendance in the Art Dept. is about 150. Catalogues may be obtained by addressing " The Librarian of Missouri University," Columbia, Boone Co., Mo.

Columbus, O. — COLUMBUS ART ASSOCIATION. — Officers : Pres., Mrs. Ezra Bliss; 1st V. P., Mrs. Henry C. Noble; 2d V. P., Mrs Starling Loring ; Treas., Mrs. N K Wade ; Sec., Mrs. Jos. Millikin. — Object : To further and encourage the study of the Arts, theoretically and practically, through the medium of lectures, teachers, l ooks, pictures, models, and in all the most approved methods of the present day, so as to bring within the reach of all persons so desiring, the means of knowledge and of improvement in the Arts. — Members : Ladies only ; annual dues, $2. Honorary members, not entitled to vote, ladies or gentlemen, $5 annually. — The Association had 55 Members and 35 Honorary Members in 1881. No report published for 1882. The Association maintains an Art School and a Library (the result of donations), and arranges lectures and readings at its meetings. — The Columbus Art School, which is the title of the school maintained by the Association, opened for its fifth year, at 15 East Long St., on Oct. 16, 1882. — Day Classes : Drawing, Decorative Design, Landscape Sketching from Nature, Elementary Life Sketch Class, Advanced Life Sketch Class, Water-Color, Oil Painting, China Painting, Wood Carving, Art Needlework. Night Classes : Free Hand Drawing, Architectural and Machine Drawing. — Students, season 1881–2, about 220, male and female. — Board of Instruction : Prof. W. S. Goodnough, Director, 161 Hamilton Ave. ; Miss Dora M. Norton, Drawing and Water-Color Painting ; Miss Fannie Edgar, Wood Carving ; Mr. Chas. E. Cookman, Oil Painting ; Prof. W. A. Mason, Modelling in Clay. — Tuition fees vary from $3 to $14 per term of three months.

Contoocook, N. H. — NEW HAMPSHIRE ANTIQUARIAN SOCIETY. — Collection of antiquities of North American Indians, ancient and modern coins, etc. The Society contemplates the erection of a building in which to arrange its collections.

Dayton, O. — LADIES' ART DECORATIVE SOCIETY. — Summit St., bet. 3d and 4th Sts. — Officers : Pres , Miss C. Brown ; V. Ps , Mrs. E. M. Wood, Mrs. O. M. Guttschall, Mrs. J. B. Thresher ; Treas., Mrs. Agnes Platt ; Rec. Sec., Mrs J. W. Johnson ; Cor. Sec., Mrs. J. A. Robert. — This Society maintains a School of Art for the purpose of furnishing a thorough course of instruction in Drawing, Painting, Composition, and Modelling. The School is open for study from life and from the antique during forty weeks of the year. Arrangements are also made for those who wish to study during the summer vacation. Isaac Broome, Director. — Terms : Painting, Modelling, or Wood Carving, $12.50 for 10 lessons ; Drawing, $5 for 10 lessons. The payment of $2 entitles students to the use of the rooms of the Society during the year. — The Miami Art Pottery in connection with the school enables students to apply their knowledge of ceramic decoration and modelling to practical use.

Decatur, Ill. — Art Class. — Sec., Miss Alice N. Roberts. (See *Central Ill. Art Union*, Springfield, Ill.)

Young Ladies' Art Class. — Sec., Mrs. Fannie J. Sedgwick. (See *Central Ill. Art Union*, Springfield, Ill.)

Denver, Col. — Academy of Fine Arts Association. — Studio Flat, Tabor Opera House. Incorporated Feb., 1882. — Officers: Pres., J. Harrison Mills, 104 Opera House; V. P., W. H. M. Cax, Leadville, Col.; Treas., Wm. G. Evans, Evans Block; Sec., Chas. I. Sturgis, C. B. & Q. R. R. Offices. Directors: Hon. Frederick W. Pitkin, State House; T. J. O'Donnell, Tabor Block, Room 6; A. T. Mills, Mills Engraving Co.; M. C. Rovira, care J. H. Mills, 104 Opera House. — This Association is the outgrowth of several earlier combinations of students, the "Art Reading Circle," the "Denver Sketch Club," and the "Kitcat." — Objects: Art teaching, the fraternization of artists and art students, and the collection of works of art for public exhibition. — Membership: The Academicians, to which grade the Directors belong provisionally, decide all art matters. No candidates have as yet presented themselves for this grade. Associates, who are elected by the Academicians, must be students of art, and pay an initiation fee of $5, and $12 a year thereafter. The Associates elect the Directors, one of whom retires annually. — Classes: First grade, Object Drawing, Perspective, Chiaro-scuro; Second, Drawing from the Antique, Black and White; Third, Study from the Life, Black and White; Fourth, Design, Color, Technique, Composition, pictorial and decorative, Modelling, Carving, Engraving on Wood and Metal, Etching, China Painting, etc. A Life Class will be organized as soon as a number of pupils are prepared to subscribe the cost of a model or models. The School proper concerns itself with only the three first grades. When color and the actual studio work begin, the students will be divided among the specialists within the Academy, who will have studios on the same floor. — Tuition, $10 to $20 per quarter. The Academic year begins Oct. 1 and ends June 1. — The Association enters upon its second year with good prospects. It has a fine Exhibition Room, only 24 by 40 ft., but beautifully designed, and large enough until a special building can be erected. A permanent exhibition will be opened in this Gallery in October.

National Mining and Industrial Exposition. — Pres., H. A. W. Tabor; Sec., S. T. Armstrong; Treas., W. A. H. Loveland; Gen. Manager, H. D. Perky; Manager Dept. of Fine Arts, J. Harrison Mills — An Art Department formed one of the features of this newly organized Exposition, which opened Aug. 1 and closed Sept. 30, and is to be repeated yearly. The catalogue enumerated 402 works of art of all kinds.

University of Denver. — 14th and Arapahoe Sts. Incorporated 1880 under the auspices of the M. E. Church. — Officers B'd of Trustees: Pres., John Evans; V. P., J. W. Bailey; Sec., Earl Cranston; Treas., J. A. Clough. Pres. of the Fac., David H. Moore, A. M., D. D. — No drawing is taught in the Preparatory Courses, and in the other courses only in the Scientific (Free-Hand, in the Sophomore year), and the Mining Engineering (in the Freshman and Sophomore years and one term of the Junior year). — *The College of Fine Arts* connected with the institution confers the degree of Bachelor of Painting. The technical work done in the Maryland Institute is the model in this department. In addition thereto there are at least two recitations per day in related branches, including modern languages, natural science, and belles-lettres. The time required for the completion of the course and obtaining the degree will depend upon the talent and application of the student. The studio is supplied with designs and casts, and the work is done by the most thorough and advanced methods. A furnace for burning decorated china adds greatly to the efficiency of the department. Wood carving has lately been added, as an art destined to command increasing attention, and to open to women new fields of delightful and remunerative employment. — Principal of the College, Miss

Ida de Steiguer; Teacher in Carving, Miss M. E. Dickson. — Tuition from $10 to $15 per quarter of 10 weeks, 2 lessons per week, according to subject. — Number of pupils last season, 60.

Elgin, Ill. — ELGIN ART ASSOCIATION. — Officers: Pres., Hon. G. S. Bowen; V. P., Mrs. J. S. Wilcox; Treas., S. E. Weld; Cor. Sec., A. W. Kenney; Sec., Mrs. H. H. Denison. — Present number of members, 50. — The Association holds an Annual Exhibition in May. Five have been held so far.

Fordham, N. Y. — ST. JOHN'S COLLEGE (Catholic) — Stephen J. Shaughnessy, Professor of Painting and Drawing. These studies are optional.

Hartford, Conn. — CONNECTICUT HISTORICAL SOCIETY. — Wadsworth Atheneum Building, 206 Main St Incorporated 1827. — Officers: Pres., J Hammond Trumbull; Treas., John F. Morris; Rec. Sec., W. I. Fletcher; Cor. Sec. Chas. J. Hoadley; Auditor, Rowland Swift. — The Society owns a considerable number of portraits, most of which have only historical interest. There is also a large collection of relics, in which the famous chest of Elder William Brewster, of the "Mayflower," has the first place.

CONNECTICUT SCHOOL OF DESIGN. — Chartered May, 1872. — Officers: Pres., J. W. Stancliff, 17 Bellevue St.; V. P., C. Conrads; Sec. and Treas., T. S. Steeler — This association, which was organized upon the dissolution of a previously existing society, known as the Hartford Art Association, has for its object the establishing of a school of art, and the holding of exhibitions and sales. The by-laws provide that there shall be two classes of members, the first professional artists, either natives or residents of Connecticut, the second honorary members. The society began under apparently favorably circumstances, but for some years past it has been dormant, although the organization is still kept up. The classes and exhibitions have been discontinued, and the casts owned by the School loaned to the Society of Decorative Art.

SOCIETY OF DECORATIVE ART. — 303 Main St. Organized June, 1877. — Officers: Pres, Miss Mary D. Ely, 668 Main St.; V. Ps., Miss Alice Taintor, Mrs. John C. Day; Cor. Sec., Mrs. A. S. Porter, 2 Wethersfield St.; Rec. Sec., Mrs. J. S. Jarvis; Treas., Mrs. F. G. Whitmore. — Objects: The promotion and diffusion of a knowledge of art among women; their training in artistic industries, and eventually the establishment of rooms for the exhibition and sale of women's work. — Any person may become a member of the Society by an annual payment of $1. — The first classes in Drawing, Painting, and Art embroidery were opened on Jan. 17, 1878, the few ladies who organized the Society pledging themselves to pay the teachers in case the sum received from pupils proved insufficient. They also assumed the rent of the studio, at $300 a year, the furnishing and care of it, and all incidental expenses for medals, etc. The Conn. School of Design kindly loaned the Society several valuable imported casts of the best works of art. Miss Taylor, Miss Wheelwright, and Miss Knowlton, of Boston, all of them pupils of Hunt, were the first teachers, followed by Miss Townsend, of Albany, who gave instruction in water-color and china painting, and Mrs. Whitney, of Hartford, in embroidery. The pupils made good progress under these teachers, and the classes were self-supporting, and have continued so ever since. The tuition fees at that time were $6 for 12 lessons in charcoal drawing, $12 for 12 lessons in water-color, china painting, or embroidery. In October, 1878, the services of Prof. J. Wells Champney, of New York, were secured, and he has been very successful in instructing and bringing forward his pupils in drawing, painting in oil and water-colors, and sketching from life. The price at present for his tuition is $15 per 12 lessons, the lessons occupying most of the day on Tuesdays, Thursdays, and Saturdays, as there are two sessions, morning and afternoon. — There are no free scholarships, but through the kindness of ladies connected with the Society, instruction has been given to several pupils, three of whom are now able to support themselves by furnishing designs to manufacturers. — On April 3, 1880, the Society held its first Exhibition and Sale, for the benefit of ladies capable of doing artistic work, and dependent on their own exertions for support. Five other sales have followed, and the Society has paid in all nearly $1,000 to contributors of this class, throughout the State, who otherwise would have had no market for their work, outside of a limited circle of friends. Thus many of the original aims and objects of the Society have been accomplished, and every day brings evidence of the stimulus it has given to art in Hartford and its neighborhood. — The financial condition of the Society is satisfactory, in so far as no debts have been incurred. But this condition could not have been secured except by the untiring energy of ladies of the Board of Managers, who have provided attractive entertainments at private houses and elsewhere, as a means of replenishing the treasury. The membership fees and the small excess from tuition fees would be wholly inadequate to make the Society self-supporting, and it has, as yet, asked no aid from the public and received no valuable donations.

WADSWORTH ATHENÆUM. — 206 Main St. Founded 1842. — Officers: Pres., Calvin Day ; 1st V. P., Wm. R. Cone; 2d V. P, Roland Mather; Sec., J. Hammond Trumbull ; Treas, J. F. Morris; Auditor, E. B. Watkinson. — This is a private association, named after Daniel Wadsworth, who gave the ground on which the Athenæum stands, and contributed freely toward the erection of the building and the acquisition of the works of art it contains. The collection known as *The Wadsworth Gallery* is rich in paintings by Trumbull, of whose work it has thirteen specimens, many of them identical [replicas probably?] with the well known Trumbulls of the Yale Art Gallery, such as "The Battle of Bunker Hill," etc., and including his first essay in painting. There are also six landscapes by Thomas Cole, including his "Mount Ætna"; Vanderlyn's "Death of Miss M'Crea"; three early works by F. E. Church ; and portraits by Stuart, Sully, Ingham, and Jewett. Among the works by foreign artists, the most noticeable are Lawrence's full length portrait of Benj. West, and an admirable portrait of a gentleman by Raeburn, printed about 1824. In the lower hall there is a collection of statuary, including several of the best works, of E. S. Bartholomew, of Hartford ("Eve Penitent," "Shepherd Boy," "Sappho"), and all his working models in plaster. — There is a catalogue of the paintings, but it is antiquated and insufficient, having been reprinted in 1863 from the original edition of 1844. — Admission, 25 cents. The Gallery is open, *for the present*, on week days, from 9 A. M. to 12 M., and 2 to 5½ P. M. in summer, to 4 P. M. in winter. Intending visitors from a distance will find it to their advantage to inquire in advance, by postal card, regarding the time of opening and closing.

Hingham, Mass. — HINGHAM ART CLUB. — Organized Oct. 1, 1880. — Officers: Pres., Wallace Corthell, P. O. address, Hingham Centre ; V. Ps., Mrs. Davis R. Hersey, Hingham Centre, and Edwin Wilder, Hingham ; Sec., Miss Ella A. Farmer, Hingham ; Treas., Chas. W. S. Seymour, Hingham ; Lior., Benj. Andrews, Jr., Hingham. — Object : The practice and cultivation of the pictorial arts. — Members pay a fee of $1 upon election. — The Club held an exhibition of the works of its own members and of loaned pictures in Aug., 1881. Probably no exhibition will be held this year.

Ithaca, N. Y. — CORNELL UNIVERSITY. — Incorporated April, 1865 ; opened Oct 7, 1868. — The University is supported by the income arising from the land scrip granted to the State under the act of Congress of July 2, 1862, the interest on an endowment of $500,000 by Mr. Ezra Cornell, and the tuition fees charged. — Officers of the B'd of Trustees : Chairm., Henry W. Sage ; Sec., Wm. R. Humphrey ; Acting Treas., Emmons L. Williams. Officers of the Fac.: Pres., Hon. Andrew Dickson White, LL. D ; Registrar, Rev. Wm. Dexter Wilson, D. D., LL. D , L. H D. ; Libr., Daniel Willard Fiske, A. M., Ph. D. — *Free-Hand Drawing* (Edwin Chase

Cleaves, B. S., Assoc. Prof. of Free-Hand Drawing) is obligatory with students of agriculture, architecture, civil engineering, mechanic arts, mathematics, and natural history; elective in all other courses. The work embraces a thorough training of the hand and eye in outline drawing, elementary perspective, model and object drawing, drawing from casts, and sketching from nature. The effort is, not to make mere copyists, but to render the student familiar with the fundamental principles. The course is largely industrial, and the exercises are arranged, as far as possible, with special reference to the drawing required in the work of the different courses. The department has a large collection of flat copies, geometrical models, casts from antique busts and parts of the human figure (see Collections below), studies from nature, and examples of historical ornament. — *The Course in Architecture* (Rev. Chas. Babcock, Prof. of Archit ; Chas F. Osborne, Asst) extends over four years, and leads to the degree of Bachelor of Architecture. It is so arranged as to give the student instruction in all subjects which he should understand in order to enter upon the practice of the art. Its object is not merely to develop the artistic powers of the student, but to lay that foundation of knowledge without which there can be no true art. — The Register for 1881-2 enumerates only 8 s ndents in architecture. Tuition fee (in all departments), $25 a term ; three terms a year. There are 128 Free State Scholarships, particulars concerning which see in the Annual Register, to be had on application to the treasurer of the University. Women are admitted on the same terms as men, except that they must be seventeen years old. — *The White Architectural Library* contains over 1,000 volumes, and the photographic gallery nearly 2,000 prints (see Collections), all accessible to the student. Several hundred drawings and about 200 models have been prepared to illustrate the constructive forms and peculiarities of the different styles. — *Museum and Collections.* The University owns the following valuable collections, mostly donations by Pres. White and others : 1. A considerable collection of casts, by Brucciani, of London. 2. About 4,000 casts of medals, medallions, and gems, principally from specimens in the Berlin Museum, with considerable additions from Italian collections ; also a number of galvano-plastic casts of the more important medals in the Berlin Museum. 3. About 2,000 large photographs illustrating the history of architecture and sculpture. Of these about 60 are devoted to Athens and other places in Greece ; 30 to Herculaneum, Pompeii, and the Greek cities of lower Italy, such as Pæstum, etc. ; 200 to Rome ; 40 to Ravenna ; 100 to Venice ; a still larger number to Florence ; 60 to Siena ; 40 to Genoa ; 40 to Orvieto ; 150 to France ; and so on through Germany, England, Spain, and Portugal. Also photographs of modern European terra-cotta work. 4. Special collections of large colored sheets, showing stained-glass decoration at sundry cathedrals. 5. A framed set of the Arundel Society's publications. 6. Sundry articles of art workmanship, and a considerable number of bronze reductions of noted statues by Barbedienne. 7. A considerable number of original pictures by modern artists, such as Eastman Johnson, Bellows, Hazeltine, Meyer Von Bremen, Wagner, Ambros, Hamman, Hiddemann, etc., bought by Prof and Mrs. Fiske, and by Pres. White. 8. A collection, now embracing six or eight specimens, but constantly increasing, of copies of noted modern pictures and portraits. Pres. White has given a commission to Mr. C. C. Burleigh, who attracted considerable attention in Berlin as a copyist, and in this country through the specimens of his work sent to the Exhibitions of the Pennsylvania Academy at Philadelphia, to reproduce a number of important paintings, including Piloty's "Galileo in Prison," at Cologne ; portraits of Frederic the Great and his sister, as children, at Charlottenburg ; a portrait of Thomasius, from the University Collection at Halle ; two portraits of Grotius, from Amsterdam ; Becker's "Coronation of Ulrich von Hutten," at Cologne ; Gallait's "Last Days of Egmont," at Berlin ; Piloty's "Wallenstein and Seni," at Munich, etc. There are also various portraits of professors and benefactors of the institution. — Many of these objects are still packed away for want of space, or scattered through the University buildings and the houses of the professors; but the authorities hope to have them all visible to the public in the Museum within a few months. The copies of modern paintings, alluded to above, are not so much intended for a gallery of fine art as for the large historical lecture-room which the authorities of the University likewise propose to have ready at no distant day. The most valuable part of the whole collection for purposes of study will doubtless be the medallions, medals, and gems. These are carefully catalogued, the gems according to the Winckelmann catalogue, published in Berlin, to which the numbers are made to correspond.

ITHACA BRANCH OF THE NEW YORK SOCIETY OF DECORATIVE ART. — Cornell Library Bldg. — Organized, 1878. — Officers : Pres, Mrs. J. C. Gauntlett; 1st V. P., Mrs. Chas. Schaeffer; 2d V. P., Miss Minnie McChain; Treas., Mrs. D. M. Stewart; Rec. and Cor. Sec., Miss Mary E. Humphrey. — Objects : The promotion and diffusion of a knowledge of decorative art among women, and their training in artistic industries. — Members : Active, who must present some work of theirs for inspection, and pay $1 initiation fee, and $1 annually thereafter; Associate, having no vote, annual dues $1; Honorary. Present number of members of all grades, 60. — The Society has organized classes in drawing, wood carving, etc., and opened a salesroom, where work by members or by outside contributors is exhibited, and orders received. An Annual Art Bazar is held in November, which is quite successful, both as regards the quality of the work displayed and the appreciation of the public.

Jacksonville, Ill. — ART ASSOCIATION. — Instituted Dec. 17, 1873 ; incorporated 1875. — Officers : Pres., D. H Harris ; V. Ps., Mrs. E. Wolcott, Mrs. I. L. Morrison ; Treas., Henry H. Hall ; Sec., Mrs. M. L. D. Keiser. — Objects : The study and appreciation of the Fine Arts, especially of the arts of design, by the formation of a public collection of art-treatises, pictures, engravings, photographs, casts, models, and such other material as may aid in this ; and furthermore by lectures, essays, and discussions on art subjects. — The annual membership fee is $1. The membership has varied from 25 to 80, the proportion of ladies to gentlemen being about as five to one. — The Association was organized in the parlor of the Ill. Female College, and owes its existence to the happy thought of Mrs. Ella O Browne, at the time teacher of art in the College. — Eight monthly meetings are held during the months of October to May inclusive, the present place of meeting being the lecture hall of the Young Men's Christian Association. The exercises at these meetings have consisted of the reading of essays by the members, selected readings, lectures by persons from other cities, discussions, and sometimes the reading of a collection of notes and gossip upon current art news, local and foreign. Whenever possible, photographs have been exhibited to illustrate the subject in hand. The range of subjects covered by these essays, etc., has been very wide, and the list of lecturers includes some names well known in the literature of art. In addition to the regular monthly meetings, fortnightly meetings have been held, since January, 1874, of a few of the members, mostly ladies, who desire to give more time to a thorough study of the history of art. Architecture has been the chief topic at these meetings. — A collection of works of art, begun some years ago, contains autotypes, heliotypes, steel engravings, and a couple of oil paintings. A few books form the nucleus of a library, for the increase of which an appropriation has recently been made. — Beginning with 1875, an Annual Loan Exhibition has been given, made up of works owned by citizens, productions of pupils and teachers in the four art schools in the city, drawings by pupils in the Public Schools, and paintings, engravings, etc., loaned by artists and dealers in St. Louis, Chicago, New York, and elsewhere. The duration of these exhibitions, the last of which was held Feb. 14 to 18, 1882, has varied from three to five days; single admission, 25 cents; season tickets from 50 cents to $1. The receipts of the eight exhibitions have been in every case greater than the expenses, the net proceeds varying from $20 to $160. (See also *Central Ill. Art Union*, Springfield Ill.)

Le Roy, N. Y. — INGHAM UNIVERSITY. — Organized at Attica, in 1835; removed to Le Roy in 1837; chartered as a Collegiate Inst., 1852; as a University in 1857. Claims to be the pioneer Female College in point of time. — Officers of the Council: Vice-Chancellor, Mrs. E. E. Ingham Staunton; Sec., Prof. P. P. Staunton. — Drawing and painting were taught in this institution as early as 1842. The *College of Fine Arts* at present connected with it owes its existence to Col. Staunton (d. 1867), the husband of the founder, who, in 1870, erected the Art Conservatory in his honor. The Art College, which is a wing of the same building, was erected in 1875. — Aim: To educate those who desire the accomplishment, or wish to follow art as a profession, and to prepare instructors for private and public schools. — Course of Instruction and Teachers: Prof. L. M. Wiles, A. M., Painting; Prof. P. P. Staunton, Drawing; Miss R. M. Shave, A P., Elementary Drawing and Water-Colors, and Oil Painting during Prof. Wiles's absence in New York, from November to May; Irving R. Wiles, A. P., Figure Painting. 1 Under-Graduate Course: Outlines of single objects; elements of linear perspective; study of light and shade, advancing to drawing from the antique; landscape, including sketching in color from nature. Those who desire to graduate from this department are required to produce a complete original picture, the materials of which have been studied from life and composed in conformity to the requirements of art. If approved by the Faculty and the Councillors of the University, it will be accepted by them, and will find a permanent place in the collection of graduating pictures. Lectures on technical matters and on the history of art by Prof. Wiles at the beginning and end of each term. 2. Post-Graduate Course: For those who have completed the Under-Graduate Course, and desire to prosecute the study of art as a specialty, a Post-Graduate Course has been formed in which they can receive a thorough training in the principles of High Art. Lectures in Artistic Anatomy, Analysis of Expression, and Philosophy of Art will be given, with practical instructions in drawing from the Living Model, in order to inculcate, as far as possible, the principles of Idealism in Portrait, Figure, and Landscape Painting. 3. Summer Class: For the benefit of teachers and others who find it more convenient to attend during the usual vacation, a Summer Term of six weeks, beginning July 6, has been arranged under Prof. L. M. Wiles. — Tuition fees: Regular courses; Full term of 6 weeks with Prof. Wiles, $30; Instruction by Miss Shave, in Oil and Water Colors, 75 cts. per lesson; full term of 20 weeks with Prof. Staunton, $85; single lessons, $1. Summer Course: $1 per day, during 5 days of the week. — Students: Although the University is for young ladies only, young men are admitted to the Art College. Season 1881–82, 108 students in the regular courses (105 females, 3 males), of whom 6 were Resident Graduates. — *The Art Conservatory* contains an inexhaustible store of materials for both artistic and scientific study, consisting of a museum of natural and artificial curiosities, and a gallery of paintings, valued at more than $50,000, and comprising Col. Staunton's best pictures, the graduating pictures painted by students, and some of the best works of eminent foreign and native artists.

Licking, O. — LICKING COUNTY PIONEER HISTORICAL AND ANTIQUARIAN SOCIETY. — Collection of Mound Builders' and Indian relics, coins, and curiosities.

Lincoln, Ill. — ART SOCIETY. — Sec., Mrs. Carrie M. Lutz. (See *Central Ill. Art Union*, Springfield, Ill.)

Louisville, Ky. — LOUISVILLE INDUSTRIAL EXPOSITION. — Officers: Pres., C. S. Snead; Sec., E. A. Maginnis. — This association holds yearly Expositions, combined with which is an art exhibition. The last took place from Sept. 5 to Oct. 21, 1882. The catalogue enumerated 333 works, by 196 artists, mostly American.

Lowell, Mass. — LOWELL ART ASSOCIATION. — Organized 1878. — Officers: Pres., Thos. B. Lawson; V. Ps., E. W Hoyt, Miss E. O. Robbins; Treas., Geo. T. Carney; Clerk, Frank N. Chase. — Object: To increase a knowledge of art and to develop a taste for it, by exhibitions, lectures, readings, or other suitable means. — Members pay an entrance fee of $1, and may be assessed $2 annually. Honorary members may also be elected. — The club has held a number of exhibitions of the works of local artists, both professional and amateur; also loan exhibitions, and the following special exhibitions: Two of etchings, ancient and modern; one of an entire set of Piranesi; one each of engravings and photographs from the works of Michelangelo, Raphael, Correggio, and Turner; and one upon the contents of the Vatican, with brief lectures upon each subject. Receptions are held during the cooler months for conversation and the exhibition of novelties and designs for manufactures. — As the city maintains day and evening schools for drawing, modelling, and designing, the Association has made no effort to establish classes.

Madison, Wis. — STATE HISTORICAL SOCIETY OF WISCONSIN. — State Capitol. Organized Jan., 1849; reorganized Jan., 1854. — Officers: Pres., Hon. C. C. Washburn, LL. D.; Cor. Sec., Lyman C. Draper, LL. D.; Rec. Sec., Robt. M. Bashford; Treas., Hon A. H. Main; Libr., Daniel S. Durrie. — The *Picture Gallery* owned by this Society contains about 120 pictures in oil and in crayon, and some portrait busts. The latest published catalogue, of Jan. 1, 1878, enumerates 113 paintings, mostly portraits and a few landscapes; and 14 busts. There is also a cabinet of antiquities, coins, curiosities, and Revolutionary relics. — The Gallery and the Library of the Society, the latter containing 45,846 vols. and 49,154 documents and pamphlets, are open, free of charge, every week day, except public holidays, from 9 A. M. to 12 M., and from 2 to 5 P. M.; during the session of the Legislature also evenings, from 7 to 9 P. M. — The Reports and Collections, published by the Society, of which 8 vols. have so far been issued, occasionally contain papers of interest to archæologists.

Manchester, N. H. — MANCHESTER ART ASSOCIATION. — Court House. — Originated Sept., 1871; organized under State law, Oct., 1874. — Officers: Pres., H. W. Herrick; Sec., F. B. Eaton; Treas., J. B. Sawyer; Auditor, A. J. Stevens. — Objects: To promote knowledge and skill in art and technology among its members, and among artists and artisans, by the establishment of an art library, the collection of paintings, statuary, models, and other works of art or science. — The members, at present about 300, are of both sexes. — Initiation fee, $1; annual assessments, not above $2. — Classes are formed to some extent in winter, the demand being chiefly for mechanical and architectural drawing. The Association owns a collection of over 50 casts, from life and from antique and modern sculptures, which is at the service of the students. Life classes have also been formed occasionally. A small fee is charged, which goes to the teachers. Lectures, illustrating the principles of art, are given occasionally. — The Library contains several hundred volumes, mostly manuals and text-books of value to the practical student. It increases steadily, and is also supplied with American and European art journals. — An Annual Exhibition is held in April, lasting usually three or four days. The exhibits largely represent industrial art, supplied by the manufacturers of the city. Oil and water-color paintings, loaned by owners or contributed by artists, are also shown, and a division is assigned to amateur work.

Maysville, Ky. — HISTORICAL AND SCIENTIFIC SOCIETY OF MASON CO. — Collection of Indian antiquities.

Melrose, Mass. — MELROSE ART CLUB — Organized Feb. 10, 1880. — Officers: Pres., Col. F. S. Hesseltine; V. P., Mrs. J. G. Adams; Sec., Robt. J. Chute;

Treas., Miss Hattie N. Andrews; Libr., Mrs. F. S. Hesseltine. — The members, of both sexes, are mostly amateurs, with only a few professional artists. Present number, 120. — A series of eight lectures, by as many lecturers, on the different periods of art, arranged in chronological order, was delivered, at the private residences of some of the members, during the season of 1881-2. At the first exhibition of the Club, held Feb. 16, 1881, in the parlors of one of the members, there were about 30 exhibitors, all of them members, with only one or two exceptions. Another exhibition is to be held in the fall of 1882. — The Club has come to be one of the popular institutions of the town. It has supplied a want that many had long felt, and has encouraged its members in the study and practice of art.

Middlebury, Vt. — MIDDLEBURY HISTORICAL SOCIETY. — Collection of aboriginal and military relics

Milwaukee, Wis. — LADIES' ART AND SCIENCE CLASS. — Milwaukee College. (Organized 1874. — Officers: Pres., Mrs. T. A Greene; Treas, Mrs. F. L. Atkins; Exec. Comm., Mrs J. MacAlister, Mrs. A. H. Vedder, Mrs. J. G. Flint, Mrs. J. H. Warner. — This Association of Ladies formed at Milwaukee College eight years ago, for the purposes of study, instruction, and discussion, grew in interest till, in 1878, it was deemed wise to assume a more definite character, on the simple plan indicated in the following Principles of Organization: 1. The Class shall be vitally connected with Milwaukee College. 2. It shall be annually organized by a ballot choice of a President, a Treasurer, and an Executive Committee of four ladies. 3. The annual fee for membership and all privileges shall be $5. 4. The funds thus accruing shall be expended by the Board of Officers in the following manner, viz.: a. Payment for the use of the College Hall as a session-room, and of the Library as a reading-room, a sum not to exceed $6 per week, during the season of meetings and Library study; b. The balance remaining after the payment for the use of the Hall and Library, and other merely incidental expenses, not including any salaries or fees of teachers, lecturers, or officers, shall be annually expended before Oct. 1, for books, pictures, casts, and such treasures, which shall be the permanent property of the College. — The subject proposed for next year is a review of Sculpture, Painting, and Architecture, by a study of the Cities of Europe. The Class meets Tuesday afternoon of each week, and the members have daily use of the special library and reading-room of the College. Excellent lantern views, eighteen feet in diameter, are almost constantly employed in the weekly session. Every important building studied, and many of the details, are illustrated on the screen, while the building is under discussion. The following topics indicate the course of study pursued last year: 1. Review of the styles earlier than the Gothic; 2. Gothic Architecture in France; 3. In Germany; 4. In England; 5. Renaissance Architecture. — Members, 78.

MILWAUKEE COLLEGE. — Chartered 1851 as the "Female Normal Institute and High School"; corporate name changed to "Milwaukee Female College," in 1853; present name assumed in 1876. The College, nevertheless, remains an institution for girls only. — Officers of B'd of Trustees: Pres., Wm. P. McLaren; V. P., Hoel H. Camp; Treas., John Johnston; Sec., W. W. Wight Pres. of the College: Chas. S. Farrar, A. M. — The College has a Primary Department, a Preparatory Department, and a Collegiate Department. In all of these departments, drawing and painting are elective studies, but lessons in "Art Criticism" form part of the regular study in the first semester of the Senior Year in the Collegiate Department. — The instruction in the *Department of Art* (Miss Frances Farrar, teacher) embraces drawing in pencil, pen, crayon, or charcoal; painting in oil or water-colors, and modelling in clay or wax. The practice consists in drawing or painting from copies, from still-life and natural forms. Particular attention given to sketching from nature, for which the students are taken to selected points affording picturesque objects and motives for landscape studies. Large studios are provided, specially designed and furnished for

the purpose. — Drawing and Sketching, tri-weekly, $15 per quarter; Painting in Oil
or Water-Colors, tri-weekly, $20. — Students in Art Department, season of 1881-2,
35; students in Art Criticism, 11. (See Ladies' Art Class above, which the students
can enter.)

MILWAUKEE INDUSTRIAL EXPOSITION ASSOCIATION. — Exposition Building. —
Officers: Pres., John Plankinton; 1st V. P., Fred. Pabst; 2d V. P., John R. Good-
rich; Treas., Chas. G. Stark; Gen. Manager, R. D. Torrey; Sec, R. P. Jennings;
Supt. of Oils and Water-Colors, Mrs. Lydia Ely Hewitt; Supt. of Black and White
Dept., Mrs. C. D. Adsit; Decorative Art, Mrs. S. S. Frackelton. — This Association
holds annual Expositions, and in connection therewith an Art Exhibition. At the
first of these exhibitions, Sept. 6 to Oct. 15, 1881, there were exhibited 452 pictures,
of which 24 were sold for $3,250, and 869 black-and-whites (including an historical
exhibition of engravings), of which 9 were sold for $260. The catalogue of the
Second Exhibition, Sept. 5 to Oct. 21, 1882, enumerated 228 oils, 128 water-colors,
and 2 pieces of sculpture, by 161 artists, and 625 engravings, etc.

MILWAUKEE MUSEUM OF FINE ARTS FOR THE STATE OF WISCONSIN. —
Exposition Building. Incorp. July 1, 1882. — Officers: Pres., Mrs. Alexander
Mitchell; 1st V. P., Wm. H. Metcalf; 2d V. P., Chas. L. Colby; 3d V. P., Mrs.
Jas. M. Percles; Sec., Wm. W. Wight; Treas., Wm Plankinton, Exposition Bldg.
— Objects: To cultivate and advance art in all its branches. For this purpose a
public collection of works of art and a School of Design are to be established. —
The members are to be Patrons, contributors of $500 or more; Fellows in Perpetu-
ity, contributors of $250; Fellows for Life, contributors of $100; and Annual Members, who are to pay $10 yearly. All these members together are to elect the Board
of Directors, of which the Directors of the Milwaukee Industrial Exposition Association are also to be members ex officiis. The Board of Directors may elect Honorary Fellows. — The Museum will occupy temporary quarters in the Exposition
Building, until the time and the opportunity shall arrive for erecting a structure of
its own. It began its activity by opening a Loan Exhibition of a few select works
of art, mostly foreign, in Sept, 1882.

Montpelier, Vt. — VERMONT HISTORICAL SOCIETY. — Small museum of
curiosities.

Nashua, N. H — NASHUA HISTORICAL SOCIETY. — Collection of historical
relics of local interest.

Nashville, Tenn. — HISTORICAL SOCIETY OF TENNESSEE. — Valuable collection of Indian antiquities; cabinet of coins; extensive museum of articles of
historical interest, including a large number of portraits of the historical characters
of the State. [No reply to inquiries.]

Newark, N. J. — NEW JERSEY HISTORICAL SOCIETY. — Cabinet of curiosities, relating to historical events and personages.

New Haven, Conn. — CONNECTICUT MUSEUM OF INDUSTRIAL ART. —
Old State House. Organized 1876. — Sec., Wm. P. Blake. — Objects: To promote the prosperity and artistic advancement of the industries of Connecticut by
establishing a museum of selected manufactures of the State, and of industrial and
applied art generally, similar in its general plan and scope to the South Kensington
Museum of London. — Collections illustrating the manufacture of fire-arms, cotton,
etc.; historical collection of pottery; art industrial objects of all kinds; life-size
groups of Swedish peasants, from the Swedish Department of the Centennial Exposition, etc. — Open throughout the year, holidays included, Sundays excepted, from
9 A. M. to 6 P. M. Admission, 25 cents No catalogue. [This institution does not
appear to be in a flourishing condition. Although the Governor of the State of
Connecticut, the Mayor of the city of New Haven, and the President of Yale College are members of the Board of Trustees, ex officiis, no public aid has been

extended to it, excepting the building, which is furnished rent-free by the city. The School of Design connected with the Museum has been discontinued.]

NEW HAVEN COLONY HISTORICAL SOCIETY. — Old State House. — Sec., Thos. R. Trowbridge, Jr. — The collection of this Society contains many interesting and valuable Revolutionary and other relics and curiosities, including a number of portraits, busts, engravings, etc. Among the portraits, that by John Trumbull of his father, Gov. Jonathan Trumbull, and a couple by S F. B. Morse, of Mr. and Mrs. David C. De Forest, are especially noteworthy. Those interested in the history of engraving in America will find, besides a number of other old prints, several specimens of the rude work of Amos Doolittle, b. 1745, d. 1832, including the "Battle of Lexington," etc. — Open free on week days. A printed catalogue of the collection can be had on application.

YALE COLLEGE. — Incorporated 1701. — Pres. of the Corp. and of the Fac., Rev. Noah Porter, D. D., LL. D., 31 Hillhouse Ave. ; Sec., Franklin B. Dexter, M. A , 76 Prospect St. ; Treas., Henry C. Kingsley, M. A., 23 Hillhouse Ave. — Instruction in Instrumental Drawing (Fred R. Honey, instructor) and in Elementary and Free-Hand Drawing (Prof. J. H. Niemeyer, instructor) is given in the Sheffield Scientific School in the introductory Freshman Year, and in the Engineering Courses. It is not included in the Courses in Chemistry, Agriculture, Natural History, and Biology, and in the Studies preparatory to Mining and Metallurgy, and the Select Studies Preparatory to other Higher Studies. In the Undergraduate Academical Department all the art instruction provided for is an Optional, four exercises a week, through the second term of Senior year, under Prof. Niemeyer in Drawing; Prof. Weir, in the Principles and Means of Art, and Prof. Hoppin, in the History of Art ; fee $18 for three months. — The Yale School of the Fine Arts, a separate department of the College, was founded by the late Aug. Russell Street, who erected the Art Building, which was opened in 1866. Faculty : The President of the College ; John F. Weir, N. A., M A , Prof. of Painting and Director of the School, 58 Trumbull St. ; Rev Jas. M. Hoppin, D. D., Prof. of the History of Art, 47 Hillhouse Ave. ; John H. Niemeyer, M. A., Prof. of Drawing, 8 Art School. — Instructors : Fred. R. Honey, in Geometry and Perspective, 14 Lincoln St. ; John P. C. Foster, M. D., in Anatomy, 109 College St. ; Harr. W. Lindsley, Ph. B., in Architecture, Cutler Building. — Aim : (1) To provide thorough technical instruction in the Arts of Painting, Sculpture, and Architecture ; (2) to furnish an acquaintance with all branches of learning relating to the History, Theory, and Practice of Art. — The courses of instruction, covering three years, provided under the heads of Practice and Criticism, may be regarded as distinct or correlative, embracing that technical and theoretical knowledge of art which is no less desirable for the critic than for the artist. In the departments of Drawing and Painting the practice of the studio is based upon the study of human form, from the antique and the living model, supplemented by lectures on Form and Proportion, Color, Chiaro-scuro, and Composition. Drawing is continued, without interruption, through the first half of the course, or until the student evinces that proficiency which will warrant advancement. Painting is continued through the remainder of the course. Students are encouraged to remain in the school and pursue advanced studies after the three years' course is completed. Perspective and Anatomy are taught in the form of lectures. Lectures are also given on the History and Philosophy of Art, and kindred subjects. Besides the Department of Drawing and Painting, there are also special Departments of Sculpture, and of Architecture, and a class in Etching. — An Exhibition of the work of the students is opened June 1, and continues through the summer. Prizes may be competed for, both in Drawing and in Painting, at the close of the course. Diplomas are only awarded to those who remain through the full course, or pass the requisite examinations. — Tuition fees, $36 for three months. Art students are admitted free to all the lectures delivered

in the school, to the collections, and to the special library provided for the Art Department — The school is open to pupils of both sexes of fifteen years or over.
Special art students in regular attendance last term, 50 (12 male, 38 female); students in drawing from the Sheffield Scientific School, 73. — The term begins Oct. 1
and ends May 31. All applications for admission to be made through the Director
before Oct. 1. No conditions of admission, save as to age and general good character. — "While the Faculty are sensible," says the last report, "of having done their
utmost to advance the interests of the school, . . . they have labored under the dis-
advantage of an insufficient income. The school is burdened with a debt [incurred,
for the most part, for the completion of the building, and like necessary expendi-
tures], the payment of the interest of which has absorbed about half the income
received through tuition fees, and thus rendered further development for the present
impossible, unless some means of relief can be provided. . . . With the discharge of
this debt the school would be able to maintain its effective and progressive course
without further assistance." The Professorship Funds with which the school is endowed amount to $75,000. — The Art Collections embrace the "Jarves Gallery of
Italian Art," numbering 120 paintings, dating from the 11th to the 17th centuries;
the "Trumbull Gallery," of works by John Trumbull, numbering 54 pictures; a collection of portraits and works of contemporaneous art, about 100 in all; and an excellent collection of about 150 casts from the antique, etc. The "Trumbull Gallery,"
which is unique for the study of this talented painter of the Revolutionary epoch,
contains some of his most important earlier works, such as the small pictures of "The
Battle of Bunker Hill," "The Death of Montgomery," "The Battle of Princeton,"
etc., and the beautiful little portrait heads which he painted as studies for his larger
works. Other important works by American artists, owned by Yale College, are
Smybert's "Family of Bishop Berkeley," Allston's "Jeremiah and the Scribe,"
Morse's "Dying Hercules," portraits by Stuart, Jarvis, Elliott, and others, and
sculptures by Bartholomew, Augur, Powers, etc. — There are no funds for additional purchases. The proceeds of the exhibition, which is occasionally varied by
transient loan collections, are applied to the incidental expenses of the school. —
Gallery open every week day, including holidays, from 9 A. M. to 12½ P. M., and
1½ to 6 P. M., June till end of Oct.; for the rest of the year only from 1 to 5 P. M.
Admission 25 cents. The catalogue has been out of print for some time, as it does
not pay. — The Peabody Museum of Natural History, the gift of George Peabody, of
London, besides its Natural History specimens, has also a collection in Archæology
and Ethnology. So far as the collections are arranged, this Museum is open to the
public every day, Sundays excepted, in term-time.

New London, Conn. — NEW LONDON COUNTY HISTORICAL SOCIETY. —
Museum of historical relics, Indian curiosities, etc

New Orleans, La. — SOUTHERN ART UNION AND WOMAN'S INDUSTRIAL
ASSOCIATION. — 203 Canal St. Chartered May 26, 1880. — Officers: Pres, Robert
Mott; 1st V. P., Gideon Townsend; 2d V. P., H M. Neill; Treas., Milton C. Ran-
dall; Sec , Jno. Crickard. Chairm. Woman's Ind. Assoc., Mrs. H W. Conner; Sec.,
Mrs. Clarence Fenner. — Objects: To advance, develop, and encourage art and
æsthetic culture in all branches, and to foster feminine skill in all departments of art
and industry. — Members (ladies and gentlemen): The original incorporators and
any one thereafter elected. Ordinary members, $10 p a.; life members, one pay-
ment of $100. Honorary members may be nominated by the president. — This
Association combines the features of a general Art Society with those of the Ladies'
Decorative Art Societies elsewhere established. It has a salesroom, in which the
work of contributors is sold on commission, and which is to be used also as a medium
for the exchange of works of art. — The School of Design, established by the Union
(for the present for women only) has classes in Drawing and Painting (day and even-

ing), Water-Color Painting, Linear Perspective, and Architectural Drawing (day and evening), painting on China and Silk, Kensington Embroidery, etc., also drawing classes for children. The tuition fees range from $4 to $6 per month Number of pupils last season, 150. Instructors last season : Miss J. Tuzo, Mr. A. Perelli, Mr. A. Molinary. The coming season Miss Tuzo's place will be filled by Miss Henr. Winant of New York. The Association is indebted to Miss Neason of Boston for a gift of $2,000, to be expended in salaries for teachers, etc. — A Free Circulating Library has also been inaugurated, by the generosity of Mrs. Field. It is worked under a system of rules drawn up by Mr. Geo. W. Cable, and the committee find it quite difficult to supply the demand for books, although donations (which are earnestly solicited) are continually coming in from all quarters. — Among the other objects of the Union are the holding of exhibitions and auction sales, the gathering of a nucleus for an Art Museum, and the publication of an Art Journal. — The first regular exhibition held by the society, exclusively for the work of professional artists, opened Feb. 17 and closed March 16, 1882. The catalogue enumerated 206 works by 95 artists, including most of the names well known in New York and Philadelphia. Of these works, which were gathered and returned free of expense to contributors, 41 were sold for $5,099. A subsequent exhibition, devoted to etchings from New York and Boston, gave great pleasure, and the sales were reasonably good.

Newport, R. I. — NEWPORT HISTORICAL SOCIETY. — Collection of Indian and local curiosities and antiquities.

REDWOOD ATHENÆUM AND LIBRARY. — Originated 1730; incorporated 1747; edifice erected 1748; enlarged 1858. — Officers: Pres., Francis Brinley; V. P., Chas. T. Brooks; Treas., Job. T. Langley; Sec. and Libr., Benj. F. Thurston — This library (23,994 vols. according to last printed report) is owned by an association of stockholders, but non-stockholders may acquire the right to use it by becoming annual subscribers. — *Art Collections.* The Library owns a number of busts, and between two and three hundred oil paintings, including many portraits of American celebrities, mostly the gift and the work of Charles B. King, an American artist, b. Newport, R. I., 1786, d Washington, D. C., 1862. Besides these there are works by Stuart, Thos Sully, J. G. Chapman, etc. One of the most interesting objects is the " Portrait of Mrs. Wanton," the wife of Joseph Wanton, governor of R. I from 1769-75. This portrait is by Robert Feke, one of the earliest native American painters of whom there is any record. Many of the canvasses are copies from paintings by the old masters. Mr. King left to the Library also a *Collection of Prints* which is thus described in the Report for 1862 : " Seven quarto volumes contain prints classified as Historical, Religious, Classical, Landscape, Portraits, Costumes, and Miscellaneous. Seven other volumes are of folio size, generally of large dimensions, and are also arranged with reference to their subjects. They include many works of the old masters : a copy of Raphael's Bible, in fifty-two plates ; some original etchings from Rembrandt ; a series from Rubens, illustrating the life and destiny of Marie de Medicis ; nine prints from the paintings of Titian, . . . and a large number of other works from the Italian, Dutch, and other schools. In portraiture will be found many of great value ; those from Vandyke and Reynolds alone making two volumes. The collection is especially rich in English engravings, published in London in the beginning of this and the latter part of the last century, and presents examples from the works of Reynolds, Gainsborough, West, Romney, Stubbs, Copley, Cosway, and other noted artists of the time, with some fine specimens of the costly line engravings issued by Boydell." Many of these prints were obtained by Mr. King while he was a student at the Royal Academy in London, and a very large proportion of them are said to be early impressions. — Open free to visitors every week day.

RHODE ISLAND CHAPTER OF THE AM. INST. OF ARCHITECTS. — Sec., Geo. C. Mason, Jr., 3 Catherine St. (See p. 1.)

New York. — AMERICAN ETHNOLOGICAL SOCIETY. — 60 Wall St. — Officers : Pres , Alex. J. Cotheal; Libr., Henry T. Drowne. — The Archæological Collections of this Society have been deposited in the American Museum of Natural History. The Peruvian Antiquities, presented to the Society by one of its presidents, the late George Folsom, are in the custody of the New York Historical Society.

AMERICAN MUSEUM OF NATURAL HISTORY. — Manhattan Square, Central Park, 77th St. and 8th Ave. Incorporated Apr. 6, 1869. — Officers : Pres., Morris K. Jesup, 197 Madison Ave. ; V. Ps., Robert Colgate, D. Jackson Stuart; Sec., Hugh Auchincloss, 17 W. 49th St. ; Treas., J. Pierpont Morgan, 219 Madison Ave. ; Supt., Prof. Albert S. Bickmore — The revenues of this Museum are derived from donations and dues paid by members, etc. The cash donations, as per last report, amounted in all to $229,018 ; but large donations have also been received in the shape of collections. The present building, which comprises only about one twelfth of the contemplated structure, was put up and is partially maintained by the city. The Museum is not devoted to the study of the lower orders of nature only, but embraces also anthropology, with its various subdivisions. — *The Archæological Department* is arranged on the gallery of the second hall or principal floor. Some of its component parts may be enumerated as follows: The most complete collection of the Ethnology of the Pacific Islands to be found anywhere. All that is left of the Squier and Davis Ohio and Mississippi Valley Collections, incl. some 60 specimens of which figures are given in "Smithsonian Contributions to Knowledge," Vol. I. All the collections made by Squier in Peru, Nicaragua, etc. The whole collection of Chas. C. Jones, Jr. (author of "Antiquities of the Southern Indians," Appleton, 1873), bought for the Museum for $7,500. A very large collection illustrating the ethnology of British Columbia, gathered by Dr. J. W. Powell, Supt. of Indian Affairs in that part of the Dominion of Canada, and presented by Mr. H. R. Bishop, of New York. The largest collection, outside of France, of prehistoric relics from that country, particularly the Somme Valley. English, Irish, and Swiss prehistoric collections. A number of minor collections are incorporated with those named. Besides these collections, all of which are on exhibition, there is a still larger collection of stone implements from various parts of the United States, east of the Rocky Mountains, owned by Mr. Andrew E. Douglass ; and a similar collection from the same area, together with the best collection of stone implements ever gathered on the Pacific Coast, owned by Mr. Jas. Terry. These private collections are in separate rooms in the building, and are accessible by application to the owners, addressed at the Museum. Together with those on public exhibition, these two collections equal in value and variety all other collections of stone implements. — The Museum also owns a few pictures, illustrating scientific subjects, among them an Arctic scene by Wm. Bradford, and a life-size portrait of an American Bison by Wm. J. Hays. — No catalogue, but most of the objects are labelled. The Museum publishes Annual Reports and Scientific Bulletins, which can be had by students on application. A consulting library, in the Superintendent's office, is also at the service of students. — Open free week days, including holidays, all the year round from 9 P. M. to half an hour before sunset. Mondays and Tuesdays are called reserved days for students, but all visitors are admitted on giving name and address. — The Museum is accessible by the Eighth Ave. horse cars, and the Harlem trains on the Sixth Ave. Elevated Railroad. Approaches for carriages and pedestrians have been made from the Fifth Ave. side of Central Park at 77th and 81st Sts. Visitors to the Park can also take the ferry at the Terrace, which will land them near the 77th St. entrance on 8th Ave.

AMERICAN NUMISMATIC AND ARCHÆOLOGICAL SOCIETY. — 25 University Bldg., Washington Sq. — Officers : Pres., Chas. E. Anthon, 1006 Fourth Ave. ; Sec., Wm. Poillon, 61 Bethune St. — Cabinet of about 5,000 coins. [Room closed, and no reply to inquiries by letter.]

AMERICAN WATER-COLOR SOCIETY. — Office, 51 W. 10th St. Organized 1868. — Officers: Pres , Thos. W. Wood, 51 W 10th St. ; Sec., Henry Farrer, 51 W. 10th St. ; Treas., J. M. Falconer, 110 St. Felix St., Brooklyn. — Object : To advance the art of painting in Water-Colors. — Members : Resident, professional artists living in the city, or its immediate vicinity; initiation fee, $25 ; no further dues. Non-Resident, professional artists living at a distance. Honorary, amateurs and connoisseurs. The two classes last named pay no fees, cannot vote, and can hold no office except that of treasurer, to which an Honorary member may be elected. There are at present 61 Resident, 22 Non Resident members; total, 83, of whom 4 are ladies. No Honorary members. — The holding of exhibitions, strictly confined to Water-Colors (although etchings have also been exhibited), is the only public activity of the Society. These exhibitions are the most important of their kind in the country. The Sixteenth Annual Exhibition will be held at the National Academy of Design from Jan. 29 to Feb. 24, 1883. The by-laws provide that "the Board of Control shall examine all works (except those made by members) sent for place in the Annual Exhibition, and order the return of such as in their judgment do not possess sufficient merit."

ARCHITECTURAL LEAGUE OF NEW YORK. — 23 E. 14th St. Organized 1881. — Officers : Pres , D. W. Willard, 57 B'way ; V. P., J. P. Riley ; Treas., J. B. Robinson ; Rec. Sec., C. I. Berg, 76 E. 54th St. ; Cor. Sec., A. W. Brunner, 24 W. 45th St. — Objects : To promote the artistic, scientific, and practical efficiency of the profession, and the means of accomplishing this end shall be : The reading of essays ; lectures upon topics of general interest ; competitions in architectural design ; exhibitions of members' work ; formation of a library ; formation of a collection of drawings, photographs, and casts ; establishment of a travelling studentship ; and any other means calculated to promote the object of the association. — Members : Active, engaged in Architectural work ; present number, 30 ; initiation fee, $5, and dues $1 per month ; finable for non-attendance. Honorary members may also be elected. — Many of the sketches by members have appeared in the "American Architect," principally designs for the regular problems which are set by the Committee on Current Work. These problems are given at each meeting, and each member is expected to send in a sketch. All the designs are hung up in the League's rooms, and the criticism of prominent architects upon them is invited. Nothing has as yet been done towards the establishment of the travelling studentship.

ARTISTS' FUND SOCIETY OF NEW YORK. — Instituted 1859 ; chartered 1861. — Officers : Pres , Thos. Hicks, 6 Astor Pl. ; V. P., Alfred Jones, care Am. B'k Note Co. ; Treas., J. M. Falconer, 110 St. Felix St., Brooklyn ; Sec., G. H. Yewell, 578 Fifth Ave. ; Honorary Medical Adviser, F. N. Otis, M. D. — Members at the time of election must reside in New York or vicinity. Present number, 91, including the elect, not yet qualified. Annual dues, $75. — The Society has three funds : 1. The Widows' Fund for the relief of widows and orphans of members. 2. The Relief Fund for the relief of disabled members. 3. The Benevolent Fund for the relief of artists, or the widows and orphans of artists, not members. The first two are maintained by the annual dues, the last is maintained by donations. — The Society holds an Annual Exhibition and Sale to which members may contribute. Out of the proceeds the dues of the contributors are paid. If the work contributed by a member brings less than $75, he must make up the amount ; if it brings over $100 the surplus is turned over to him. The next, or Twenty-Third Annual Sale will be held in February, 1883. The services of the auctioneer at these sales are given gratis. — This Society claims to be the most successful benevolent organization in existence of those maintained by artists only.

ART STUDENTS' LEAGUE. — 38 W. 14th St. — Founded June 2, 1875 ; incorporated Feb. 8, 1878. — Officers : Pres., Wm. St. J. Harper, 11 E. 14th St. ; V. Ps., Miss A. B. Folger, Fred. Juengling ; Cor. Sec., G. Fitz Randolph ; Rec. Sec., Miss E.

L. Sylvester; Treas., B. N. Mitchill. The majority of the Board of Control must be students actually at work in the Life Classes; one of the Vice-Presidents must be nominated by the ladies. — Objects: The establishment and maintenance of an Academic School of Art, which shall give a thorough course of instruction in drawing, painting, and sculpture; the cultivation of a spirit of fraternity among Art Students. — The active members must be artists and students who intend to make art a profession; applicants for membership are required to work three months in the Life Class, before they can be elected. Present number of members, over 100. Honorary members may also be elected. The fixing of the annual membership fee is left to the Board of Control. — Classes (opened for the season 1882-3 on Oct. 2; close May 26, 1883): Drawing, Painting, or Modelling from life; Painting from Draped Model or Still-Life; Drawing from the Head; Drawing from the Antique; Sketch Class; Composition Class; Lectures on Perspective; Lectures on Artistic Anatomy. Both sexes taught together, except in the Life Classes The Classes are open for study from the life and the antique, every day in the week, morning, afternoon, and evening, during eight months in the year. — Instructors: Drawing and Painting, Morning Life Class, Morning and Afternoon Antique Class, and Composition Class, T. W. Dewing; Drawing and Painting, Evening Life Class and Evening Antique Class, Wm. Sartain; Drawing and Painting, Afternoon Life Class, and Classes in Drawing from the Head, C. Y. Turner; Painting Classes, Wm. M. Chase; Artistic Anatomy, J. S. Hartley; Perspective, Fred. Dielman. — Tuition fees: For students, not members of the League, the fees vary from $120 for the full term of eight months, six full days each week in the Painting Class, downward, according to time and subject. Members of the League pay less, and the Board of Control may relieve any student from the payment of class dues for a limited time, provided satisfactory reasons therefor are presented in writing. — Students of both sexes can enter any class immediately, upon submitting specimens of work which show the necessary proficiency. The requirements are as follows: Applicants for admission to the Life Classes must submit a drawing of a full-length nude figure from cast or life; for the Painting Class, a painting from life or still life; for Class in Drawing from the Head, a drawing of a head from cast or life; for the Antique Class, a drawing from cast; from the Composition Class, an original design; for the Sketch Class, apply to Sketch Class Committee. Number of students, season 1881-2: Life Classes, 88; daily average, 87 (37 ladies). Painting Classes, 77; monthly average, 67 (majority ladies). Antique Class, 152; average, 70. Sketch Class, average, 80. Composition Class, about 50. Total number of students entered during the season, 313, an increase of 25 over the previous season. — The collections belonging to the League consist of casts, studies, etc., and a library. — The peculiar feature of this school is that it is entirely under the control of the students, through the Board of Control elected by the members of the League. Practically, therefore, the students themselves appoint their teachers. The League has all along been quite successful, and the season of 1881-2 was the most prosperous the society has known since its organization. The treasurer in his last report estimated that the total cost of maintaining the classes would be about $8,000 for the school year. The total receipts, including surplus from last year, will exceed $11,000, an increase of $800 over the preceding season. The balance from last season of $1,500 has been added to the surplus fund, making the total amount invested in government and other bonds $5,000 par value, which amount is held as a reserve fund to guarantee the permanence of the school — Monthly evening receptions are given during the season, at which the work of the students is exhibited, together with other works of art. For further information address "The Art Students' League," 38 W. 14th St., New York.

ASTOR LIBRARY. — 34 Lafayette Pl. — Founded and endowed by John Jacob Astor; incorporated Jan. 18, 1849. — Officers: Pres., Alex Hamilton; Sec., Henry Drisler, 48 West 46th St.; Treas., John Jacob Astor; Libr., Frederick Saunders. —

The Library has no special art collections, but is very rich in works on archæology, architecture, the industrial arts, decoration, etc.; books of reference on art, and art manuals; illustrated works on the great galleries of Europe, etc. All the more important art journals of Europe are regularly received. — The Library is for reference only, and under no circumstances can books be taken away. — Open daily, except Sundays and holidays, from 9 A. M. to 5 P. M. from April to the end of July, and from the beginning of Sept. to end of Oct.; to 4.30 P. M. in Nov.; to 4 P. M. in Dec., Jan., and Feb.; and to 4.30 P. M. in March. Closed from end of July to beginning of Sept.

CENTURY CLUB. — 109 East 15th St. — Organized Dec., 1846. — Officers: Pres., Daniel Huntington, P. N. A., 49 East 20th St.; 1st V. P., Gilbert M. Speir, 9 East 34th St.; 2d V. P., Henry A. Oakley, 20 Fifth Ave.; Sec., A R. Mac-Donough, 19 Madison Ave. — This Club was formed by members of the old "Sketch Club," a private social club composed of artists, literary men, and art amateurs of the day. It remains true to its artistic traditions, counting not only a large number of artists among its numbers, but taking a lively interest in everything pertaining to art. The Club has a valuable permanent collection, in which the following painters and sculptors are represented: A. Bierstadt, Eug. Benson, H C. Bispham, J. F. Cropsey, Thos. S. Cummings, T. Colman, C. P. Cranch, F. O. C. Darley, W. P. W. Dana, A. B. Durand, C. T. Dix, Paul Duggan, J. W. Ehninger, Chas. L. Elliott, Regis Gignoux, F. Guenet, H. P. Gray, R. Swain Gifford, W. J. Hays, Thos. Hicks, D Huntington, R. W. Hubbard, E. L. Henry, W. J. Hennesey, Winslow Homer, A. C. Howland, Geo. Hess, C. C. Ingham, Jones, J. A. Jackson, Eastman Johnson, J. F. Kensett, Louis Lang, E. Leutze, Lancret, H. A. Loop, W. J. Linton, Wm. S. Mount, E. J. Man, L. R. Mignot, Jervis McEntee, H. D. Martin, Powers, C. S. Reinhart, Rondel, T. P. Rossiter, Jas. A. Suydam, R. M. Staigg, J. B. Stearns, Launt Thompson, E. Terry, G. Trumbull, Jr., L. Voelkert, J. F. Weir, M. Waterman, T. W Wood, W. Whittredge. Besides these originals, there are also a number of engravings, casts, photographs, etc. As the Club is not open to strangers, the collection can only be seen upon personal introduction by a member. For the monthly meetings held during the winter season, loan collections of works of art are gathered, and these remain on view the Sunday and Monday following the Saturday on which the meeting is held. To these exhibitions visitors are admitted on presenting the card of a member.

CHAMBER OF COMMERCE. — 63 William St. — Sec., George Wilson. — The Chamber owns a number of portraits, including some good specimens of the work of early American artists, as follows: — Matthew Pratt : full length of Lt.-Gov. Cadwallader Colden, painted for the Chamber in 1772 (the price paid to Pratt for this portrait was £37); J. S. Copley : Henry White (copy by an unknown artist); John Trumbull : full length of Alex. Hamilton, first Sec. of the Treasury, painted in 1792, and DeWitt Clinton; Henry Inman: DeWitt Clinton; H. P. Gray: Joshua Bates (copy after Eddis), and Isaac Carow (from a miniature); D. Huntington: John Murray (after Trumbull), Robert Lenox (after Jarvis), John C. Green (replica), John Sherman, Sec of the Treas., and S. B Ruggles; Thos. Hicks: Elias Hicks (replica), John Alsop copy from unknown original), John Cruger (from a miniature), Thos. Tileston, Pelatiah Perit (replica); Vinc. Colyer: Theophylact Bache (copy of a crayon by St. Memin); T. P. Rossiter : Jas. Boorman, Jas. Brown, Jas. G. King; Fagnani : Richard Cobden and John Bright, both from life. Unknown artists : Wm. Walton, Duke of Bridgewater, Jonathan Goodhue (marble bust). — The rooms of the Chamber are open, free to all visitors, on week days during business hours.

CHARCOAL CLUB — 14 and 16 W. 14th St. (at the Gambier Gallery). Organized April 12, 1882. — Officers: Pres., Chas. Volkmar, Tremont; V. P., F. Rondel, Sr., 1298 B'way ; Treas., Jos. Clare, Booth Bldg., 6th Ave. and 23d St.; Sec., Geo.

4

R. Hahn, 236 W. 25th St. — Objects : To secure the artistic improvement of its members by sketching and drawing from draped and nude models, still-life, etc., and to promote social intercourse. — Members : Active members, limited to 21, who must practise art as a profession. Honorary members, unlimited. Initiation fee, $10, monthly dues, $2, for both classes. Honorary members excluded on study nights, nor can they vote or hold office. Present number, 16 active, 7 honorary. — Meetings in winter, every Tuesday evening. In summer, one Sunday each month to be devoted to an excursion for sketching and out-of-door enjoyment. The social meetings, every fourth week, to be inaugurated by a half-hour address or paper to be read by a member on some art subject.

City Hall. — Broadway, opposite Murray St. — The Governor's Room, in the old City Hall, contains a collection of portraits of governors of the State, mayors of the city, and national celebrities which are well worth seeing, on account of the artistic and historical interest attaching to them. Among the painters whose work is represented here are John Trumbull (1756–1843), Vanderlyn (1776–1852), J. W. Jarvis (1780–1840), Samuel Waldo (1783–1861), S. F. B. Morse (1791–1872), Geo. Catlin (1796–1872), Henry Inman (1801–1846), C. L. Elliott (1812–1868), H. P. Gray (1819–1877), Weimar, A. H. Wenzler, W. H. Powell, Whitehorne, Mooney, Spencer, Robt. W. Weir, Wm. Page, D. Huntington, Thos. Hicks, F. B. Carpenter, J. H. Lazarus, and Mrs. Anna Lea Merritt. Many of these artists are represented by several specimens, Vanderlyn by four, Inman by six, Elliott by five, including one of his best larger works, the portrait of Gov. Bouck, dated 1847. The canvas by Morse is the full-length portrait of Lafayette, which he was commissioned to paint when the Marquis visited the United States in 1824 on an invitation by Congress. — The Governor's Room is open free to visitors all the year round, except on Sundays and holidays, from 10 A. M. to 3½ P. M. — The city owns a number of other interesting portraits, but as they are hung in the Mayor's office, and other rooms in constant use, they are not generally accessible.

College of Archæology and Æsthetics. — 120 E. 105th St. Incorporated 1880. — Officers : Chancellor, Hon. Amos K. Hadley, 237 E. 79th St. ; Vice-Chan. and Dean, Rev. J. W. Henry Canoll. — This institution comprises : I. The Philosophical Department, composed of the Fellows (electors) and Colleagues (associate members), who meet in sections for the reading and discussing of original essays and the presentation of facts relating to the history and the technicalities of the fine arts and various handicrafts. II. The Polytechnic Department, in which the strictly æsthetic arts are taught, including modelling, music, English versification, and literary criticism. — The College is self-supporting, and makes no appeals to the public for financial aid. Its museum and principal offices are at 120 E. 105th St., where free lectures are frequently given. The museum is open to the public, without charge, on Thursday evenings. It contains collections of ancient and modern pottery, numerous idols and religious symbols, antique books and manuscripts, laces and mediæval tapestry, mosaics, cameos, and gems. It affords peculiar advantages in studying the analogies of the arts. — Life Members, constituting the Fellows of the College, are elected only on especial nomination ; tickets, $100. Colleagues, entitled to all the privileges of the Philosophical Department, are elected on nomination of the Dean. The securing of an annual matriculation ticket is thereafter required, for which the fee is $1. Corresponding Members, having the privilege of presenting essays for discussion and requiring reports thereon, entitled also to replies to questions on art technics, are elected to annual membership. They are required to take a matriculation ticket, for which the fee is $3. — Pupils are admitted to the Polytechnic Department on application to the Dean. Fees in all branches of this department are moderate. The canons of the College prohibit the exactment of dues, fines, and assessments. They require that, as far as may be practicable, the institution shall be an unostentatious, liberal school of the æsthetic arts and cognate literature. — Inquiries and applications should be addressed to the Dean, Prof. Canoll, 120 E. 105th St. [From written information furnished by the Rev. J. W. Henry Canoll. There appear to be no printed catalogues or reports. Names of teachers not given.]

COLUMBIA COLLEGE. — Officers B'd of Trustees : Chairm., Hamilton Fish, LL. D., 251 E. 17th St.; Treas., Gouvern. M Ogden, 9 W. 10th St.; Clerk, Gerard Beekman, 5 E. 34th St.; Pres. of College, Fred. A. P. Barnard, S. T. D., LL. D., L. H. D., 63 E. 49th St. — *The School of Mines*, E. 49th St., cor. Madison Ave., established in connection with this College in 1864, offers six courses of study, viz.: Mining, Engineering, Civil Engineering, Metallurgy, Geology and Palæontology, Analytical and Applied Chemistry, and Architecture. Drawing, in its practical application to the subjects involved, is taught throughout the whole of each course (four years), with the exception of that in Chemistry, in which it is omitted in the third year. — *The Course in Architecture* was established in the year 1881, under the direction of Prof. Wm. R. Ware, formerly of the Massachusetts Institute of Technology, of Boston. This course is intended for those only who wish to pursue the study of architecture in the most thorough manner, and no students will be received who do not propose to take the entire four-years' course, with all the literary and scientific studies which may be laid down for the training of a scientific and thoroughly educated architect. (For a detailed exposition of the course, see the "Circular of Information," issued by the School of Mines.) — The school is well supplied with drawing models for the use of students, consisting of a large collection of flat models and of plaster casts (including casts from antique statuary) ; the Olivier models, forming all mathematical surfaces by silk threads, and admitting of a variety of transformations ; also other models, illustrating general and special problems of descriptive geometry, shades and shadows, and stone cutting ; photographs of plaster casts and of parts of machines for use in free-hand drawing ; drawings of machines and parts of machines for studying and copying; also, landscapes in crayon and in water-color for instruction in sketching ; and models of machines of all sorts.

COOPER UNION FOR THE ADVANCEMENT OF SCIENCE AND ART. — 7th St., cor. 4th Ave. — Founded in 1857 by Mr. Peter Cooper, and since sustained by his generosity, and a few small donations by others. Total expenditures, from organization to end of last term, $1,549,192. — Officers : Pres., Peter Cooper, 9 Lexington Ave.; Treas., Wilson G. Hunt, 331 Broadway ; Sec., Abram S. Hewitt, 9 Lexington Ave.; Curator, J. C. Zachos ; Clerk, W. H. Powell. — Besides its Free Library (about 16,000 vols., for reference only), Free Reading Room, Free Lectures, Free School of Telegraphy for Women, and Free Night Schools of Science, the Cooper Union maintains several Art Schools. — *The Free Art School for Women.* (Clerk, Mrs. M. B. Young.) Aim : To afford instruction in the Arts of Design to women, who, having the requisite taste and natural capacity, but are unable to pay for instruction, intend to apply the knowledge acquired in the institution to their support, either by teaching or pursuing Art as a profession. — Classes: Elementary drawing from objects ; Cast drawing ; Life drawing from draped model ; Normal designing class ; Oil painting ; Retouching and coloring photographs ; Porcelain painting ; Wood engraving. The classes are in session from beginning of October to end of May. Hours of study from 9 A. M. to 1 P. M. daily, except Saturdays and Sundays. Pupils may remain for practice until 4 P. M. — Teachers : Mrs. Susan N. Carter, Prin.; R. Swain Gifford, Oil, painting; John P. Davis, Wood engraving ; Miss C. E. Powers, Normal drawing ; S. A. Douglas Volk and J. Alden Weir, Life and cast drawing ; G. D. Brush, Cast drawing and composition ; Mrs. M. C. B Ellis, Crayon photographs ; W. W. Scott Photo-color ; Miss A. A. Wood, China painting ; Wm. H. Goodyear, Lecturer on art. — Tuition free; pupils must provide their own materials, etc. Orders for wood engraving and other work, to be executed by the students and graduates, are taken at the school, and the earnings, which amounted to $29,003 57 last season, go to the students who have done the work. — Students: Females only; ages from 16 to 35. Written reference must be given as to character, fitness, and inability to pay. For formalities of application, see circular to be obtained at the office of the Cooper Union. Pupils in the wood-engraving class not taken for less than three years. Number of students, season of 1881-2: Applied for admittance, 1,442; admitted, 755 (of whom 45 in wood-engraving class); remained at end of term, 715. — Money prizes varying from $5 to $50, silver and bronze medals, and honorable mentions are awarded at the Annual Exhibition in May. Certificates are given for drawing, painting (of two grades in these studies), normal drawing, and photo-crayon. — *Afternoon or Amateur School.* This department forms an exception to the rest of the institution, as the students are required to pay. — Classes: Elementary, cast and life drawing, from draped model, $15 for 30 lessons of 2½ hours each; Oil painting, $15 dollars for 20 lessons, 2 hours each (G. D. Brush, teacher); China painting, $3, 6 lessons; Designing class, $15, 30 lessons; Wood engraving (for particulars apply to Mrs. M. B. Young, Clerk of Women's Art School). The profits derived from this school go towards the maintenance of the free classes. — Students, female only, over 100. — *The Free Night School of Art.* Aim: Practical instruction, bearing on some useful employment in which the arts of design and drawing are the principal or accessory occupations. — Teachers and subjects taught: Mechanical drawing, J. A. Saxton, A. M., and Edm. Maurer; Architectural drawing, Edw. C. Miller and Emil Maurer; Perspective, Benj. Braman; Cast drawing, Wm. W. Scott; Form drawing, J. A. McDougall, Jr.; Ornamental drawing, Max Eglau; Figure and rudimental drawing, Geo. W. Maynard; Decorative designing, Theo. Baur; Modelling, Nic. Rossignoli. — The classes are in session from 7 30 to 9 30 P. M. Term begins Oct. 1, ends Apr. 15. — Tuition free, but pupils must provide materials. — Students, male only, must be at least 15 years old For formalities of application see "Rules and Regulations," to be obtained at the office of the Cooper Union. Number of students, season of 1881-2: Admitted during the term, 1,227; remained at close of term, 729. — Honorable mentions and prizes, and certificates of two grades, are awarded at the end of the term. A reception and exhibition of drawings deemed worthy of showing is given in May. — The teaching in the classes is supplemented in all the departments by lectures delivered by the instructors and others — A small gallery of photographs has lately been added for the use of the female students, comprising excellent examples from the early masters, Giotto, Cimabue, etc., and from Holbein, Velasquez, Titian, etc. During the past year Mr. Abram Hewitt has presented to the school a collection of beautiful casts. A set of the Elgin marbles and of various Greek statues, and Florentine bas-reliefs from originals by Donatello, Della Robbia, and others, fill the long corridor on the floor occupied by the Women's School with most inspiring examples of the art work of other times. The library, specially gathered for the use of this school, contains only 305 vols.; nevertheless the Principal says of it, "I believe it to be the most useful art library I have seen in this country."

GENERAL SOCIETY OF MECHANICS AND TRADESMEN OF THE CITY OF NEW YORK. — Mechanics' Hall, 18 E. 16th St. Chartered March 14, 1792. — Officers: Pres., John J. Tucker, 37 W. 12th St.; 1st V. P., Daniel Herbert, 215 E. 48th St; 2d V. P., John H. Rogers, 405 E. 83d St.; Treas., Jas. J. Burnet, 89 E 10th St.; Sec., Thos. Earle, Mechanics' Hall; Chairm. School Comm., Anthony O. Rowe, 360 West St.; Sec. School Comm., Augustus Meyers, foot of Horatio St. — This wealthy Society, organized, as its name indicates, by mechanics and tradesmen, for the purposes of benevolence, founded a *School for the Instruction and Improvement of Apprentices*, in which reading, writing, and arithmetic were taught, at a time when the public-school system was as yet undeveloped. Upon the establishment of these institutions, the course of instruction in the School of the Society was changed, and Architectural, Mechanical, and Free-Hand Drawing, together with Book-keeping and Penmanship, were substituted for "the three R's." The subjects last named were, finally, also dropped, and the school is now simply a *Free Drawing School.* — Teachers: John C. Babcock, Supt.; Henry Van Kuyck, Free-Hand drawing; C. H. Randolph, Elementary class; C. Otto Fichte, Advanced class; Jos. Crampton, Mechanical drawing; Jos. Monckton, Machine drawing; W. S. Purdy, Architectural drawing; Miss Lucy Stone, Ladies' class. — Term, 6 mos., begins the latter part of September, and ends in March. — Tuition absolutely free; materials supplied at cost. — Pupils last term, about 240 boys and young men; 60 females. Conditions of admission, good character; those working at some trade as apprentices or journeymen preferred. — Aim: To make mechanics more proficient in their trade by means of the art of drawing, and to train designers for the art industries. — The School is reported to be in a very prosperous condition. In the Ladies' Class, which has been in existence only about eight years, drawing from objects and designing are the principal studies; but these studies are also encouraged in the male classes. "The Ladies' Class," says the last annual report of the Chairman of the School Committee, "is an interesting feature of the School; some of the last year's pupils have developed excellent taste in designing, and found employment at good wages; others are reaching still higher." — Besides its School, the Society maintains a Free Library (about 60,000 vols.), and Reading-Room, and during the winter season arranges courses of lectures for its members and their families. Free Scholarships in Columbia College and in the University of New York are in the gift of the Society.

LADIES' ART ASSOCIATION. — 24 W. 14th St. Founded 1867; incorporated 1877. — Officers: Pres., Mrs. E. J Sterling, 29 Bedford Ave., Brooklyn; V. P's., Mrs. Jessie Curtis Shepherd, 54 W. 26th St., Miss Sara Rachel Hartley, 301 W. 4th St., Mrs. E. F. Coe, 668 Fifth Ave., Mrs. Florence I. Duncan, 912 Arch St., Phila.; Treas., Miss Charlotte J. Howells, Flushing, L. I.; Cor. Sec., Miss Martha Allason, 327 E. 58th St. — Objects: To promote the interest of Women Artists, and to found a central point of union and reference for its members; to provide instruction (1) for those already engaged as teachers of drawing and painting in schools and colleges, (2) in painting on porcelain and those departments of decoration which prove the most readily remunerative as a profession, (3) for boys and girls up to the age of fifteen in art industrial education, (4) for artists in study from life and nature; to enlarge facilities for non-residents, whose stay in New York is limited, and whose study needs direction; to provide a way for students to pay for art education by the Labor-Note System; to secure a building in which studios connected with apartments may be hired to members. — Members: Active, *i. e.*, professional women artists, $2 annually; Associates, *i. e.*, women art students, $3 annually; Subscribing Members, any lady or gentleman interested in art, $5 annually. Teachers of any specialty may become Subscribing Members on payment of 30 cents a month. Strangers may be introduced to the privileges of the rooms by members for $1 per month. There are also Honorary Members. Candidates for active membership must submit an original work of art to the Executive Committee. — The Association is supported by the dues of members, the small tuition fees paid by the pupils, and donations. — Classes and Teachers: Teachers' Class, drawing and painting, ———; Drawing and painting, J. Roy Robertson; Animal and landscape painting, A. Hochstein; Drawing from cast, Annie Morgan; Crayon and photo-crayon, Mrs. Blanca Bondi Robitscher; Copying heads in oil, Harriet C. Lane; Landscape in water-colors from nature, Mary J. Huygue; Perspective, E. C. Field; Children's Class, Alice Donlevy; Porcelain painting, Camille Piton; Botanical drawing, Sophie J. Knight. Opportunities for summer study, either independently or under a teacher, are afforded to those who wish to utilize part of their vacation. — Students: Female only, except in the Children's Class. The number varies from 80 to 100. A small fee is charged to students, but those who cannot pay are admitted on the Labor-Note System, an arrangement peculiar to this Association. Under it the student binds herself to do a certain amount of work for the Association, within a certain time, as an equivalent for the tuition given. Three scholarships have been established by Mrs. W. Jennings Demorest, Mrs. Edward Moran, and Mrs. Jane Russell. — During the last season a number of lectures were delivered by Dr. C. West on "Japanese Art" and "Art in the Stone Age"; A. Duncan Savage, "Greek Sculptures in the Cypriote Collection"; F. E. Tryatt, "How the Moon had her Portrait painted," and "American Pottery"; Sarah Rachel Hartley, "Peculiarities of Light," and others. At the monthly meetings art matters are discussed, and technical questions are submitted to specialists. — The erection of a Studio Building for Women is one of the principal objects of the Association. The first step towards the carrying out of this idea was taken on May 1, 1881, when a large room was hired, to be used as a class-room, while the apartments formerly occupied by the Association in the same building were let as studios to ten ladies. — The Association owns a small collection of books on art and education, illustrated books, casts, photographs, etc.

LENOX LIBRARY. — 1001 Fifth Ave., 70th and 71st Sts. — Founded by the late Mr James Lenox, who erected the building at a cost of about $1,000,000, endowed the institution with $250,000, and gave nearly the whole of the collections at present contained in it. Opened to the public in 1877. — George H. Moore, Sec. and Supt. — The Art Gallery, according to the last printed catalogue, spring 1882, contains 147 paintings, 18 works of sculpture, and 59 paintings on porcelain, enamels, mosaics, etc. (these latter exhibited in the rooms on the ground floor). The following are some of the artists represented in the collection. American artists: A. Bierstadt, Geo L. Brown, J. G. Chapman, F. E. Church, Thos. Cole, J. S. Copley, A. B. Durand, W. J. Hays, G. P. A. Healey, D. Huntington, H. Inman, J. W. Jarvis, J. F. Kensett, Chas. R Leslie (8 specimens), S. F. B. Morse, Wm. S. Mount, G. S. Newton, Jas. Peale, Rembrandt Peale, Gilbert Stuart (5 specimens), John Trumbull, John Vanderlyn, Thos. Ball, Thos. Crawford, Hiram Powers. European artists, old: Andrea del Sarto, Le Brun, Jacob Ruysdael, Salomon Ruysdael, European artists, modern: F. de Braekeleer, Sr., Sir A. Calcott, Wm. Collins, John Constable, Paul Delaroche, Leon y Escosura, Thos. Gainsborough, Sir Francis Grant, Carl Hübner, José Jimenez, Sir Edwin Landseer, J. B. Madon, Geo. Morland, J. L. E. Morgenstern, Wm. Mulready, M. Munkaczy ("Milton dictating to his Daughters," presented to the Library by Mr. Robert Lennox Kennedy), Peter Nasmyth, Sir Henry Raeburn, Sir Joshua Reynolds, David Roberts, H. Salentin, J. M. W. Turner (3 specimens), P. Van Schendel, Eug. Verboeckhoven, Horace Vernet, C. Wanters, Sir David Wilkie (7 specimens), Ed. Zamacois, E. Barrias, John Gibson, C. D. Rauch, Sir John Steell, etc. — The Library is exceedingly rich in incunabula and old illustrated books, valuable to the student of the history of engraving. A large number of these, together with a collection of old illuminated MSS, are exhibited in cases in the rooms on the lower floor. — Open to the public, until further notice, every Tuesday, Friday, and Saturday, except during the month of August, from 11 A. M. to 4 P. M. No person admitted without a ticket, which will be mailed to applicants free of charge. Address the Superintendent by postal card, at the Library. — Catalogues for sale; price 15 cents.

METROPOLITAN MUSEUM OF ART. — Central Park, Fifth Ave., and 82d St. — Inaugurated at a meeting held Nov. 23, 1869. Chartered Apr. 13, 1870. — Officers: Pres, John Taylor Johnston, 8 Fifth Ave.; V. Ps., Wm. C. Prime, 38 E. 23d St., D. Huntington, 49 E. 20th St.; Treas., Henry G. Marquand, 21 W. 20th St.; Sec. and Director, L. P. di Cesnola, 107 E. 57th St.; Libr., Wm. L. Andrews, 16

E. 38th St. — Objects: Establishing and maintaining a museum and library of art, encouraging and developing the study of the fine arts and the application of arts to manufactures and practical life, advancing the general knowledge of kindred subjects, and to that end furnishing popular instruction and recreation. — Members: The original incorporators, the Patrons and Fellows, and all persons duly elected, are life members of the corporation; new life members are elected by the corporation upon nomination of the Trustees. Annual members and Honorary Fellows may also be elected by the Trustees. The contribution of $1,000 entitles the contributor to be a Patron in perpetuity, with the privilege of appointing a successor; $500, a Fellow in perpetuity, with privilege of appointing a successor; $260, a Fellow for Life. Any person giving twice the value of the amounts named in works of art, if accepted, may be elected to either of the above degrees by the Trustees. Annual members pay $10 a year. Number of members, etc, Dec. 31, 1881: Patrons, 184; Fellows in Perpetuity, 134; Fellows for Life, 113; Honorary Fellows, 29; Annual Members, 526. Assessments may be laid on members of the Corporation, not to exceed $50 annually, as determined from time to time by the Trustees. (Such an assessment was laid in 1873.) — The government consists of the officers, 21 Trustees, and, *ex officiis*, the President of the Department of Public Parks, the Comptroller of the City of New York, and the President of the National Academy of Design. The officers are elected annually from among the members. The Trustees serve for seven years, and three are elected annually, also from among the members. — The Museum is dependent for support on the annual membership fees, which up to Dec. 31, 1881, amounted to $28,-179.50 in all; the receipts at the door on the two pay days, which, up to the same date, amounted to $36,453.91 (including the proceeds of the Centennial Exhibition held for the benefit of the Museum in 1876); the appropriations made by the city of New York; and donations in cash (by Patrons, Fellows, etc) and in works of art. The receipts for catalogues, etc., are offset by the cost of making and printing them. The city, authorized by act of Legislature of Apr. 5, 1861, put up the building now occupied by the Museum (which is only a small part of the structure as it is eventually to be) at a cost of nearly $500,000 This building, which remains the property of the city, is given rent-free so long as the Museum fulfils the conditions of its charter. The collections remain the property of the corporation, which can vacate the building at any time, upon giving due notice. The city was also authorized to expend certain moneys in keeping the building in repair, in installing the collections therein, and in maintaining them. Up to Dec 31, 1881, the city had expended upon the Museum, for these purposes the sum of $165,343.96. These appropriations, however, are not sufficient for current expenses, and are precarious, as they can be withheld or reduced at any time. The building having already become too small for the collections, the Legislature, in 1881, passed a bill authorizing the city to expend $240,000 additional, in four yearly instalments of $60,000 each, in extending it; but this bill failed to receive the approval of the governor. Another bill, subsequently passed and approved by the governor, authorized the expenditure of $60,000; but the Board of Apportion, ment declined to place the amount in the tax levy, and the act is no longer operative. The total of paid-in subscriptions to the funds of the Museum, according to the Twelfth (last) Report, amounted, on Dec. 31, 1881, to $459,589.80 According to the same report-the Museum on that date found itself in debt to the amount of $16,000. — This debt was, however, paid off by subscriptions received in January, 1882, so that it has now no liabilities. The works of art donated up to Dec. 31, 1881, are valued at $197,790.50. There is no endowment for purchases, and whenever a new acquisition is to be made, the friends of the Museum must be appealed to. "The members of the Museum," says the last Report, "have reason to congratulate themselves on its sound financial condition. They possess property, and are exhibiting for the instruction of the public, works of art which their private generosity has gathered, whose value in money, estimated at cost, is upwards of $600,000, and they owe no debt of any kind but grateful acknowledgment to one another of the cordial unanimity and determination of purpose which have led to our present condition of prosperity."—Of the purchases made by the Museum, the most important are as follows: A collection of 175 paintings, mostly by Flemish and Dutch artists of the 16th and 17th century, but including also some old Italian, French, and German pictures, costing about $145,000; Kensington reproductions, $3,160.76; Cesnola Collections of Cypriote Antiquities, $130,750.71; MacCallum Collection of Laces, $2,445; Collection of Babylonian Cylinders, $496 71; Avery Collection of Oriental Porcelain, $35,000; Collection of Antique Glass, $15,000; King Collection of Antique Engraved Gems, $6,000. Some of these collections were purchased with funds specially donated for the purpose, as for instance the Antique Glass, for which the money was supplied by Mr. Henry G. Marquand, while Mr. John Taylor Johnston provided the means to buy the King Collection of Gems. The following are some of the larger donations of works of art, with the names of the donors: Collection of Central American Pottery, etc., N. Y. Chapter of Amer. Inst. of Arch ; Thirty-eight oil paintings, the last summer studies executed by John F. Kensett, Thos. Kensett; Collection of Greek Vases, etc., Samuel G. Ward; Collection of Japanese Coins, etc., J. Carson Brevoort; 85 water color paintings by Wm. T. Richards, Rev. E. L. Magoon, D. D.; Collection of Ancient American Pottery, and another of old Venetian Glass, Henry G. Marquand; Collection of old Venetian Glass, etc., J. J. Jarves; Collection of 690 Drawings, etc., by old masters, Corn. Vanderbilt; Collection of Architectural Casts, Rich. M. Hunt; Collection of Peruvian Pottery, W. W. Evans; Collection of Egyptian Casts, and Collection of Ancient Coins, Jos. W. Drexel; Miscellaneous collection of works of art, valued at $50,000, bequeathed by Stephen Whitney Phœnix; Collection of casts of ivories, Alph. Duprat, etc. Besides these more extensive collections, the list of donations registers the gift of many smaller ones, and a large number of single pictures, statues in bronze and marble, objects of industrial art, etc.—The library is as yet small, but has lately received from Mr. Heber R. Bishop an endowment fund of $2,000, and a friend of the Museum has agreed to contribute $75 each year for subscriptions to periodicals.—The Museum has published a series of twelve etchings by Jules Jacquemart from paintings in its possession, and some of the antique jewelry of the Cesnola collection has been reproduced by Tiffany & Co. Photographs of some of the objects in the Museum are for sale at the door.—Besides the permanent exhibition of the collections owned by the corporation, there are two Loan Exhibitions each year, of paintings, and objects of industrial art, etc., loaned by private owners. The plan of lending for exhibition in different cities selections from the cabinets of the Museum, which, according to the Seventh Report, has been approved by the Trustees, has not yet been carried into execution.—The Museum was opened in a temporary gallery, 681 Fifth Ave., on Feb. 21, 1872. The year following it removed to a more commodious building, 128 W. 14th St. The transfer of the collections to the present building was accomplished in March and April, 1879; the opening occurred March 30, 1880.—The total number of visitors for the six years from 1873 to 1879 was 353,421. During the last year of the Museum's occupancy of the 14th St. building, there were 26,137 free, and 3,795 paying visitors. From the day of the opening of the new building, to April 30, 1881, a period of thirteen months, the visitors are given as 1,191,796 free and 8,577 paying. The last annual report, covering the period to Dec. 31, 1881, contains no statement of the number of visitors. From figures obtained at the Museum, the number of visitors, which are now counted automatically by means of turning stiles, footed up 105,386 free and 5,554 paying, total 110,940, for the six months from Jan. 1 to June 30, 1882.—The Museum publishes eight catalogues or "hand-books," which are for sale at the door, to wit: 1. Pictures by Old Masters, 10 cents. 2. Potteries of the Cesnola Collection, 10 cents. 3. Sculptures of the Cesnola Collection, 10 cents. (4 has been dropped.) 5. Oriental Porcelains, 10 cents. 6. Loan Collection, 10 cents. 7. Collection of Casts from Ivory Carvings, 10 cents. 8. Vanderbilt Collection of Drawings, 10 cents. 9. Engraved Gems, 15 cents. — The Museum is open daily, legal holidays included, except Sundays, and from April 15 to May 1, and Oct. 15 to Nov. 1, from 10 P. M. to one half hour before sunset. Admission on Mondays and Tuesdays, 25 cents; on other days free. (*Technical Schools of the Museum*, see below.)

NATIONAL ACADEMY OF DESIGN. — W. 23d St., cor. 4th Ave. Instituted 1826; Incorporated 1828. — Officers: Pres., Daniel Huntington, 49 E. 20th St.; V. P., Thos. W. Wood, 51 W. 10th St.; Cor. Sec., T. Addison Richards, National Academy; Rec. Sec., H. W. Robbins, 51 W. 10th St.; Treas., Alfred Jones, Am. B'k Note Co. — Members: Academicians, limited to 100, at present 92; Associates, at present 81, of whom 3 are ladies; Fellows for Life, contributors of $100 to the Fellowship Fund, at present 620; Fellows in Perpetuity, contributors of $500 to Fellowship Fund, 95 at present living. — *The Schools of the Academy* consist of an Antique School and a Life School. Aims and methods: In the Schools of the Academy, the principles and practice of art are taught chiefly through the study of the antique sculpture and the living model, both nude and draped, by means of lectures upon anatomy, perspective, and other subjects, through portrait, sketch, and composition classes, and in such other ways as may from time to time be provided. — The schools are open from the first Monday in October until the middle of May, daily, Saturdays and Sundays excepted, from 8 A. M., with morning, afternoon, and night sessions, either or all of which may be attended by the students. The life class begins on the third Monday of October. — Teachers: Lemuel E Wilmarth, N. A., Professor in Life and Antique Schools; C. R. Smith, Assist. in Antique School; J. Wells Champney, A. N. A., Lecturer on Anatomy. — *All* students must first enter the Antique School. Qualifications: Fair practice in study from plaster cast, to show which a shaded crayon drawing of part of the human figure must be exhibited to the School Committee. Students in the Antique School may be advanced to the Life School on showing to the Council an approved drawing of a full-length statue made in the Antique School, during the current session. Oil and water, colors, as well as crayons, may be used in the studies in both the Antique and Life Schools, when permitted by the professor. The duration of the course of study depends entirely upon the capacity and the progress of the student — Students of both sexes are taught together, except in the Life Classes. Total number, season of 1881-2, 190 (males 120, females 70). Number in each class: Antique, all students; Life, 50; Sketch, 40. — Lectures delivered last season: On Anatomy, by J. Wells Champney, A. N. A.; Perspective, Prof. E. L. Wilmarth, N. A.; Greek and Roman Costume, F. D. Millet, A. N. A. — All students are required to pay an annual entrance fee of $10, and must provide their own materials. Otherwise the instruction is free. — The "Elliott Medals," silver and bronze, are awarded in the Antique School; the "Suydam Medals," silver and bronze, in the Life School. Honorable mention is also accorded. An exhibition of the drawings which are specially made in competition for these prizes, and of other selected work by the students, usually held in the Lecture Room of the Academy, near the close of the session. — *Collections*: The Academy owns the portraits of all its Associates, and one work by each Academician, the presentation of these on election being one of the conditions of admission. It is also in possession of a collection of foreign and American pictures (bequeathed to it by Jas. A. Suydam, an American artist who died in 1865), and numerous other works of art. None of these are accessible, however, and most them are packed away, for lack of room. The Academy has, besides, an excellent collection of casts for the use of its schools, and a library. — *Exhibitions:* A

most important part of the activity of the Academy is found in its Exhibitions, which
have been held regularly since its organization, and of which there used to be two each
year, one in spring, the other in winter. The Winter Exhibition was abandoned
some years ago, but is to be revived this year, in the shape of a Special Autumn
Exhibition, to be held from Oct 23 to Nov. 18. — The building occupied by the
Academy, which is its property, was built from the plans of Mr. P. B. Wight, and
opened to the public in 1865. — For a history of the institution, see Thos. S. Cummings, N. A., " Historic Annals of the National Academy of Design." Phila. : Geo.
W. Childs. 1865.

NEW YORK CHAPTER OF AM. INST. OF ARCHITECTS. — Sec., A. J. Bloor, 335
Broadway. (See p. 1.)

NEW YORK ETCHING CLUB. — Organized Nov., 1878. — Officers : Pres., Henry
Farrer, 51 W. 10th St. ; Sec. and Treas., J. C. Nicoll, 51 W. 10th St ; Exec.
Comm., F. S. Church, 58 E. 13th St , Thos. Moran, 166 W. 55th St., F. Dielman, 51
W. 10th St. — Object : To advance the art of " Free-Hand Etching." — Members :
Resident, etchers resident in the city, or its immediate vicinity ; initiation fee, $10 ;
annual dues, $3. Non-resident, etchers living at a distance ; can neither vote nor
hold office, and are exempt from fees Present number of members, 36 (28 resident,
8 non-resident), one of whom is a lady. — The only public activity of the Club, so far,
has been the holding of exhibitions, the next of which will occur, in conjunction with
that of the American Water-Color Society, at the Academy of Design, from Jan. 29
to Feb. 24, 1883.

NEW YORK HISTORICAL SOCIETY. — 170 Second Ave. — Instituted 1804. — Offi-
cers : Pres., Frederic de Peyster ; 1st V. P., Hamilton Fish ; 2d V. P., Benj. H.
Field ; For. Cor. Sec., John Wm. Draper ; Dom. Cor. Sec., Edw. F. de Lancey ;
Rec. Sec., Andrew Warner ; Treas., Benj. B. Sherman ; Libr., Jacob B Moore ;
Chairm. of Comm. on Fine Arts, A. B. Durand. — Members : 481 resident, 641 life,
610 corresponding, 210 honorary ; total, 1942. — Art Gallery and Museum of the
N. Y. H. Soc. Besides a very valuable library (abt. 70,000 vols. not counting the
pamphlets, maps, newspapers, and MSS.), the Society owns the following collections
bearing upon Archæology and Art : 1. The Abbott Collection of Egyptian Antiquities, 1127 numbers ; 2. A Collection of Paintings, 791 numbers, comprising the
Bryan and the Dürr Collections of Old Masters, the Luman Reed Collection, the
Collection of the former New York Gallery, and a large number of single pictures
donated by artists and others [the Bryan and Dürr Collections afford the best and
most complete illustration of the History of Painting, from Christian Byzantine Art
down to that of our own time, to be found in the country, many of the specimens, all
of them presumably originals, being of excellent quality ; the History of Painting
in the U. S., from early colonial times to about the middle of this century, is
nowhere else so abundantly illustrated, especially as regards portraiture] ; 3. A
Collection of Sculptures, principally American, 57 numbers ; 4. The Lenox Collection of Nineveh Sculptures, 13 pieces ; 5. A Collection of American Antiquities,
at present packed away, for want of space ; 6. The nucleus of a Print Collection,
about 250 choice engravings, mostly by modern Italians, such as Raphael Morghen,
Volpato, etc., made by Luman Reed, the generous art patron of New York during
the first half of the century, and a volume containing all the engraved work of Asher
Brown Durand. — The rooms are open daily, from 9 A. M. to 6 P. M., except on
Sundays, legal holidays, and during the month of August. — The Historical Society
is a private association, but its policy is very liberal, and visitors, especially strangers,
can easily gain access by application to the librarian at the building, or by a card
or note of introduction from a member. No admission fee. Catalogues may be
obtained at the desk in the library. — The Society owns the building in which it is
located. It is very prosperous, having no debts, no mortgages on its building or col-

lections, and no outstanding bills. It has several funds, amounting in all to $74,050, some of which were given for special purposes, such as the publication of works of history, etc. The building erected as a Library, and not as an Art Gallery, is unfortunately but ill suited to the display of paintings, etc., and it is therefore the desire of the Society to provide, as soon as possible, another building, offering the requisite exhibition facilities.

NEW YORK TURNVEREIN. — Turnhalle, 64-68 East 4th St. — Officers: Pres., Anton Weidmann; Chairm. of School Comm., Jacob Heintz; Sec of School Comm., Gustav Scholer. — The School of the Turnverein was established in 1852, at first for gymnastic exercises only, to which reading and writing in German, singing, bookkeeping, drawing, modelling, and needle-work were added later. The aim of the school is: 1. Thorough and harmonious development of the body by gymnastic exercises; 2. The preservation of the German language and German customs; 3. Technical and artistic education by means of free-hand drawing, geometrical drawing, perspective, and modelling in clay. — The sessions of the classes begin at 4 o'clock in the afternoon, and there is also a Sunday school. Most of the pupils are boys and girls who attend the public schools, or young people already engaged in earning a living. The total number of pupils, in May and June last, was 973, of whom 175 were girls. The pupils pay 50 cents a month for instruction in gymnastics, which is obligatory. All other subjects are elective and are taught free. The school is supported by the small tuition fee charged, and by the interest on an invested fund of $9,000. — The Drawing and Modelling Classes are in charge of H. Metzner, 212 East 83d St. (who is also the Principal of the whole school), assisted by F. Eifler and R Singer. There are 12 classes in Free-Hand Drawing (2 of these for girls and 2 for young men), and one each in Geometry, Perspective, and Modelling. Number of pupils in drawing, abt. 600 boys and 150 girls; in modelling, 20, all grown up. The Classes in Needle-Work are attended by 120 girls. In the lower Drawing Classes, wall charts are used, prepared by the principal, and showing in the first stage straight and curved lines, angles, triangles, and squares, and thence progressing to simple geometrical forms, simple vessels, natural leaves, etc. These are succeeded by ornaments from the flat, and object drawing from geometrical models. In the higher classes ornament drawing in advanced stages is continued, and figure drawing is added. The more talented pupils draw from casts. All the drawing is done in lead pencil or crayon. The school owns a collection of about 600 models and casts, including antique busts, reliefs, statues, etc., which were bought of the widow of the late sculptor Plassmann.

PERMANENT EXHIBITIONS. — Permanent exhibitions are to be found at the galleries of the art dealers, among the most important of whom are the following: — The American Art Gallery, Kurtz Building, 6 E. 23d St., Madison Sq., Jas. F. Sutton, Proprietor. American Works of Art only; admission to gallery, 25 cents; open from 9 A. M. to 6 P. M., in winter also from 8½ to 10 P. M. — S. P. Avery, 86 Fifth Ave., near 14th St. Mostly foreign works of art; open free from 9 A. M. to 6 P. M.; closed from end of July to beginning of Sept. — Cottier & Co., 144 Fifth Ave. Principally decorative art work and furniture; also paintings, etc., mostly foreign; open free — M. Knoedler & Co. (Goupil & Co.), 170 Fifth Ave., corner 22d St. Foreign and American paintings, etc.; admission to gallery, 25 cents. — Adolph Kohn, 166 Fifth Ave. Foreign paintings; open free. — Gustav Reichard, 226 Fifth Ave. Foreign and American paintings, etc; open free. — William Schaus, 749 Broadway. Foreign paintings, etc.; open free.

SALMAGUNDI SKETCH CLUB. — Organized 1870; incorporated Feb. 23, 1880. — Officers: Pres., Jos. Hartley, 301 W. 4th St.; V. P, Chas. Volkmar, Tremont, N. Y. City; Rec. Sec., Sid. Osborne, 2 Neilson Pl.; Cor. Sec., F. M. Gregory, 19 University Pl.; Treas, A. C. Morgan, 58 E. 49th St. — Object: The encouragement of originality in its members, by the frequent submission of original sketches to mutual criticism; and the advancement of the interests of art in black and white by public exhibitions. — Members : Active, artists, either professional or amateur ; candidates must submit an original work, which, on election, becomes the property of the Club; entrance fee, $10; monthly dues, $1. Honorary, who need not be artists; annual dues, $5. Present number of members, 35 active, 2 honorary. — Every active member is expected to furnish a sketch at each weekly meeting, illustrating a subject previously selected by majority vote Whoever fails to do so, without good reason, at four successive meetings, may be dropped. — A yearly reception is given by the Club, to which gentlemen only are invited — The Club has successfully inaugurated the holding of *Black and White Exhibitions*, the fifth of which will open at the Academy on Dec 2, 1882. The by-laws provide that "the Art Jury [one of the standing committees] shall decide what works shall represent the Club, and what works shall be admitted to the exhibitions."

SOCIETY OF AMERICAN ARTISTS. — Organized 1878. — Officers: Pres , J. Wyatt Eaton, 80 E. Washington Sq ; V. P., A. H. Thayer, 52 E. 23d St.; Sec., Will H. Low, 152 W. 57th St ; Treas., J. Carroll Beckwith, 58 W. 57th St. — Object: The advancement of the Fine Arts — Members : Active only. Present number, 63, of whom 4 are ladies. — The only public activity of the Society, thus far, has been the holding of exhibitions. the Fifth of which was open, at the American Art Gallery, Kurtz Building, from April 6 to May 20, 1882. The Sixth Exhibition will be held at the same place in April, 1883. The constitution provides that " the Committee on Exhibition shall consist of the Board of Control and the Hanging Committee, and a majority shall decide as to the acceptance of any works of art." The following additional provisions are contained in the by-laws : " Space in exhibitions shall be allotted to pictures and other works of American artists in Europe, and the selection of such works of art shall be made by committees appointed by the Board of Control. Invitations to artists, not members of the Society, to submit pictures for exhibition, shall be issued only by the Committee on Exhibition."

SOCIETY OF AMERICAN WOOD-ENGRAVERS. — Organized Feb. 14, 1882. — Officers: Treas., John P. Davis, 109 W. 34th St.; Sec., Frederick Juengling, W. 161st St, second door east of Morris Ave. No president; chairman elected at each meeting. — Object : The advancement of Art in Wood Engraving. — Members : None but actual wood-engravers ; but any members of five years' standing, who may relinquish engraving after that time, may remain in the Society. Assessments may be levied, or dues established, by a two-thirds vote of all the members. The by-laws require every member, upon election, to subscribe $25 toward the general fund, subject to the call of the Treasurer. Present number of members, 9. — The Society proposes to publish a portfolio of proofs from blocks specially engraved by the members for the purpose.

SOCIETY OF DECORATIVE ART. — 28 E. 21st St. Organized March, 1877 ; incorporated March, 1878. — Officers: Pres., Mrs. Wm. T. Blodgett, 11 E. 12th St.; V. Ps., Mrs. J. E. Zimmerman, Mrs. H. G. De Forest, Mrs. Richd. M. Hunt, Mrs. U. W. Ireland ; Treas., Geo. C. Magoun, 10 E. 37th St.; Sec., Mrs. Frederick R. Jones, 312 E 18th St.; Asst. Sec., Mrs. G. A. Custer; Supt. and Book-keeper, Miss K. Stewart. — Objects : The reception, exhibition, and sale of artistic and decorative work ; the promotion of decorative art, and instruction in artistic and decorative work and industries. — The membership of the Society consists of Voting, Associate, and Honorary Members. — The Voting Members, who alone have the right to vote, and whose number is limited to 30, consist of the original incorporators, and such others as may be elected by the Board of Managers. Any person may become an Associate Member by an annual payment of $5. Besides the members, there are also " Annual Subscribers," who are accorded the privilege, in proportion to the amount of their subscription, of nominating a pupil or pupils to the free classes, and of designating poor needle-women, etc., as recipients of the charity of the Society, which is dispensed in the shape of materials furnished for work to be done. According to last report, there were 411 such subscribers.—The activity of the Society consists in the maintenance of classes, of a lending library, and of sales and work rooms for the taking and execution of orders and the sale of articles sent by "contributors" (i. e., needle-women, artists, etc., all over the country); the holding of sales at well-known summer resorts; the arrangement of competitions and exhibitions, etc. — *Classes:* Artistic embroidery (pay class, $5 for 6 lessons; free class for professional students, nominated by subscribers); Painting on China: Underglaze, teacher, Miss M. V. Mead, Limoge, Mr Chas. Volkmar (mostly paid pupils, $2 a lesson); Water color, decorative work only, teacher, Miss M. V. Mead (paying pupils only, individual lessons, $1 50; in classes of not over six, $1 per lesson); Object drawing in charcoal and pencil for children and young people: Teacher, Miss Amanda Brewster ($8 for 12 lessons of 1½ hours each). Classes are also held during July, August, and September at various summer resorts. The free classes have been full during all the year, and the more competent graduates have found instant and remunerative employment. — *The Lending Library* is used as a means of instructing distant workers, to whom books, patterns, designs, etc., are sent by mail, — an advantage which is highly appreciated by them. The last report acknowledges a gift of $150 for the Library, and expresses the hope that it may prove a suggestion to others. — *The Sales-Rooms and Work-Rooms* are reported to have been prosperously active during the past year. "The work of the Needle-Work Department," says the Report, "continues both in quantity and quality to be steadily progressive. Aside from the financial aid given through the work-rooms, this department has become a centre of instruction, from which many skilled workers have gone forth, both as independent teachers and as aids to anxiliary societies." The articles contributed, or sent for sale, by outside workers, are examined by a committee, and those approved are accepted. According to last Report, out of 4,677 articles sent during the year, 2,310 were rejected. Contributors whose articles are rejected may, by request, receive special criticism and advice. A commission of 10 per cent is charged on the sales of contributed articles; and as the commissions received in 1881, according to the treasurer's report, amounted to $3,142, it follows that sales to the amount of $31,420 must have been made. Twenty-six women were also assisted by sending them work. "This work has been sent," says the Report, "to North Carolina and South Carolina, Virginia, Maryland, New Jersey, Massachusetts, New York, and Connecticut; in almost all instances to obscure towns, and in many cases to invalids, to whom it brought pleasure and interest as well as profit." —*Competitions and Exhibitions.* The last exhibition held by the Society, in May, 1881, was one of Competitive Prize Designs, in connection with a Loan Exhibition, at which $1,300 were distributed in prizes. — This Society was the first to conceive the idea of combining education in decorative art with honorable aid to struggling and deserving women, and is the parent society of the various associations of like title now existing in the U. S. and Canada All its operations are carried on in the interest of its pupils, workers, and contributors. Its income is mainly derived from membership dues and annual subscriptions, tuition fees, profits on materials sold and orders executed, and commissions on sales. "The success of the work thus far has been entirely due to the personal efforts of the working members of the Society, some of whom, since its foundation, have given daily to its advancement many hours of thought and active labor. It has had no large donations, no legacies, no capital, nothing but the determination to succeed in the work of educating women in marketable art industries which inspired its organization five years ago."

TECHNICAL SCHOOLS OF THE METROPOLITAN MUSEUM OF ART. — 214 and 216 E. 34th St. — Officers: Museum Comm. on Art Schools and Industrial Art,

Robert Hoe, Jr., 11 E. 36th St.; Wm. L. Andrews, 16 E. 38th St.; Wm. E. Dodge, Jr, 262 Madison Ave ; J. T. Johnson, 8 Fifth Ave.; Sec. of Comm. and Manager of Schools, Jno. Buckingham, 162 Second Ave. — Aims : These Schools form part of the system of art education for which the Museum was established. The value of technical education in foreign schools being evident in the prices commanded by workmen who have had these advantages, it is proposed to furnish the facilities, not hitherto attainable in this country, for a combined artistic and practical experience in the branches taught. — The last term began Oct. 4, 1881, and ended May 31, 1882. — Classes : 1. Drawing and Designing ; instructors, Ernest Gilles and B. Palladino ; fee for the course, $6; number of pupils on roll, 59. 2. Modelling ; instructor, Jos. Smith ; fee, $10 ; number of pupils, 30. 3. Carriage Drafting and Construction (under special direction of the Carriage Builders' National Assoc.) ; instructor, John D. Gribbon; fee, $5; pupils, 49. 4. Fresco Decoration ; instructor, C. C. Pyne ; fee per month, $4; pupils, 7. The above classes meet in the evening, from 7.30 to 10. 5. Day Class in Tempera Decoration for Women (Object : To furnish instruction to young women seeking a means of support in practical, remunerative production); instructor, W. Ostrander ; fee for the course, $15; pupils, 18. Total number of pupils on roll, 163. — The fees charged are only intended to cover the cost of materials used. The school has an invested fund of $50,000, the gift of Mr. G. F. T. Reed, and receives $1,200 p. a from the Carriage Builders' National Association. Part of the deficit of last year was covered by a Special Subscription of $500, and a cash payment of $3,335.84 by the Museum, leaving a balance of $1,233.36 to be provided for.

TILE CLUB. — 58½ W. 10th St. — Organized fall of 1877. — This Club is a rather informal association of artists, musicians, etc., without constitution and by-laws, and even without officers. The Club meets every Wednesday evening during the winter season, when part of the evening is devoted to the decoration of tiles, plaques, etc. The members act as hosts in turn, the host of the evening providing the tiles and materials, as well as the plain fare which the traditions of the Club allow, receiving in return the artistic product of the evening's labors. The Tile Club has been made famous by the articles descriptive of its summer excursions, written and illustrated by members, which have appeared in "Scribner's Monthly." Messrs. Harper & Bros. are now producing in its behalf an important artistic publication under the title of "Harper's Christmas Pictures and Papers, done by the Tile Club and its Literary Friends."

YOUNG MEN'S CHRISTIAN ASSOCIATION. — 52 E. 23d St., cor. 4th Ave. — Officers : Pres., Elbert B. Monroe; V. P., Cornelius Vanderbilt; Cor. Sec., R. R. McBurney; Rec. Sec, J. V. Van Woert, Jr.; Treas., Waldron P. Brown; Libr., Reuben R. Pool. — The Association owns and is the depository of a number of paintings, which have been distributed throughout the various rooms, but are accessible to all visitors. Prominent among them are, the series of three large allegorical landscapes, "The Cross and the World," by Thos. Cole ; a mountain gorge with a waterfall, by Kensett, a very good specimen ; "Peace and Plenty," an immense landscape by Geo. Inness, dated 1865; a very good portrait of John Howard, the philanthropist, attributed to Gainsborough; Rossiter's portrait group, "American Merchants"; and three pictures by Federigo Nerly (Friedrich Nehrlich), a German artist. — The Library (over 18,000 vols.), for reference only, contains a very good and quite extensive collection of books on the various branches of art, with a preponderance of architecture and the decorative arts; illustrated works on the great European galleries ; illustrated art journals, etc. It possesses also the nearest approach to a *Collection of Prints* to be found in any public institution of the city of New York, including the collection of about 8,000 engraved portraits, many of them by celebrated engravers and in good impressions, arranged in 35 folio volumes begun by John Percival, Earl of Egmont, and completed by John T. Graves, purchased for $1,600; a collection of imitations of drawings in aquatint, etc, such as were so popular in the last century; several volumes with old Dutch etchings, etc. — The rooms of the Association, as well as the Library, are open week days, including holidays, from 8 A. M. to 10 P. M.; Sundays from 1½ to 10 P. M. Admission free.

Northampton, Mass. — SMITH COLLEGE. — Founded by Miss Sophia Smith, of Hatfield, Mass., who bequeathed for that purpose property amounting now to over $500,000. — Officers: Pres. of B'd of Trustees and of Fac., Rev. L. Clark Seelye, D. D.; Treas., Hon. Geo. W. Hubbard. — Object: To furnish to young women means and facilities for education equal to those afforded in our colleges to young men. The College is not intended to fit woman for a particular sphere or profession, but to perfect her intellect by those methods which philosophy and experience have approved, so that she may be better qualified to enjoy and do well her work in life, whatever that work may be. It is to be a Woman's College, aiming not only to give the broadest and highest intellectual culture, but also to preserve and perfect every characteristic of a complete womanhood. — No preparatory department is connected with the institution. The standard of admission and the standard of instruction are in accordance with its legitimate collegiate work. — The study of art in any form is not obligatory in the College, but the students are admitted gratuitously to all lectures in the *School of Art*, which forms a separate department. The aim of this School is to furnish an opportunity for the progressive study of drawing, painting, and sculpture. Its privileges are accorded to all regular students who may elect to use them. Special students are admitted, if they are sixteen years of age, and have pursued courses of study equivalent to those required for graduation from a standard High School. They will be expected, unless excused by the President, to take, under the direction of the Faculty, at least two collegiate studies in those branches which they are qualified to pursue. Lectures will be given to all the students upon Architecture, Sculpture, Painting, and Household Decoration. — Teachers: Prof. John H. Niemeyer, of Yale College, Drawing and Painting; Prof. Richd. H. Mather, D. D., of Amherst College, History of Sculpture. — Terms: One lesson a week, $30 a year; $20 a half-year. To special students, $40 and $25. — Number of students according to last report, October, 1881, 16, of whom 7 were special. — *Art Gallery.* The collections owned by the College embrace several hundred antotypes, illustrating the history of painting in chronological sequence; a collection of casts from the antique, from architectural details, etc.; and a collection of original oil paintings, embracing the works of the most distinguished American painters. Through the generosity of Mr. Winthrop Hillyer a new Art Gallery has just been erected, 180 by 50 feet, designed exclusively for the collections and for studios. The building has been constructed with special reference to the exhibition of works of art, great pains having been taken to avoid cross lights. The lower floor, devoted to sculpture and to studios, is 18 ft. high, with the exception of a long corridor, which is 20 ft. high. In the upper story there are galleries for oil paintings (26 ft. high, and 25 by 54 ft. in dimension) and for the exhibition of architectural specimens. These are surrounded by a corridor 12 ft. wide arranged for the exhibition of smaller pictures, and to give opportunity for a free circulation of air through the entire building.

Norwalk, O. — FIRELANDS HISTORICAL SOCIETY. — Cabinet of Indian and other relics.

Peoria, Ill. — LADIES' ART SOCIETY. — Rec. Sec., Miss Alice M. Dodge; Cor. Sec., Miss Minnie E. Bills. (See *Central Ill. Art Union*, Springfield, Ill.)

Philadelphia, Pa. — ACADEMY OF NATURAL SCIENCES. — S. W. cor. 19th and Race Sts. Organized March 21, 1812; chartered March 24, 1817. — Officers:

Pres., Jos. Leidy, M. D., 1302 Filbert St.; V. Ps., Thos. Meehan, Germantown, and Rev. H. C. McCook, D. D., 125 N. 21st St.; Rec. Sec. and Libr., Edw. J. Nolan, M. D , 1418 N. 18th St.; Cor. Sec., Geo. H. Horn, M. D., 874 N. 4th St.; Treas , Wm C. Henszey. — The *Museum* of the Academy is mainly filled with specimens illustrating zoölogy, botany, mineralogy, etc., although anthropology, including archæology, ethnography, and ethnology, is also within its province. The archæological and ethnographic collections are as yet limited, but are constantly increasing by gifts. The following are the more important components of these collections as at present constituted : The Peale collection of stone implements, made by Franklin Peale, one of the sons of Chas Wilson Peale ; Prof. S. S. Haldeman's collection of stone implements, pottery, etc. ; a small collection of Egyptian and Greek antiquities ; the Poinsett Collection of Mexican antiquities, mainly pottery and small sculptures ; a collection of Peruvian pottery, and some specimens of Nicaragua pottery presented by Dr. J. F. Bransford. — The *Library*, which is quite extensive, includes a valnable collection of works on Roman, Greek, and French antiquities, among which is a complete set of Piranesi. A series of portraits of presidents and benefactors of the Academy is hung in the Library. — Open daily, except Sundays and holidays, from 9 till sunset. Admission to Museum, 10 cents ; students admitted free on application to the secretary, Dr. E. J. Nolan, or to the curator in charge, Mr. Chas. F. Parker. The archæological collections are not in the main museum, but can be seen on application to the officer in charge. They are not included in the " Guide to the Museum " (published 1876), for sale at the door.

ARTISTS' FUND SOCIETY. — Incorporated April 29, 1835. — Officers : Pres , I. L. Williams, 1334 Chestnut St ; V. P., Geo. C. Lambdin, 1520 Chestnut St.; Sec , F. DeB. Richards, 1520 Chestnut St. ; Treas , Samuel Sartain, 210 Franklin St — Objects : The relief of such artists or their families as may be, by the by-laws, entitled to pecuniary assistance, and such modes of promoting the cultivation of skill, the diffusion of taste and the encouragement of living professional talent in the arts of painting, sculpture, architecture, and engraving, as may best conduce to the primary purpose of benevolence. — There are four classes of members (both sexes) : Members of the Board of Control (initiation fee, $50, in cash or in a work of art; annual dues, $3), professional artists who have resided in or near Philadelphia for one year ; Associates, gentlemen and ladies residing in Philadelphia or vicinity, who shall pay an annual contribution ; Life Members, who pay $100 on election, and Honorary Members, distinguished non-resident artists. — The Board of Control, in which all the powers of the body are vested, consists of the original incorporators and such other persons elected by them from among the members. — The Society has two funds, the Benevolent Fund and the Trust Fund. The former is sustained by dues, sales of works of art contributed by members and others, interest on investments and donations. Appropriations may be made from this fund for the relief of sick and disabled members, and the heirs of deceased members are paid about $100 out of it. The Trust Fund consists of voluntary contributions which are placed to the credit of the member contributing. The interest derived from this fund goes to the Benevolent Fund, but the principal is paid over to the heirs of the contributor upon his or her death — In its earlier years, under the presidency of John Neagle, this Society included a large majority of the resident artists among its members, and up to the year 1845 furnished, with some few exceptions, all the annual exhibitions opened in Philadelphia. Its last annual exhibition in 1845 was held in conjunction with the Penn. Academy of Fine Arts, the Society having, in the year 1840, made an arrangement with that institution, by which they had erected a separate exhibition gallery in front of the building of the Academy. After the fire in the Academy in 1846, the Society led a very quiet life until 1862-3, when occasional receptions and exhibitions were gotten up. In the year 1866 the suite of galleries on the second floor of 1334 Chestnut St. was leased, free exhibitions were arranged and a series of sales held, the amount realized over $100 on each work sold going to the contributor. The venture was not successful, however, and at the end of its three years' lease the Society found that the proceeds of the annual sales and the money received from annual contributors (of whom there were then about 100, at $10 each) had been swallowed up by the expenses. Since then all exhibitions have been abandoned, and under its present by-laws, as remodelled in 1877, the Society has taken a fresh start, with a good outlook for the future.

FAIRMOUNT PARK ART ASSOCIATION. — 524 Walnut St., room 18. Incorporated Feb. 2, 1872. — Officers: Pres., A. J. Drexel, S. 39th, cor. Walnut St; V. P., Chas. H. Rogers, York Road; Treas., Jas. L. Claghorn, 222 N. 19th St.; Sec., John Bellangee Cox, 524 Walnut St. — Objects: To embellish Fairmount Park with fountains, statues, busts, and similar ornaments, such as good taste shall dictate, and the Commissioners of the Park sanction. — Members (both sexes): Annual, $1 initiation fee and $5 p. a.; Life, $1 and one payment of $50; Honorary. Present number: Honorary, 7; Life, 123; Annual, 814. — The income is derived from membership dues and donations. Funds in hand according to last printed report: Permanent Fund, $10,052.57; General Fund, $6,628.40; Meade Memorial Fund, $14,684.20. — The Association has thus far presented 13 works of art to the Park; and has voted to contribute $5,000 to the Meade Memorial Fund, of which it is the Trustee, and to become a contributor to the fund for a statue to General Reynolds, started by Mr. Jas. E. Temple. It has also resolved to create a fund for the erection of a Garfield monument in Fairmount Park.

FRANKLIN INSTITUTE OF THE STATE OF PENNSYLVANIA FOR THE PROMOTION OF THE MECHANIC ARTS. — No. 15 South Seventh St. — Officers: Pres., W. P. Tatham, 1420 Walnut St.; Sec., Wm. H. Wahl, 1436 N. 13th St.; D. S. Holman, Actuary. — *Drawing School of the Institute.* Aims and Methods: The main feature of the School has been the teaching of such drawing as would be useful in the workshop and applicable to construction as well as to ornamentation, and thus a large part of the instruction has been devoted to the geometrical principles of drawing, but the demonstration and application of these principles have always been made to conform with the practice of the best engineers and architects, while proper manipulation and correct technicalities have been rigidly enforced, so that the student would learn how to properly use his hands and his instruments; how to give clearness and beauty to his work, and at the same time obtain a knowledge of geometrical forms and their projections, intersections and developments, and finally, learn to make working drawings of machine or architectural constructions. In this course, the use of copies has been almost entirely avoided, the student being required to make his drawings accurately to scale, either from free-hand sketches, or from the drawing on the blackboard by the preceptor, who spends part of his time there and part with the student in giving individual instruction and criticism. Importance is attached to the free-hand sketches of the student, and the value of this accomplishment is always kept in view. The class of exclusively free-hand drawing has been small, but the progress has been very satisfactory. — Classes and Teachers, etc.: Junior Class, teacher, Carl Barth; Intermediate Class, Victor Angerer; Senior Mechanical Class, Wm. H. Thorne, Principal; Architectural Class and Free-Hand Class, W. L. Price. Two terms of 16 weeks each; Winter from Oct. to Jan.; Spring from Jan. to May. The next Winter term begins Oct. 2, 1882. Hours of attendance, Tuesday and Thursday evenings from 7½ to 9½ P. M. The full course extends over two years, but special subjects may be selected by sufficiently advanced pupils. Students are required to do home work. — Pupils: Winter Term, 1881-2, 166; Spring Term, 1882, 123. — Tuition Fee, $5 per term of sixteen weeks. Pupils must provide their own apparatus and materials. Twelve free scholarships, from the

5

B. H. Bartol Fund, are awarded each year to pupils who have successfully completed their first term. Students also have the free use of the library of the Institute. — Certificates of proficiency, graded according to merit, are given to those who have completed the full course of two years. — This Drawing School has been in operation for more than half a century, and the Institute is now so crowded for room, that a subscription has been set on foot for a building fund of $200,000. — For tickets to the School and further information apply to D. S. Holman, Actuary, at the rooms of the Institute.

HISTORICAL SOCIETY OF PENNSYLVANIA. — 822 Spruce St. — Organized Dec. 2, 1824. — Libr., F. D. Stone. — Collection of portraits, paintings, and engravings of historical interest, and of Indian and other antiquities. A catalogue was published in 1872.

INDEPENDENCE HALL AND NATIONAL MUSEUM. — Old State House, Chestnut, bet. 5th and 6th Sts. — In the old State House of Pennsylvania, the Second Continental Congress, sitting in the east room on the first floor, adopted the Declaration of Independence on July 4, 1776. This room, since known as *Independence Hall*, was restored to its original state as far as possible about ten years ago, and upon its walls was placed a collection of portraits, all of them absolutely authenticated, of the men who signed, voted upon, or debated the Declaration in this very chamber. A large number of these portraits are originals by Chas. Wilson Peale, which formerly belonged to his Museum, others are copies after Copley, Trumbull, Stuart, etc. A descriptive catalogue, price 25 cents, is for sale at the Hall. — The western room, on the same floor, formerly the Judicial Hall of the Colony of Pennsylvania, is occupied by the *National Museum*. Besides many relics of great interest and value, illustrative of the history of Pennsylvania, this Museum contains also a number of paintings, among them "Penn's Treaty with the Indians" and a portrait of Chief Justice Allen, both by Benj. West, and quite a large number of crayons by Sharpless, including portraits of Mr. and Mrs. Washington, John Adams, Jefferson, Madison, and other personages of distinction. There is no catalogue of this Museum. — Open free, all the year round except Sundays, from 8½ A. M. to 5 P. M. — The statue of Washington in front of the building is by J. A. Bailly.

LADIES' DECORATIVE ART CLUB. — 1512 Pine St. — Organized Dec., 1881. — Officers: Pres., Chas. G. Leland; Sec., Mrs. James Mifflin; Treas., Miss Elizabeth Robins. — The great aim of this Club is to have its members taught something serious in the way of Design and Art, a little deeper than the present fashion of making something merely pretty. All facilities and help will be given for the production of objects of art for purposes of sale or otherwise, and opportunity given to those who wish systematic study, with a view to making it a profession. — Membership limited to 200 (the Club is full); terms, $25, which entitles members to one lesson a week in each department of the school maintained by the Club. — Classes and Teachers: Preliminary Drawing, Designing in Monochrome, and several minor arts, Chas. G. Leland; Painting from Still-Life, Casts, Flowers, Living Models in Costume, etc., J. Liberty Tadd; Modelling from Still-Life, Fruit, Flowers, the Living Model, etc., J. Liberty Tadd; Different Styles of Pottery, Limoges, High or Low Relief, Underglaze Painting, etc., J. Liberty Tadd; China Overglaze Painting, Miss E. D. Paul; Wood Carving, H Uble; Repoussée. It is proposed to have a Life Class, for which an extra charge will be made. Term from Oct. 15 to June 1. — The Club occupies an entire house devoted to the different classes, a salesroom, library, etc. Lectures and exhibitions are also to be provided.

NUMISMATIC AND ANTIQUARIAN SOCIETY. — S. W. cor. 18th and Chestnut Sts. — Incorporated, Feb. 19, 1858, as the Numismatic Society of Philadelphia; present name adopted in 1865. — Officers: Pres., Eli K. Price, LL. D., 709 Walnut St.; Cor. Sec. and Treas., Henry Phillips, Jr., 200 S. 5th St.; Curator of Numismatics, Robt. Coulton Davis, Vine, cor. N. 16th St. ; Curator of Antiqu., Francis Jordan, Jr., 4212 Chestnut St. ; Libr., Phil. Howard Law, 115 S. 17th St. — Object : To encourage and promote numismatic science and antiquarian research. — Members : Resident (initiation fee, $5, diploma fee, 50 cents, annual dues, $5, or $50 in commutation of all fees) ; Corresponding ; Honorary. — Besides a Library, the Society has also a cabinet of coins and medals, Grecian, Mexican, and other American antiquities, pottery, engravings, etc., which is open to members only. The coins and medals, however, have been placed on exhibition at the Pennsylvania Museum of Industrial Art, Memorial Hall, Fairmount Park, together with similar collections belonging to the Library Company of Philadelphia, and the American Philosophical Society. For some description of these collections see Henry Phillips, Jr., " Notes upon the Collection of Coins and Medals," etc., Phil., 1879 (reprinted from the Proceedings of the American Philosophical Society), and " Additional Notes upon the Collection of Coins and Medals," etc. (read before the American Philosophical Society, Oct. 3, 1879), which can be obtained at Memorial Hall. — The Numismatic and Antiquarian Society of Philadelphia is the oldest of its kind in the U. S.

PENNSYLVANIA ACADEMY OF THE FINE ARTS. — N. Broad, cor. Cherry St. — Organized Dec., 1805; incorporated March 28. 1806. — Officers : Pres., James L. Claghorn, 222 N. 19th St. ; Treas., Edward H. Coates, 116 Chestnut St. ; Sec., Geo. Corliss ; Chairm. of Comm. on Instruction, Fairman Rogers, 202 S. 19th St. ; Curator of the School and Libr., H. C. Whipple. — Objects : To promote the knowledge and enjoyment of, and cultivation in, the Fine Arts in the city of Philadelphia, by the establishment of schools and other methods of instruction ; by books and other publications ; by the establishment of a gallery, or galleries, of paintings or sculpture ; and by such other methods as in their judgments may seem proper. — Membership is confined to the stockholders, at present over 1,100, who elect the President and a Board of Directors. Liberal patrons of the Academy and distinguished friends of art may be elected Honorary Members by the Board ; distinguished artists may be elected Professional Honorary Members in the same way. Present number of Honorary Members, 96. — The funds with which the Academy has been established were raised entirely by subscription. Its capital is limited to 10,000 shares at $100 each, and of these 3,456, representing a value of $345,600, have been subscribed and paid for. The income is limited to admission and tuition fees, and donations. The Academy has also the following invested funds, given for specified purposes : Temple Trust Fund, $55,000, the interest to be used for purchases at the exhibitions of the Academy ; Phillips Bequest, $12,000, for the maintenance of the Phillips Collection ; Charles Toppan Prize Fund, $8,000 ; and Mary Smith Prize Fund, $2,000. — Exhibitions. Two or more exhibitions are held every year. The regular Annual Exhibition, held in spring heretofore, is in future to be held in autumn. At the exhibition of last autumn 26 works, valued at $9,858 were sold, out of 428 works exhibited by 272 artists. The Fifty-Third Annual Exhibition opens Oct. 23 and will continue until Dec. 9, 1882. At this exhibition the Mary Smith Prize of $100 will be given to the best painting in oil or water colors by a resident Philadelphia lady artist, and the two Charles Toppan Prizes, of $200 and $100 respectively, will be awarded for the two best pictures by students of the Academy. At the Fifty-Fourth Exhibition, to be held in the autumn of 1883, special prizes will be given in the "Temple Competition in Historical Painting," the details of which will be found in the chapter on " Coming Exhibitions." — Collections. The last edition of the Catalogue of the Permanent Collection of the Academy, dated 1881, enumerates 259 paintings and 60 pieces of sculpture (not including the casts used in the schools), acquired mostly by donation and bequest. Some of the pictures bear the names of old masters, and among the later acquisitions there are a number of large canvases by well-known European artists, such as

Wittkamp, Janssen, Bouguereau, Kaulbach, Hermans, etc. The interest centres, however, upon the paintings by American artists, in which the collection is very rich, standing, in this respect, next to that of the N. Y. Historical Society, and rather surpassing it in variety of subject. Among the artists represented may be named : Stuart, Trumbull, Sully, West ("Death on the Pale Horse," "Paul and Barnabas," "Christ Rejected"), Allston ("Dead Man Restored to Life"), the Peales, Vanderlyn ("Ariadne"), Leslie, Neagle, Shaw, Doughty, Mount, Inman, Rothermel, Shüssele, Leutze, May, Gray, Huntington, etc. Generous patrons have lately begun to increase the collection by works of American artists of the younger generation bought at the exhibitions held at the Academy. In this way have been acquired the paintings by Robert Wylie, Picknell, R. Koehler, presented by Mr. Jos. E. Temple, and Dana, presented by Mr. Atherton Blight. The sculptures also include many works by earlier American artists, such as Rush, Frazee, Clevenger, etc. — *The Phillips Collection of Engravings*, left to the Academy by its former owner, with the fund alluded to above, contains about 60,000 impressions, and is the largest public collection of its kind in the U. S. — Besides these collections there is a *Library* of works on art of about 1,000 volumes. Open every week day, throughout the year, from 9 A. M. to 6 P. M.; admission 25 cents. Sundays, open free, from 1 to 6 P. M., on tickets obtainable at the Academy during the week. Strangers from out of town are admitted without tickets. Catalogues, 10 cents. — *Schools of the Academy*. Aims : The Academy does not undertake to furnish detailed instruction, but rather facilities for study, supplemented by the occasional criticism of the teachers; and the classes are intended especially for those who expect to be professional artists. — Instructors : Director, Thomas Eakins ; Asst. Prof. of Painting and Drawing, Thomas Anshutz ; Prof. of Artistic Anatomy, W. W. Keen, M. D.; Demonstrator of Anatomy, John Wallace. — The Course of Study is believed to be more thorough than that of any other existing school. Its basis is the nude human figure. In the anatomical department, the advanced students dissect. Animals are also dissected from time to time, and a living horse is used as a model in the modelling room. Classes : Men's Life (day and evening); Women's Life ; Antique (day and evening); Portrait, Sketch, Lectures on Art Anatomy, Dissecting Room Study. Lectures are also given on Perspective and Composition. School Year from first Monday in October to last Saturday in May. — Any person of good character, of either sex, and over fifteen years of age, giving satisfactory proof of proficiency, will be admitted as a student. Number of students, season of 1881-2, 129 men, 106 women ; total 235, of whom only 208 (117 men, 91 women) remained at the end of the term. — Tuition fees : The Directors having decided to make a charge for admission, instead of having the instruction free, as heretofore, the following rates have been established. Full season, all privileges, $48 ; one month, all privileges, $8 ; Antique Class, one month, day and night, $4 ; Night Life Class, one month, $4. — The only prizes given are the Charles Toppan Prizes, alluded to above. Competitors must be students of two years' standing, and the terms of the fund especially provide that drawing shall be first taken into account by the examiners. — The Schools of the Academy are amply furnished with the necessary casts, etc., and the accommodations provided for them are admirable. Correspondence on matters connected with the Schools should be addressed to H. C. Whipple, Curator. — The Pennsylvania Academy of Fine Arts is the oldest institution of the kind in the U. S. For some details of its history see "The First American Art Academy," reprinted from "Lippincott's Magazine" (not dated), in which may also be found representations of the former building of the Academy erected in 1806, and demolished in 1870, and of the elegant structure at present owned and occupied by it, the work of Messrs. Furniss & Hewitt.

PENNSYLVANIA MUSEUM AND SCHOOL OF INDUSTRIAL ART. — Museum, Memorial Hall, Fairmount Park; School, 1709 Chestnut St. Incorp. Feb. 26, 1876.— Officers of B'd of Trustees: Pres., Wm. Platt Pepper, 1730 Chestnut St.; V. Ps., Frederic Graff, 1337 Arch St., Phil. C. Garrett; Treas., Thos. Cochran, 320 Chestnut St.; Sec., Dalton Dorr, 2104 Locust St. The Governor of the State and the Mayor of the City are *ex officiis* members of the Board, upon which the State Legislature, the city Councils, and the leading scientific and artistic bodies of the city are also represented. — Object: The establishment of an institution like the South Kensington Museum and School in London. — Members (both sexes) of the corporation according to last report, Nov. 30, 1881: Contributing, who have paid at one time $200 or upwards, 38; Life, who have paid $100 at one time, 168; Annual, who paid $10 for 1881, 86: total, 292. — *The Museum.* The building occupied, rent free, by the Museum, is the Memorial Hall, erected as an art gallery for the Centennial at the joint expense of the State of Pennsylvania and the city of Philadelphia. The income of the Museum is limited to membership dues, tuition fees from the pupils of the School, donations, and a yearly appropriation by the City Councils of $10,000 for the maintenance and repair of the Hall, which is given on condition that the Museum shall be open free to the public. Until this appropriation was made, the annual receipts, including the admission fees then charged, were so insufficient that the necessary repairs could not be made, and the building was rapidly going to decay. The need of an endowment fund, however, not only remains, but is more urgent now than ever before, if the educational work of the School is to be developed, and permanency is to be given to the Museum. There are no funds for purchases, and the constant growth of the collections is due to gifts and deposits on loan. No money has as yet been received for the purpose of creating a fund, but the Trustees have secured a sufficient number of pledges of subscription, conditioned on the raising of a specified amount, to encourage them to persevere in their efforts. The total value of gifts in money and objects received so far, according to the balance sheet of Nov. 30, 1881, amounts to $67,717.20. — The nucleus of the present collections was formed by purchases made at the Centennial Exhibition with funds subscribed for the purpose, to which were added donations by exhibitors at the same exhibition. Very valuable donations have since been made by private individuals (Wm. S. Vaux, bequest of Greco-Italian and ancient American pottery; the Moore Memorial, given by Mrs. B. H. Moore in memory of her husband, consisting of over 1,000 objects in pottery, enamels, metal work, etc.), and the collections have been largely increased by loans. The character of the Museum is distinctively art-industrial and technical, covering a wide range of time and of nationalities. A few paintings by American and foreign artists are included in the Moore Memorial. — A "Guide to the Museum" (price 5 cents), giving a general idea of the collections and their location in the building, is for sale at the door, where may also be obtained a catalogue of the "India Collection" and "Notes on the Collection of Coins" (by Henry Phillips, Jr.), deposited in the Museum by the Numismatic and Antiquarian Society. Photographs of objects in the Museum can likewise be bought at the catalogue stand. A slip inventory of the collections has lately been completed, and the publication of a series of descriptive catalogues was to have been begun this year. — During the three years, 1878, '79, '80, when an admission fee was charged, the total number of visitors was only 42,000. From Jan. 1, 1881, when the entrance fee was abolished, to Nov. 30, 1881, the number of visitors was 128,556. — Open daily throughout the year, Sundays and holidays included, from 9.30 A. M. to 5.30 P. M. in summer, and 4.45 P. M. in winter, except Monday mornings. [The Director or Curator of the Museum is not named in the Report.] — *The School.* Aim: To furnish such instruction in drawing, painting, and modelling as is required by designers and workmen in the various constructive and decorative arts, and to serve as a training-school for teachers of these branches. — The course of study embraces drawing and painting from models, casts, draperies, and still-life; plane and descriptive geometry; projections, with their application to machine drawing and to building construction; shadows, perspective; modelling and casting; historical ornament and original design. Instrumental drawing is taught by means of class lessons or lectures, and lectures are also given upon anatomy, structural botany, historical ornament, the harmony of color, etc. The complete course of study embraces three years, but graduates may continue in the school for advanced study. — Teachers: L. W. Miller, Principal; H. F. Stratton, Assistant; W. W. Keen, M. D., Lecturer on Anatomy; Horace F. Jayne, Assistant Lecturer. — Tuition Fees: Day Class, $18 per term of 18 weeks; Night Class, three times a week, $5 per term of 18 weeks. Two terms each year. The attendance of regular students is required only on four days of the week, from 9 till 1 o'clock. The Board of Trustees have placed at the disposal of the Board of Public Education five free scholarships. Graduates may continue in the School for advanced study without payment of fees, on condition that they will devote a certain amount of time to teaching in the School. — Students (both sexes) must be not less than fifteen years of age. No previous knowledge of drawing is necessary. Number of students, 1881–2, 82 (63 males, 29 females). — Certificates are given upon the completion of the Course in Drawing, in Painting, and in Modelling. Those who have received the three certificates are awarded the full diploma of the School. — An exhibition of the work of the students was made in the Rotunda of Memorial Hall during the summer vacation, and a series of drawings, illustrating the course of study, has been placed permanently in the North Corridor.

PERMANENT EXHIBITIONS of works of art, both foreign and American, will be found at the galleries of *Messrs. Jas. S. Earle & Sons*, 816 Chestnut St, and *Mr. Chas. F. Haseltine*, 1516 Chestnut St.

PHILADELPHIA CHAPTER OF THE AM. INSTITUTE OF ARCHITECTS. — Sec., Edward Hazlehurst, 508 Walnut St. (See p. 1.)

PHILADELPHIA SCHOOL OF ART NEEDLE-WORK. — 1602 Chestnut St. — Founded 1879; incorporated 1881. — Officers: Pres., Mrs. T. Dundas Lippincott, 509 South Broad St.; Secr., Mrs. Caspar Wister, 1303 Arch St.; Treas., Miss Fanny Clark, 2037 DeLancey Pl. — Principal, Miss Frances Tate Lawe, formerly of the Royal School of Art Needle-Work, London. — Orders are taken in the Salesroom, to be executed by the pupils taught in the School. Originally started with a contributed fund of $1,800, the school has since been self-supporting. For the year ending Mch. 8, 1882, the receipts, of which $7,142.03 went to the workers, exceeded the expenses by $1,036,83, with a stock of materials, etc., on hand, valued at $5,247.09. Those desirous of entering the School as workers are required to pay an entrance fee of $10, which entitles them to the necessary instruction, and a place in the workroom at the first vacancy. — Instruction to others, daily from 10 A. M. to 4 P. M., 12 lessons, $10; 6 lessons, $5; 1 lesson, $1. — The School holds an exhibition in May.

PHILADELPHIA SCHOOL OF DESIGN FOR WOMEN. — S. W. cor. Broad and Master Sts. — Founded 1847; incorp. 1853. — Officers of B'd of Directors: Pres, Jas. L. Claghorn, 222 N. 19th St.; V. P., John Sartain, 728 Sansom St.; Sec. and Treas., F. O. Horstmann, 3925 Chestnut St. — Object: The instruction of women in decorative art, and the various practical applications thereof to industrial pursuits. Particular attention is given to those who may wish to adopt teaching as a profession. — The corporation consists of Life Members, who have paid $50 or more at one time; and Annual Members, who pay $5 p. a. The members, of both sexes, elect the Board, consisting of twelve gentlemen, who in turn appoint a Board of (12) Lady Managers. Number of Life Members, according to last report, 129; Annual Members, not given. — This School was founded in 1847 by Mrs. Sarah Peter, wife of the British consul at Philadelphia. It then passed into the care of the Franklin Institute for a short time, until it assumed corporate existence under its present charter. Its income is derived from the contributions of members, tuition fees, an annual appropriation made by the State Legislature, and donations. It has never been attempted to render it self-sustaining, since that could only be done by raising the tuition fee to an amount which would impair its usefulness. — The School is organized into seven classes: A. Preparatory course B. Ornament, with its subdivisions. C. Landscape. D. Human figure (including the study of antique statuary, draperies, etc). E. Modelling. F. Wood engraving, drawing on wood, lithography, and etching. G. China decorating. The regular course occupies three years. The various technical courses are taken by students who wish to devote their whole attention to a thorough preparation for special professional employment. A standard of admission is required for these special courses. Those who do not meet the requirements, enter the preparatory course, for which no previous knowledge of drawing is required. Regular courses of lectures on art subjects are delivered before the Scoool, and art literature has been made an additional study. — Teachers : Miss Elizabeth Croasdale of South Kensington, Principal ; Chas. Page, Designing, Modelling, and Lithography ; Peter Moran, Landscape in Oil and Water-Colors ; Stephen J. Ferris, Drawing from Life in Charcoal, Oil, or Water-Colors, and Drapery ; Herm. Faber, Antique Drawing, Anatomy and Composition ; Geo. P. Williams, Wood Engraving ; Albrecht Jahn, China Decorating ; Geo. C. Lambdin, Flower Painting in Oil and Water-Colors ; Emma W. Fullerton, Perspective ; Mary M'Allister, Light and Shade, Time Sketching, Drawing from Nature, Analysis of Plant Form, and Color ; Sara C. Pennypacker,Geometry, Free-Hand, Object Drawing, and Elementary Design ; Prof. Wm. H. Goodyear, Lecturer on Historic and Decorative Art. — Tuition, $20 per term of five months ; two terms each year. To those requiring preparation for special classes, $5 per term extra ; to those desiring instruction from more than one master in the higher branches, $10 per term extra. In consideration of the appropriation made by the State, ten pupils are accepted annually from the advanced classes of the Philadelphia Girls' Grammar and Normal Schools. Eleven perpetual free scholarships have also been established by patrons of the School, who have given $1,000 each. Another scholarship, founded by Mrs. Wm. J. Horstmann, is awarded annually, as a prize. — Students, females only, must be at least thirteen years of age. Number of pupils, season of 1881-2, 293. — The Diploma of the School is granted to those students only who complete the subjects of study, and pass the examinations in Classes A, B, C, and D. Certificates as teachers are given upon examination. — Besides the scholarship awarded annually, as mentioned above, three gold medals, founded by Mr. Geo. W. Childs and Mr. Jas. L. Claghorn, are given each year. — The spacious building at present occupied by the School, the former Forrest Mansion, was purchased 1880 for $45,000, and $60,000 have since been expended upon it for improvements. It embraces a well-lighted gallery for the statues possessed by the School, with school-rooms adapted to the special needs of each class, a large lecture-room and conservatory, with ample grounds, to which the students can resort for recreation. The copies of masterpieces of art, casts of ornaments, drawings, valuable books, etc. (of which a partial list is given in the Report), obtained at a cost of $5,000, are, so it is claimed, superior in number and arrangement to those possessed by any similar institution in the country.

PHILADELPHIA SKETCH CLUB. — 1328 Chestnut St. — Organized Nov. 20, 1860, as "The Crayon Sketch Club"; present name adopted Dec. 3, 1861. — Officers : Wm. J. Clark, Jr., 108 South 3d St. ; V. P., Henry T. Cariss, 1328 Chestnut St. ; Sec., Geo. Wright, 1520 Chestnut St. ; Treas., Geo. D. McCreary, 137 South 2d St. — Objects, etc. : Social intercourse among artists, students of art, and amateurs, and artistic practice. The association is distinctively a students' club, and efforts have always been made to maintain this character. At each weekly meeting impromptu sketches, single figures in action, are made from subjects given out by the Executive Committee. Besides these, monthly studies are required, from subjects announced in advance, as essays in composition and treatment of subject, and annual studies, from subjects chosen by the Club, or by the artist, as may be determined. — Members : Artists, art students, and amateurs are eligible; students and amateurs must submit sketches for approval by the Committee. Present number of members, 70. — Prizes : In former years money prizes were occasionally given by individual members or friends of the Club; latterly, the prizes have consisted of a photograph or a photogravure from a modern picture for the best original monthly study, and an autotype from an old master for the best original study submitted at the annual meeting in January. — The Club arranged an Exhibition of Works of American Artists at the Academy in the winter of 1865-6, and published, in 1874, "The Sketch Club Portfolio," a collection of designs, without text, in monthly parts. From 1873-76, after the demolition of the old Academy of Fine Arts, and before the opening of the new building, a Life Class for drawing from the nude was conducted under the auspices of the Club, with Mr. Thos. Eakins as instructor. Lectures on anatomy were delivered before the class in the winter of 1874-5. This class (open to males only) was a great success, and the applications from non-members, who were admitted on payment of a small fee, were so numerous that many had to be refused. — A peculiar feature of this Club is its *Relief Trust*, of which Messrs. Geo. D. McCreary, 137 South 2d St., and W. Moylan Lansdale, 709 Walnut St., are the Trustees. This fund, applicable to the relief of members only, in case of sickness or where assistance is needed to pay burial expenses, is sustained by a small annual assessment and by donations. In case the Club ceases to exist, it is provided that the fund shall be paid over to the Academy to be applied by that institution to the relief of artists and students, or to the Pennsylvania Hospital.

PHILADELPHIA SOCIETY OF ARTISTS. — Galleries, 1725 Chestnut St. — Officers : Pres., Jas. B. Sword, 1520 Chestnut St. ; Sec., Newbold H. Trotter, 1520 Chestnut St.; Treas., C. H. Spooner, 1520 Chestnut St. — Members : Active, professional artists; Contributing, annual dues, $5; Life, $25. Present number of members : 36 Active (of whom two are ladies) ; Contributing and Life, 263 (ladies and gentlemen). — The exhibitions of the Society, which, so far, have been its only public demonstrations, were held at the Penns. Academy of Fine Arts, until the inauguration in 1881 of the galleries on Chestnut, near 17th St. The Fourth Annual Exhibition will be held from Dec. 30, 1882, to Jan. 27, 1883. A Special Sketch Exhibition opened Nov. 4, and a Water-Color Exhibition will probably be held in February, 1883.

PHILADELPHIA SOCIETY OF ETCHERS. — Organized June, 1880. — Officers : Pres., Peter Moran, 1322 Jefferson St. ; Sec., J. Neely, Jr., 617 Market St. ; Treas., Stephen J. Ferris, 4035 Oregon St. — Objects, etc. : The advancement of the art of etching; social intercourse at the monthly studio meetings ; and a quarterly exchange of etchings among the members. — Present number of resident members, 8. — The First Exhibition of the Society will open at the Penns. Academy of Fine Arts on Dec. 27, 1882.

SOCIAL ART CLUB. — 1811 Walnut St. — Officers : Pres., Caspar Wister, M. D., 1303 Arch St. ; V. Ps., Geo. S. Pepper, 1819 Walnut St., Francis W. Lewis, M. D., 2016 Spruce St.; Treas., Wm. Henry Eisenbrey, 1717 Locust St. ; Sec., Thos. DeWitt Cuyler, 704 Walnut St. — Objects : The promotion of literary, artistic, and antiquarian tastes among the citizens of Philadelphia, and such kindred purposes as the Club may from time to time determine, by establishing and maintaining a library and reading-room, and a collection of works of art and antiquities, either by loan or otherwise. — Membership, limited to 400 : Resident members, who alone have the right to vote, $100 initiation fee, and $25 annually ; non-resident, $50 and $15. No person under twenty-three years of age can become a member.

SPRING GARDEN INSTITUTE. — N. E. cor. Broad and Spring Garden Sts. — Organized and incorp. 1851. — Officers: Pres., John M. Ogden, 446 Marshall St.; V. P., John Baird, 1705 N. Broad St.; Treas., W. Hobart Brown, 1911 Park Ave.; Sec., Addison B. Burk, 1024 Brown St.; Chairm. Comm. on Drawing Schools, Jas. H. Windrim, 817 N. Broad St. — Object: The moral and intellectual improvement of young persons. — Members: Stockholders, $10 per share, each share subject to $2 annual tax; Stockholders *in perpetuo*, $50 free of further tax; Stockholders for life, $30 free of further tax. There are also Annual Subscribers (adults), $6 p. a., and Junior subscribers (minors), $4 p. a. These subscribers have the use of the library, and the right to attend a night class two sessions per week. Membership as per last report: 36 In Perpetuo, 725 Life, 96 Stockholders, 149 Annual, 540 Junior Subscribers; total, 1546 (male and female). — The general expenses of the Institute, and the costs of its lectures and entertainments, are about paid by the revenues of the property, by admission fees at entertainments, etc., and by the Journal published by the Institute. Its other work, including the Library (about 12,000 vols.), the Drawing Schools, and the Mechanical Handiwork Classes, is not fully paid for by the fees, dues, etc., and recourse must therefore be had to contributions. Extra expenses having been incurred last year in refitting the rooms of the Drawing Schools, etc., extra efforts were also made to obtain contributions, and with very gratifying results, the receipts from this source amounting to $16,420.46, of which $7,000 have been invested as an Endowment Fund. It is proposed to increase this fund to $30,-000. — *The Drawing Schools of the Institute:* Night Classes in Free-Hand Drawing (from the flat, simple objects, and casts), Mechanical and Architectural Drawing, six nights each week for six months of the year. The teachers are practical draughtsmen employed in large industrial establishments. The attempt to teach the principles of design has met with success. Lectures on Architecture were delivered last season by Prof. W. H. Goodyear, and it is proposed to institute other lectures on perspective, principles of composition and design, harmony of color, etc. These classes are attended by the "subscribers." — Day Classes for giving instruction in oil and water-color painting, china painting, modelling in clay, over and under glaze decoration, and others of the higher branches of art, under Prof. W. A. Porter. They are attended only by people of leisure (mostly ladies), whose fees, $20 per term of about 20 weeks, pay expenses when the classes are full. The school is provided with a kiln. It is proposed to add other branches of the ceramic art, glass painting, etc., as soon as the growth of the school justifies it. — Pupils in Night Classes, total, 458. The applications for admission far exceed the capacity of the room. — The schools have become employment agencies for the pupils, and the Directors report that, as a result of the instruction given, many of the pupils have already obtained desirable situations, and others have been advanced in their chosen profession.

Pittsburgh, Pa. — PITTSBURGH SCHOOL OF DESIGN FOR WOMEN. — Bank Block, 173 Wood St. — Incorporated 1865. — Officers: Pres., Chas. J. Clarke; Treas., Geo. A. Berry; Sec., John B. Jackson. — Object: The systematic training of young women in the practice of art, and in the knowledge of its scientific principles, with the view of qualifying them to impart to others a careful art education, and to develop its application to the common uses of life, and its relation to the requirements of trade and manufactures. — The course lasts from two and a half to four years, depending on the industry of the student. It begins with drawing from the flat, from lines to the entire human figure; progresses to drawing from models and casts, the study of composition and design in ornament, perspective, color, etc., and ends with painting in oil and water-color from nature, and such other work as may be necessary in connection with design. Lectures are given on Geometry, Botany, Perspective, Anatomy, and the Principles of Design. Provision has also been made for instruction in architectural and mechanical drawing, and for instruction in special branches. — Teachers: Annie W. Henderson, Prin.; Olive Turney, Drawing and

Painting; Agnes D. Jamison, Drawing. — There are two sessions, lasting from the second Monday of February and of September to the last day of January and of June respectively; classes meet daily, except Saturday and Sunday. Besides these regular classes there are also Saturday classes for women, and in connection therewith a class for boys from 8 to 15 years of age. — Fees for session of 5 months : Elementary Course, $15 ; Figure and Landscape, in oil, each, $25 ; Saturday Painting Class, $12.50; Saturday Drawing Class, $10 ; China Decorating, $20. — A number of free scholarships have been founded by contributors to the funds of the school. — An annual exhibition is held, and bronze, silver, and gold medals may be competed for at the close of each school year. — Number of students in attendance at date of last printed Report, Sept., 1881 : Women's Classes, 107 ; Boys' Class, 12. — The receipts from tuition, at present rates, do not meet more than 50 per cent of the necessary current expenses of the School, the institution relying on the intelligent liberality of its friends to sustain it. It is nevertheless hoped that the annual contributions to the school fund will ultimately be large enough to allow of making the instruction free to all. The attendance is increasing yearly. [No response to requests for later information.]

Pittsfield, Mass. — LADIES' ART ASSOCIATION. — 8 South St. — Organized 1880. — Officers : Pres., Mrs. Theodore Pomeroy ; V. Ps., Mrs. J. M. Stevenson, Mrs. C. B. Redfield ; Treas., Miss F. W. Stevenson ; Sec., Miss M. W. Redfield. — Objects : 1. To raise the standard of woman's work ; 2. To find a good market for it, and to do away with the unpleasantness and trials ordinarily connected with the disposal of work ; 3. To aid, by establishing new industries, and by showing what is salable and desirable ; 4. To establish free classes, that may help to direct many into desirable ways of earning a livelihood. — Any person may become a member by paying an annual fee of $1. — The salesroom established by this Association has been quite successful. During the season from June 1, 1881, to Jan. 1, 1882, it paid to contributors, over and above all commissions and expenses, $1,071.21. The articles taken on sale from members and outside contributors (commission, 10 per cent) comprise all sorts of artistic and decorative work, old furniture, etc., and homemade cake, preserves, jellies, etc. Orders are also taken. — All correspondence to be addressed to Mrs. M. C. Buell, the lady in charge.

Plymouth, Mass. — PILGRIM SOCIETY. — Cabinet of relics of the Pilgrims, pictures, engravings, etc.

Portland, Me. — PORTLAND SOCIETY OF ART. — 507½ Congress St. — Organized 1882. — Officers : Pres., Jas. P. Baxter, Portland Packing Co. ; 1st V. P., Francis H. Fassett, 93 Exchange St. ; 2d V. P., Henry B. Brown, 400 Danforth St. ; Treas., Wm. E. Gould, First Nat'l B'k ; Sec., Wm. S. Lowell, 513 Congress St. ; Lib., Hubbard W. Bryant, 218 Middle St. — Objects : To encourage a knowledge and love of art, through the exhibition of art works and lectures upon art subjects ; the acquisition of an art library and works of art, such as paintings, statuary, and engravings, and the establishment of an art school and museum. — The membership, at present about 200, is not limited by either profession or number. — The Society held its First Annual Exhibition from June 15 to Aug. 15. The catalogue enumerated 226 works by 143 artists. Four pictures were sold.

SPECIAL EXHIBITIONS are held periodically at the store of *H. G. Hewes*, 593 Congress St. The last of these was an exhibition of water-colors, open from June 8, 1882, to about the middle of July, with contributions by artists in New York, Boston, Philadelphia, etc.

Poughkeepsie, N. Y. — VASSAR COLLEGE. — [Instruction in drawing, painting, etc., is given in this College ; Henry Van Ingen, professor. According to report, a professorship of engraving was also to be established. No response to repeated requests for information.]

Princeton, N. J. — COLLEGE OF NEW JERSEY (PRINCETON COLLEGE). — Officers: Pres. of the B'd of Trustees and of the Fac, James McCosh, D. D., LL. D.; Clerk of B'd of Trustees, Elijah R. Craven, D. D.; Treas., Rev. Wm. Harris, A. M.; Clerk of the Fac., John T. Duffield, D. D.; Lib., Frederic Vinton, A. M.; Registrar, Henry N. Van Dyke, A. M. — According to the last published catalogue (1881-2), the only department in which drawing is taught is the John C. Green School of Science, which is connected with the college; Frederick N. Willson, C. E., Instructor in Drawing. The pupils in the General Course in Science are regularly engaged in the drawing-room in the Freshman year (Elements of Industrial Drawing, Projections, and Descriptive Geometry), Sophomore year (Descriptive Geometry, Shades, Shadows, and Perspective), and Junior year (Free-Hand Drawing). No provision for drawing is made in the Senior year. In the special courses which may be taken up in the second year, drawing, confined to topographical and map drawing, is taught only in the Course in Civil Engineering. There is, however, a course of lectures on art subjects every winter, which is open to the whole College. The lecturers for the last four winters were, Gen. L. P. Di Cesnola, Mr. Wm. C. Prime, Prof. John F. Weir, and Prof. C. E. Norton. At the last meeting of the Trustees, Prof. Allan Marquand was appointed lecturer on the History of Art, and it is believed that the friends of the College will soon provide a fire-proof building, to serve as a museum for the objects which the College already possesses and is likely to receive in the near future. — *The E. M. Museum of Geology and Archæology*, Prof. Arnold Guyot, Director, Prof. Wm. Libbey, Jr., Vice-Director, is classified in the three general departments of Geology, Palæontology,'and Archæology. The Archæological Department contains an extensive collection of specimens of prehistoric implements of the palæolithic age, from Switzerland, France, Denmark, etc.; remains of the mound builders, and a large collection of recent Indian relics from Alaska and the West.

PRINCETON SKETCH CLUB. — This is an association of about three professors and twenty students of Princeton College, which has a room in the College, hires its own instructors, and meets twice a week for art study. The instructor last winter was Mr. J. W. Alexander. It gave a First Annual Reception on June 16, 1882. The "Bric-à-Brac" and the "Tiger," both College publications, are illustrated by members of the Club. [Names of officers, etc., asked for, but not given]

Providence, R. I. — PROVIDENCE ART CLUB.— 35 North Main St.—Organized 1880. — Officers: Pres., Wm. B. Weeden; V. P., Robt. E. Hallworth; Sec., Courtl. B. Dorrance; Treas., Geo. W. Whitaker. — Objects : To unite and promote the interests of the artists of Rhode Island, and to cultivate and combine social interests with those of art. — Members, of both sexes: Professional, artists by profession ; Associate, not practical artists. Initiation fee, $6 ; annual dues, $6, payable by all members alike, all of whom are entitled to vote. Present number, over 200, of whom about 6 per cent are artists. The constitution provides that at least two thirds of the Executive Committee must be professional artists. — Lectures on art and other subjects, concerts, etc., are given during the winter, and two exhibitions are held yearly. The last Spring Exhibition, April 17 to May 13, 1882, contained 195 works, of which 15 were sold for $915.

PROVIDENCE ATHENÆUM. — Incorporated 1836. — Officers : Pres., Wm. Gammell; V. P., Alex Farnum ; Treas., Stephen H. Arnold ; Sec., Wm. M. Bailey, Jr.; Lib., Daniel Beckwith. — The Athenæum is a private library (number of vols., Sept. 1, 1881, 39,574), owned by an association of stockholders. Non-stockholders may, however, obtain its use as Annual Subscribers, and strangers can be introduced by stockholders. — The *Art Collections* of the Athenæum are small, consisting of three busts and eight paintings Among the latter are portraits of James Gates Percival, by Alexander ; Washington Allston, by Chester Harding ; and John Hampden, by

James Gandy, an English artist of the 17th century, said to have been a pupil of Van Dyck. There is also a "Cavalier of the Time of Charles I.," by Van Dyck; a "Girl Reading," by Sir Joshua Reynolds; and Edward G. Malbone's celebrated miniature, "The Hours," on ivory, 6 by 7 inches. (Some of these pictures were stolen in the year 1881, but were subsequently recovered.) — The library is open every week day from April 1 to Oct. 1 from 9 A. M. to 7 P. M., and from Oct. 1 to April 1 from 10 A. M. to 9 P. M. Transient visitors are admitted on application.

R. I. Historical Society. — Waterman St., opp. Hope College. — Officers: Pres, Zachariah Allen; V. Ps., Wm. Gammell, Francis Brinley; Sec., Amos Perry; Treas, Richmond P. Everett. — The *Cabinet of the R. I. Historical Society* contains about twenty-five oil paintings, a number of busts, about one thousand engravings, woodcuts, photographs, etc., mostly portraits, and a large number of historic memorials of various kinds. As the special object of the Society is local history, the art collections are mainly designed to illustrate this subject. Of special interest to the student of the history of art in America is the portrait of Rev. John Callender (b. 1706, d 1748), by Robert Feke, the earliest native colonial painter of ability of whom a positive record is left. — The Cabinet is open free to all orderly visitors, daily from 10 A. M. to 1 P. M., and from 2½ to 5 P. M., Saturday afternoons, Sundays, and legal holidays excepted.

R. I. School of Design. — Hoppin Homestead Bldg., 283 Westminster St. — Organized 1878. — Officers: Pres., Hon. C. B. Farnsworth; V. P., Hon. Rowland Hazard; Sec., Miss Sarah E. Doyle. — Object: To furnish such instruction in Drawing, Painting, Modelling, and Designing, as required by artisans generally, that they may more successfully apply the principles to the mechanical arts and industries; the systematic training of students, enabling them to become successful art teachers, and the general advancement of art culture. — This School was orignated by an association of which any person may become an annual member by the payment of $3 a year, or a life member upon the payment of $100. The income consists of tuition fees, membership dues, donations, and the interest of the "Hospital Trust Co. Centennial Fund," which yielded $1,500 last year. The State Legislature has also appropriated $500 for the year 1882 towards the support of the School, and the city of Providence has turned over to it the appropriation for evening drawing schools. The association is slightly in debt. — The Course of Instruction embraces Elementary Free-Hand Drawing and Design; Free-Hand from copy, models, and casts, in pencil, crayon, stump, India ink, and charcoal; Geometrical and Applied Design; Elementary Class for Mechanics (architects, carpenters, engineers, machinists, tinworkers, jewellers, ship-builders, etc., etc.); Oil and Water-Color Painting; China Painting. — Instructors: E. Rose, 32 Hammond St., Principal; Miss E. Carter, G. W. Whitaker. Assistants: W. Woodward, E. Woodward. Curator: Miss H. C. Hall. — Tuition fees: Day Students, $20 each term (two terms a year); Evening Students, $6; Children (Saturday Class), $4; China Painting, $3 for 6 lessons; Special Classes, special terms. — Number of pupils, both sexes, season of 1881-2: Day pupils, 47; evening, 76; Saturday, 60; afternoon, 10: total, 193, including 48 pupils who availed themselves of the opportunity to study in the school offered by the city.

Quincy, Ill. — Quincy Art Association. — 413 Hampshire St. — [The officers of this Association, according to a circular issued in 1879, were at that time as follows : Pres., Miss Hannah E. Davis; V. P., Mrs. D. A. Kelsey; Sec., Miss Lettie Long; Treas., Mrs. A. D. Munson. The same circular announces classes in drawing, sketching from nature, painting on china, in oil and water-colors, and in pastel, wood-carving, fret-sawing, mechanical drawing, and embroidery; teachers, Miss Hannah E. Davis and Miss Mary Long. Conversations, lectures, exhibitions, etc., are also promised. — No reply to requests for later information.]

Richmond, Va. — Richmond Art Association. — Studio and Office, over Express Office, 819 E. Main St. Decorating Room and Furnace, 731 E. Main St. — Organized 1878. — Officers: Pres., Miss M. J. Morris, 206 W. Grace St.; V. P., Miss Agnes Laird; Sec., Miss Lottie Price; Treas, Miss Mary Crenshaw. — Members, both sexes, about 85 at present, are divided into two classes, viz.: Members of the Art Class, entrance fee $1, annual dues $6; and Associate Members, $5 annually. — The Art Class Course includes drawing, composition, and design; members must be fifteen or over. Instruction, under special terms, is also given in painting in oil and drawing, teachers, W. L. Sheppard and J. Elder; architecture, M. Dimmock; water-colors, Miss Alicia Laird; painting on porcelain, Miss M. J. Morris. There is besides a preparatory class for pupils under fifteen. Artist in charge of furnace, Gustav Friede. The classes have been well attended, and the furnace has been used with decided success. — The Association arranges monthly reunions, sketching parties, and other entertainments, and holds Annual Exhibitions. The fifth of these, May, 1882, although much smaller than the one of the year previous, is reported to have been one of the most excellent ever held, and to have shown great improvement of home talent. — No attempt has lately been made to extend the activity of the Association, as it is burdened with a debt, which is to be discharged before any new undertakings are entered upon. It is hoped that this object will be accomplished in about a year.

Virginia Historical Society. — Westmoreland Club House. — Organized Dec. 29, 1831; chartered Mch. 10, 1834. — Officers: Pres., Alex. H. H. Stuart, Staunton, Va.; V P's., Conway Robinson, Washington, D. C., W. W. Corcoran, Washington, D. C., Wm. Wirt Henry; Cor. Sec. and Libr., R. A. Brock; Rec. Sec., Geo. A. Barksdale; Treas., Robt. T. Brooke. — Present membership: 30 Honorary, 63 Corresponding, 52 Life, 447 Annual; total 592. Annual dues, $5; no entrance fee; life, membership, $50. — The Society, besides a number of engraved portraits, relics, etc., has a collection of twenty-eight portraits in oil, including the following: Pocahontas (two), Earl of Essex, Capt. George Percy, Lord Culpepper, George Washington, Martha Washington, Patrick Henry, Peyton Randolph, George Mason, Thomas Jefferson, Lafayette, Arthur Lee, Edmund Pendleton, John Marshall, Duke de Lauzun, Gerard, John Randolph of Roanoke, Hugh Nelson, Comm. Oliver H. Perry, Gov. Wm. B. Giles, Black Hawk, and Rev. M D. Hoge, D. D. — The portraits may be inspected any week day between 9 A. M. and 3 P. M., when the Librarian is in attendance.

Rochester, N. Y. — Powers Art Gallery. — Established by D. W. Powers in 1875. — One of the objects of this Gallery is to show, in copies, and explain the noted paintings of the old masters side by side with the best examples of recent art. — The catalogue registers 487 titles, including 34 illustrated works (such as the Musée Royale, Musée Français, Munich Gallery, Dresden Gallery, Turner Gallery, Claude's Liber Veritatis, etc.), and 6 pieces of statuary. The rest are oil and water-colors, comprising copies after Allori, Andrea del Sarto, Boucher, Biliverti, Bassano, Battoni, Ann. Caracci, Correggio, Carlo Dolci, Ferrari, Guercino, Guido, Gargiuoli, Honthorst, Mad. Le Brun, Raph. Mengs, Michelangelo, Murillo, Carlo Maratti, Raphael, Leopold Robert, Sassoferato, Titian, Tintoretto, Paul Veronese, Joseph Vernet, etc. Pictures by the following are catalogued as originals: Bonifacio, Boucher, Carletto Cagliari, Canaletto, Polidoro da Caravaggio, Caravaggio, Honthorst, Sigmund Holbein, P. Liberi, Pieter de Laar, Salvator Rosa, Rosa da Tivoli, Tiepolo (6 entries), Zuccarelli, etc. There are also modern European pictures by O. Achenbach, Bruck-Lajos, Breling, C. Brecker, Bouguereau, Chierici, Diaz, Delacroix, Dubufe, Carl Hoff, Kowalski, Knaus, Leon y Escosura, Meissonier, Carl Müller, Meyer von Bremen, Pallizzi, Peerus, Piot, Romako, Riedel, Roybet, Anton Seitz, Hugo Salmson, Schenck, Carl Sohn, Simler, Schreyer, Trayer, F.

Voltz, Vibert, Worms, Zimmermann, etc. The American artists represented are Wm. II. Beard, A. F. Bunner, J. J. Enneking, J. M. Falconer, R. Swain Gifford, S. R. Gifford, Edw. Gay, D. Huntington, Eastman Johnson, Geo. McCord, Geo. H. Story, T. W. Wood, etc. The sculptures include "The West Wind," by Thos. Gould, and "Joy," by Thos. Ball. [The very confused catalogue contains many names of artists unknown to fame, some of which are no doubt rendered unrecognizable by the outrageously careless spelling. It fails also to give information as to terms of admission, etc., and the requests for information on these points have remained without reply.]

    ROCHESTER ART CLUB. — Savings B'k Bldg., Rooms, 24, 25, and 27. — Organized 1877; incorporated Mch. 4, 1882. — Officers : Pres., John Guernsey Mitchell, 31 Savings B'k Bldg. ; V. P., Jas. Hogarth Dennis ; Sec., Horatio Walker, 48 Elwood Bldg. ; Treas., John Z. Wood. — Object: The cultivation and advancement of the Fine and Industrial Arts and the promotion of social intercourse among its members. — Members are of three classes : Resident, artists of Rochester and vicinity (6 at present), in whom are vested all the powers of the Club; Non-resident, artists at a distance (7 at present) ; and Honorary, amateurs and connoisseurs, neither of whom can vote or hold office. Resident and Honorary members pay an initiation fee of $10. — Every [resident ?] member must submit a specimen of his own handiwork for exhibition in the rooms of the Club within two months after election, and is liable to forfeiture of membership upon failure to contribute to the Annual Exhibition. — This association had its origin in the meetings, begun in 1872, of a few artists for the purpose of drawing from life, but the Club was not actually formed until 1877. At the beginning of the year 1882 it was reorganized under the present constitution, and incorporated. The first exhibition was held in 1879, followed by the second in 1880. The third took place at Powers Hall, April 19 to 21, 1882. The (illustrated) catalogue enumerates 174 works. — Classes in Drawing and Oil Painting, Charcoal Drawing, Drawing and Painting in Water-Colors, Sketching, and Drawing from the Figure were opened in the fall of 1882, and lectures on Composition, Perspective, etc. are also to be given. Instructors : Miss Ida Taylor, and Messrs. J. H. Dennis, Horatio Walker, and John Z. Wood. Terms vary from 35 cents to $1.25 for single lessons, and $1 to $4 per month, one lesson weekly, or $7 p. m., two lessons weekly.

    ROCHESTER ART EXCHANGE. — 191-196 Powers Bldg. — Organized Feb. 2, 1880. — Pres., Miss Lois E. Whitney ; V. Ps., Miss Mary Butts, Mrs. D. W. Powers, Miss Cunningham, Mrs. M. B. Anderson, Mrs. Wm. S. Kimball ; Treas., Mrs. Elmer Smith ; Sec., Miss Belle Clark ; Cor. Sec., Miss Belle Watson. — Objects : To provide for the exhibition and sale of decorative art work of any description, which shall be of sufficient excellence to be accepted, and for training in artistic industries. — Any person may become a member by an annual payment of $1.50. — The activity of this association is similar to that of the Decorative Art Societies organized in other places. During the past two years it has supported a free class in charcoal drawing, and one in Kensington embroidery. In the former there was an average attendance of 47 pupils. The embroidery class was also well attended, as were those in water-color, for figure and flower painting. A special summer class in china painting was very successful. A commission of 10 per cent is charged on the amount of sales made for contributors.

    Salem, Mass. — ESSEX INSTITUTE. — Plummer Hall, 134 Essex St. — Incorporated 1848. — Officers : Pres., Henry Wheatland ; V. Ps., Abner C. Goodell, Jr., Daniel B. Hagar, Fred. W. Putnam, Robt. S. Rantoul ; Sec., Geo. M. Whipple ; Treas., Geo. D. Phippen ; Aud., Richd. C. Manning ; Libr., Wm. P. Upham ; Curator of Archæology, Fred. W. Putnam ; Curator of Painting and Sculpture, F. Hunt. — The Essex Institute was formed by the union of the Essex Historical and the Essex County Natural History Societies. Its objects embrace Science, History,

Horticulture, and Art. — Present number of members, about 340. Membership is secured by election and the payment of an annual fee of $3. Life membership, $30. — The *Art Library* consists of 318 vols. of the choicest selection, including the best current issues upon painting, sculpture, architecture, ceramic decoration, etc., and is constantly increasing. (The whole number of volumes in the library of the Institute, June, 1881, was 58,900.) — The *Art Exhibitions* began in Feb., 1875, with a collection mostly of copies of paintings by the old masters, which was succeeded in November by a Second Exhibition of Paintings, in connection with the first ceramic display ever attempted in the city. In December of the same year an Exhibition of Antique Articles was held, gathered from the rich stores of colonial furniture, etc., still owned in Salem. Other exhibitions were held in June, 1879, April, 1880, May, 1881, and May, 1882, and are to be continued annually. The exhibits are confined almost entirely to the work of local artists and amateurs, and include paintings, drawings, etchings, embroidery, ceramic decoration, etc. The sales at these exhibitions, amounted to $150 in 1881, and to $195.15 in 1882. — The *Art Collections* consist of about 80 paintings, a very considerable collection of busts of men of local reputation, many rare and choice engravings and prints, large and well-arranged collections of coins and medals, and the best existing collection of relics and curiosities illustrative of the history, characteristics, arts, and industries of Essex County. Among the paintings are two portraits of Governor Endicott (1588–1665), copied from likenesses painted from life; a portrait of Rev. John Rogers, by Smibert; portraits of Timothy Fitch and wife, by Copley; a portrait of Alexander Hamilton, by Trumbull; and others by Jas. Frothingham, Chester Harding, Francis Alexander, etc.; several old views in and about Salem; and a few old Dutch and Flemish pictures. — A place is also given to art in the *Lectures* arranged by the Institute during the winter season. — Open free, every week day, excepting holidays, from 8.30 A. M. to 1 P. M., and from 2.30 to 6 P. M. in summer, to 5 P. M. in winter. A guide, entitled "Plummer Hall: Its Libraries, its Collections, its Historical Associations," is for sale at the office, price 15 cents. This guide contains a descriptive list of the paintings. There is no catalogue of the other collections, which are labelled.

PEABODY ACADEMY OF SCIENCE. — East India Marine Hall, 161 Essex St. — Endowed in 1867 by George Peabody, of London. — *The Museum* embraces the Ethnological Collection of the East India Marine Society, the Natural History, Ethnological, and Archæological Collections of the Essex Institute, and additions to these made since the endowment of the Academy. It is very strong in the archæology of North and South America, and more particularly so in that of Essex County, including Indian implements, etc. In the ethnology of China, India, the South Sea Islands, etc., its collection is probably unrivalled in the country. There is also to be seen at the Academy a collection of portraits, 14 in all, of old East India merchants and ship-masters. — Open, free, from 9 A. M. to 12 M., and from 1 to 5 P. M., daily, Sundays excepted.

PUBLIC BUILDINGS. — At the *Court House*, Federal St., cor. Washington, may be seen the portrait of Chief Justice Shaw, one of the best works of the late Wm. M. Hunt; the portrait of Judge Lord, by Frederic P. Vinton, and a portrait of Judge Putnam. In the *City Hall*, Washington St, there is a portrait of Washington, copied by Frothingham from an original by Stuart, in the Aldermen's Room; and in the Council Chamber another Washington, copied from an original by Stuart, by his daughter, Miss Jane Stuart; and a portrait of Lafayette, copied by Chas. Osgood from the original by Morse in the City Hall at New York.

SALEM ART CLUB. — Organized 1880. — Officers: Pres., Miss Louisa Lander; V. P., Miss M. L. King; Treas., Miss Nellie Pierce; Sec., Miss Anna G. Endicott. — The Club has established a school in which the following branches are taught: Charcoal, Miss Louisa Lander and Miss S. E. Smith, teachers; Oils, Miss S. E.

Smith; Water-Colors, Miss L E. Merrill; China Decorating, Miss Minnie Barton and Miss M. I. King. — The members of the Club, studying in the classes, number about 50, and there are as many Honorary Members.

San Francisco, Cal. — San Francisco Art Association. — 430 Pine St. — Organized Mch. 28, 1871. — Officers: Pres., Col. A. G. Hawes; 1st V. P., F. Marion Wells, 757 Mission St.; 2d V. P., Horace Fletcher, 520 Commercial St.; Sec., D. P. Belknap, 604 Merchant St.; Asst. Sec., J. Ross Martin; Treas., Lovell White. — Objects: The promotion of painting, sculpture, and the fine arts in general, and the establishment of a School of Design.— The membership, both sexes, unlimited, consists of Life Members, who pay $100; Contributing Members, initiation fee $2, monthly dues $1; and Honorary Members. Present number of members: 150 Life; 440 Contributing; 9 Honorary. Members are elected by the Board of Directors. — The resources of the Association consist of the dues of members, and the tuition fees of the pupils in the School of Design, averaging $375 a month. — The *California School of Design*, which is maintained by the Association, has the following classes, Regular: Crayon Drawing, antique and portrait, $24 per term of three months (three terms each year), or $10 per month; Oil Painting, still-life and portrait, $30 per term, or $12 per month. Special: Portrait Class, $5 per month; Sketch Class, $2 per month; Landscape Class (study from nature, excursions in the country every Wednesday), $4 per month. The special classes are open without charge to all regular pupils who are sufficiently advanced. The Director gives semi-weekly lectures to pupils and such members of the Association as choose to attend on anatomy, perspective, color, etc. Director, Virgil Williams; Assistant, Chris. Jorgensen. — Pupils must be 14 years or over. Both sexes are taught together. Average number, 78. — Two prizes, the Avery Gold Medal for excellence and progress in oil painting, and the Alvord Gold Medal for best full-length crayon study from cast, are awarded to pupils of the regular classes at the end of each school year. Pupils who intend to teach art are entitled to a certificate from the Director, specifying the course of study pursued and the medals received, and giving the opinion of the Director as to the qualifications of the recipient. — It is claimed that the collection of casts and other material belonging to the Art Association is unsurpassed by any in America. — *Exhibitions.* Annual Exhibitions are held of works of local artists, and of work done by pupils of the schools; also occasional loan exhibitions, including foreign paintings, etc.

San Francisco Chapter of the Am. Inst. of Architects. — Sec., Geo. H. Wolfe, 240 Montgomery St. (See p. 1.)

Society of Decorative Art of California. — 631 Sutter St. — Organized Jan., 1881. — Officers: Pres., Mrs. Jas. R. Pringle, 1820 Clay St.; V. P's., Mrs. L. L. Baker, Mrs. F. F. Low, Sutter and Gough Sts., Mrs. Hall McAllister, 517 Mason St., Mrs. J. L. Rathbone, Palace Hotel; Treas., Mrs. Geo. W. Gibbs, 16th and Capp Sts.; Rec. Sec., Mrs. J. G. Kittle, 525 Harrison St.; Cor. Secs., Miss Kate M. McLane, 438 Bryant St., Mrs J. C. Merrill, 14 Stanley Pl. — Objects: To establish rooms for the exhibition and sale of women's work; the diffusion of a knowledge of decorative art among women, and their training in artistic industries. — Annual membership, $5; Life membership, $100. Present number of members, 190. — The income of the Society is derived from dues, donations, tuition fees, commissions on sales and orders (10 per cent), interest on life membership fund, and the proceeds of exhibitions. — Classes: Art Needle-Work, Miss Fanny Grant, teacher ($5 for 6 lessons; $1 a single lesson in class; $2.50 a private lesson of two hours); Decorative Design and Water-Colors, Mr. Jules Godart, teacher ($12 a month, $2 for single lessons); Children's Saturday Morning Class, Miss Ingalsbe, teacher ($5 for 6 lessons). Pupils may be of both sexes, but so far they have all been of the female sex, except in the Children's Class. Number of paying pupils, from Aug., 1881, to Feb., 1882, 80; free pupils, nominated by members, 9. — The Society held a very successful Art Loan Exhibition in April, 1881, including paintings, engravings, and objects of industrial art of all kinds, the proceeds of which netted $3,453.21. For the first two weeks of Nov., 1882, a Competitive Exhibition of Embroideries and Designs for Embroideries has been announced, at which $445 will be distributed in prizes. — On the whole, the experience of the Society, thus far, is reported to have been promising, and it is hoped that it will soon be enabled to extend the activity of its school by adding classes in additional subjects.

Springfield, Ill. — SPRINGFIELD ART CLUB. — Sec., Miss Margerie Constant. (See next entry.)

CENTRAL ILLINOIS ART UNION. — Organized May 26, 1880. — Officers: Pres., Charles Ridgely, Springfield ; Sec., Mrs. M. L. D. Keiser, Jacksonville. — The credit of originating this association belongs to Mrs. Col. Latham, of Lincoln. At her instance, the Art Society of Lincoln, in the spring of 1880, extended invitations to several similar associations to send delegates to an informal meeting at the place named. About twenty representatives of half a dozen societies responded, and spent a pleasant and profitable day or two in a highly artistic atmosphere, with several essays, a few speeches, and much social converse. The whole affair was so thoroughly enjoyed, that in order to insure its repetition a formal organization was agreed upon. The constitution adopted at the second meeting, held in Springfield in 1881, is here given entire : " I. The name of this Association shall be *The Central Illinois Art Union.* II. It shall be composed of representatives from the Art Societies of Central Illinois, — each Society to be represented by five delegates. III. The officers shall be a President, one Vice President from each Society, a Secretary, and a Treasurer. IV. The term of office shall be one year. V. The officers shall be nominated at the annual meeting by a committee appointed for that purpose, and shall be elected by the oral vote of a majority of delegates present. VI. The Secretary of the Union shall be chosen from the place where the next annual meeting is to be held. VII. Regular meetings of the Union shall be held annually on the third Wednesday in May. Special meetings may be called by the President at the request of representatives of a majority of the Societies. VIII. The place of holding the annual meeting shall be chosen by the committee on nominations, subject to the approval of the Union. IX. At the annual meeting a paper shall be presented by each Society, — the reading of said paper not to occupy more than thirty minutes. X. When deemed practicable, a Loan Exhibition shall be held in connection with the annual meeting. XI. The Secretary of each Society shall send to the Secretary of the Union, on or before the first of May, each year, a full report of the work of the Society during the year, — embracing names of officers, number of meetings, lists of topics, essays, readings, lectures, or other exercises, of works of art procured, of books used, and such other information as may be valuable in the study of art. XII. The Secretary of the Union shall make an annual report compiled from the reports of the Societies, and summarizing their work. XIII. Other Art Societies may be admitted to the Union on the vote of three fourths of the delegates present at any annual meeting." The third meeting for the present year was held at Bloomington. Next year's meeting will again be held at Springfield. — The Union is composed of the following Societies: *Historical and Art Society,* Sec., Margaret M. Templeton, and *The Palladen,* Sec., Mrs. Gertrude Fifer, both at Bloomington ; *Art Class,* Sec., Miss Alice N. Roberts, and *Young Ladies' Art Class,* Sec., Mrs. Fannie J. Sedgwick, both at Decatur ; *Art Association,* Sec., Mrs. M. L. D. Keiser, Jacksonville ; *Art Society,* Sec., Mrs. Carrie M. Lutz, Lincoln ; *Art Society,* Cor. Sec., Miss Minnie E. Bills, Peoria ; *Art Club,* Sec., Miss Margerie Constant, Springfield. [This association is inserted under the heading " Springfield," as the president of the year resides there.]

6

Springfield, Mass. — Springfield Art Association. — First Nat'l B'k Bldg., 349 Main St., opp. Court Square. — Organized Jan., 1879. — Officers : Pres., E. C. Gardner ; V. Ps., E. Morgan, W. W. Colburn, G. S. Merriam; Aud., E. C. Rogers; Cor. Sec , Chas. Bill; Treas., A. N. Brown; Clerk, Wm. F. Ferry. — Object : To furnish opportunities for education that shall be of value, not merely as a pleasant accomplishment, but as a preparation for industrial and artistic pursuits, enlarging in a practical way the means of dignified and honorable self-support for young men and women. — Members pay $10 annual dues, which entitles them to free admission to all lectures and exhibitions given during the year and to the privilege of using the rooms and casts at any time, when the regular classes are not in session. The payment of $25 secures a transferable membership ticket, entitling the holder to instruction in any of the classes for one year. — The classes established by the Association (Willis S. Adams, Instructor) embrace Elementary Drawing to Drawing from the Antique and from Life, Design, Perspective, etc., and Painting in Water-Colors, on China, and in Oil. Instruction is also given in Art Needle-Work. The School is in session from Oct. 1 to June 1. Tuition fees vary for members and non-members, and according to time and subject. — Number of pupils, season of 1881-2, 50 (21 males, 29 females). — Monthly art receptions are held during the school year, at which the work of the students is exhibited. Several public lectures on art are usually arranged in the winter season, by persons prominent in the department of art on which they lecture, and an Annual Art Exhibition or Fair is held, also in the winter season.

Special Exhibitions of "Pictures selected from the Studios of New York" are held annually in February at *Gill's Art Galleries*, Jas. D. Gill, Prop., cor. Main and Bridge Sts. Admission, 25 cents. For the rest of the year the Gallery is open free.

St. Johnsbury, Vt. — St. Johnsbury Athenæum. — Founded 1870; opened 1871. — Officers: Horace Fairbanks, Edw. T. Fairbanks, Andrew E. Rankin, Franklin Fairbanks, Trustees ; Mrs. Abbie McNeil, Libr. — The Athenæum building contains a library (about 10,000 vols.), a lecture hall, and an *Art Gallery*. The paintings, of which there are about 50, and the statuary gathered in this gallery, have been selected with a view to forming a collection of choice specimens of representative artists. The following are among the more prominent paintings : "The Domes of the Yosemite," by A. Bierstadt ; "Woods of Assohochan, Catskills," Jervis McEntee ; "On the Plains, Colorado," W. Whittredge ; "South Mountains, Catskills," S. R. Gifford ; "Under the Elms," Jas. M. Hart ; "Hiding in the Old Oak," J. G. Brown ; "The Emigrant Train, Colorado," Saml. Colman ; "Marine, after a Storm," M. F. H. De Haas; "Sheep," Verboeckhoven ; "Italian Girl," Kaulbach ; "St. Ursula," Gabr. Max; "View in Holland," Achenbach ; "Up for Repair," Guez; "The Halberdier," J. Beaufain Irving ; "Autumn on the Delaware," J. F. Cropsey ; "Cattle," Hartmann ; "Aspasia," Coomans. In the same hall have been placed a number of standard illustrated works on art, including Ruskin, Mrs. Jameson, Owen Jones, Lübke, etc. ; Roberts's "Egypt and the Holy Land," the " Musée Français," "Musée des Antiquités," etc. — The institution was founded and is sustained by Mr. Horace Fairbanks. It has a permanent endowment fund of $30,000. — The Library and Reading Rooms are open free daily, Sundays excepted ; the Art Gallery is open free on Tuesdays and Fridays. Hours from 8½ A. M. to 12 M., and from 2 to 6 P. M.

St. Louis, Mo. — Missouri Historical Society. — The establishment of a cabinet of antiquities, relics, etc., is one of the objects of this Society.

Pen and Pencil Club. — Organized 1870. — Officers: Pres., W. R. Hodges, 2115 Walnut St. ; V. P., Mrs. M. J. Lippman ; Sec. and Treas., Mrs. A. C. Walker, 2809 Washington Ave. — Object: Art and literary culture. Meets at the residences of members. Present number of members, about 40.

St. Louis Academy of Sciences. — Collections illustrating the archæology of the country. The Archæological Section of the Academy published " Contributions to the Archæology of Missouri. — Part I. Pottery." (Salem : Geo. A. Bates, 1880.)

St. Louis Art Society. — This Society has placed on permanent exhibition in the Public School Library a collection of 3 oil paintings, 21 engravings, 10 casts of statuary, and 151 autotypes. [Further information promised, but not sent.]

St. Louis Künstler-Verein (St. Louis Artists Society). — 108 S. 4th St. — Organized Feb. 19, 1878. — Officers : Pres., Herm. Marquardt, 106 S. 8th St. ; V. P., Wilh. Mackwitz, 120 N. 3d St. ; Sec., Adolph Schenk, 108 S. 4th St. ; Treas., L. Hock, 217 S. 2d St. — Object : Harmonious co-operation among artists in the social and practical relations of life, and more especially the encouragement of the art of the country. — Members : Active, professional artists, initiation fee, $2, monthly dues, 25 cents; Passive, amateurs and connoisseurs, initiation fee, $4, monthly dues, 25 cents. Present number, 35 active and 25 passive members. — At the meetings of the Club some one of the members delivers a lecture, and this is followed by a discussion. Most of the members are Germans, and all the proceedings are conducted in German.

St. Louis School and Museum of Fine Arts (Art Department of Washington University). — Officers B'd of Control : Pres., Jas. E. Yeatman ; Sec., Edwin C. Cushman ; Director, Halsey C. Ives. — The St. Louis School of Fine Arts was organized May 22, 1879. The establishment of an art school upon a broad and permanent foundation has always been part of the plan of Washington University. For more than twenty-five years art instruction has been embodied in the course of studies followed by many of the classes. In 1875 special students were admitted to the Drawing Department, and class and public lectures were given by Prof. Ives on Art History. The same year an evening school was opened. From this time the growth of the department was so marked, and the work of the students had assumed such a degree of importance, that it was deemed advisable to reorganize the Drawing Department. The Directors of the University therefore passed an ordinance on May 22, 1879, establishing it as a special department, the objects of which were set forth as follows : " The object of said department shall be instruction in the Fine Arts ; the collection and exhibition of pictures, statuary, and other works of art, and of whatever else may be of artistic interest, and appropriate for a public gallery or art museum ; and in general the promotion by all proper means of æsthetic and artistic education." — The School furnishes instruction in drawing, modelling, painting, artistic anatomy, perspective and decorative design, including study from the draped and nude model. Full-time students are privileged to take up the study of French, German, and English History and Literature in classes of the Undergraduate Department as regular school work. Ladies are not required to work with University students who come to the School for instruction, but are given places in rooms set apart to the use of art students. — Instructors : Prof. Halsey C. Ives, Director ; Carl Gutherz, Paul E. Harney. Howard Kretschmar, Edmund Eugler ; Assistants in Evening Class, John H. Fry, Chas. S. Holloway, Arthur L. Smith. — There are two terms in the year, from October to February, and from February through the rest of the academic year. The rooms are open daily from 9 A. M. to 5 P. M. — Classes for drawing from the antique and from life meet four evenings in the week, from Nov. to May. Students may enter any class upon submitting examples of work showing the necessary skill. — Tuition for term, admission to all classes and lectures, $40 ; half-time students (3 days per week), $25. Special rates for special students. Evening Classes, $3 per term of 12 weeks. — Students enrolled in the Art School on Dec. 1, 1881 (the date of the last Report obtainable), 200 ; at the same time there were 350 students from other departments of the University receiving instruction either in the Art School or from its teachers. — The School is fully equipped with models, casts from the antique, etc. A collection of several hundred autotype reproductions from sketches, studies, and paintings by celebrated masters from the 15th century to the present time may be used by the students upon application to the Director. There is also a collection of 1,041 carbon prints, illustrating the historical development of art, and including the following six divisions: Prehistoric and Ethnographic, Egyptian, Assyrian, Grecian, Etruscan and Roman, Mediæval. The Museum (see below) is free to the students at all times, while open, and an Art Library is being formed for their use. From time to time class and public lectures are given upon the History of Art, for the illustration of which more than 1,400 views are available — *The Museum of Fine Arts* was founded by Mr. Wayman Crow, in memory of a deceased son. The building, which cost about $150,000, was dedicated and transferred to the Board of Control of the University on May 10, 1881. Subscriptions toward an endowment fund of $100,000 were started at the same time. The Museum contains a carefully selected collection of casts from antique and mediæval sculptures (348 examples according to last Report); several works in marble and in bronze; a collection of paintings; rare engravings; etchings; and other objects of art and art industry. Examples are being added, when feasible, with a view to affording the student the best possible opportunity for pursuing the study of art history. — Open daily, except Sundays, from 9.30 A. M. to 5 P. M. Admission 25 cents.

St. Louis Sketch Club. — 615 Chestnut St. — Organized about 1877. — Officers: Pres., Almon B. Thomson, 513 Olive St.; V. P., J. R. Meeker; Sec. and Treas., W. S. Eames, 293 Washington Ave. — Objects: The cultivation of sociability among artists and members, and the development of the creative faculty. — Members: Regular, who must qualify by presenting a satisfactory original sketch; Privileged, members of the press, art patrons, and those specially devoted to the advancement of art; Associate, friends of the fine arts. Only Regular members can hold office or vote. Regular members pay an initiation fee of 50 cents, and the same amount monthly. Associate members are expected to contribute to the support of the Club at pleasure. Present number of members, about 20 Regular and 60 Associate and privileged. — Meetings are held every Wednesday, from October to June. At the first meeting of each month every Regular member must present an original sketch illustrating a subject announced the month before. On these evenings one of the members acts as host, providing a simple entertainment, and becomes the owner of the sketches presented. The other meetings are devoted to business, impromptu sketching, etc.

Students' Sketch Club. — Organized Feb., 1882. — Officers: Pres., A. B. W. Hodges, 2115 Walnut St.; V. P, J. B. Longman; Sec. and Treas., S. M. Cady, 1430 Papin St. — Composed of students of the Art School. The members, of whom there are twelve at present, meet every two weeks for the illustration of a given subject. Any member who fails to produce a sketch is fined $1. This rule is strictly enforced.

St. Paul, Minn. — Minnesota Historical Society. — Collection of pictures, Indian curiosities, etc.

Syracuse, N. Y. — Artists' League. — Organized 1881. — Pres., Prof. N. A. Wells, 5 Harlow Block. [No reply to inquiries]

Æsthetic Society. — Organized 1873. — Pres., H. S. Gutsell. — This Society, organized by students of the College of Fine Arts connected with Syracuse University, holds meetings for mutual improvement and for æsthetic and social culture. During the spring and fall terms sketching excursions are made by the Society. Last year the Italian schools of painting were thoroughly studied by essays written by members upon all the chief masters, illustrated by extensive collections of photographs. [No response to request for details.]

Portfolio Club. — Organized 1875. — Pres., Mrs. Thomas Hooker. [No reply to inquiries.]

SOCIAL ART CLUB.—Organized Nov., 1875. — Officers: Pres., Mrs. Mary Hicks; V. P., Mrs. Henry C. Leavenworth; Sec., Mrs. Louise V. L. Lynch; Cor. Sec., Mrs. Geo. N. Crouse; Treas., Mrs. Edwin S. Jenney; Libr., Mrs. Henry Gifford.— Object: To cultivate the study of art in its various relations, by reading, discussions, essays, and such practical work as may be suggested. — Members, ladies only: Regular, limited to 40, annual fee, $3; Associates, limited to 15, annual fee, $5 — Honorary members may also be elected. Every vacancy is promptly filled, and applicants are always waiting for admission. — The Club has pleasant rooms, well supplied with pictures, art publications, etc. At the weekly meetings essays are read by members, on art and its history. In this manner were studied during the past year, Roman architecture, the ruins of Pompeii and Herculaneum, Etruscan art, Greek and Roman sculpture, Greek and Roman coins, pottery and porcelain, animal forms in ornamental art, Greek and Roman painting, etc. The Club owns a collection of about 200 engravings, wood-cuts, autotypes, heliotypes, photographs, and chromolithographs (published by the Arundel Society, of which the Club is a member), of which 161 are framed. The published catalogue of this collection shows that it illustrates the art history of Europe from the fifteenth century downwards, and includes some valuable engravings by Dürer, Carracci, Calamata, Morghen, Longhi, Desnoyers, F. Müller, and others.

SYRACUSE UNIVERSITY. — Organized 1870. — Officers B'd of Trustees: Pres, Francis H. Root, Delaware Ave., Buffalo; 1st V. P., Hon. Geo. F. Comstock, LL. D.; 2d V. P., Erastus F. Holden; Sec., Rev. D. W. C. Huntington, D. D.; Treas, Thos. J. Leach; Gen. Agent, Rev. E. C. Curtis, 727 Irving St. Officers of Gov't: Chancellor, Rev. Chas. N. Sims, 646 Irving St.; Dean of Coll. of Lib. Arts, John R. French, LL. D., 728 Chestnut St.; Dean of Coll. of Fine Arts, Geo. F. Comfort, A. M., 383 East Ave. — Three colleges are organized and in active operation, viz, the College of Liberal Arts, the College of Medicine, and the College of Fine Arts. Other colleges are to be organized as circumstances may permit. All the colleges are open to women on the same terms as men. — The College of Liberal Arts has four courses, Classical, Latin Scientific, Scientific, and Civil Engineering. Students in the Scientific and Latin Scientific Courses are required, and students in the Classical Course may elect, to attend the classes in the College of Fine Arts two hours a week during one term in Free-Hand Drawing, Mechanical Drafting, and Architectural Drafting. Students in the Scientific Course are also required to attend classes in Perspective Drawing two hours a week during the first term of the Sophomore year. Weekly lectures are given on Æsthetics during the first term, and on the History of the Fine Arts during the second and third terms of the Senior year. The appliances of the College of Fine Arts are employed to illustrate these lectures. — The College of Fine Arts. Opened 1873. — Faculty: Geo. F. Comfort, A. M., 383 East Ave, Dean and Prof. of Æsthetics and the History of the Fine Arts; Newton P. Wells, M. P., 5 Harlow Block, Prof. of Drawing; Frank Beard, West Adams St., Prof. of Painting; Ward V. Ranger, Prof. of Photography; Edgar M. Buell, B. Ar., 63 East Castle St., Instr. in Archit. Drafting; E. Ely Van De Warker, M. D., 45 Montgomery St, Lecturer on Artistic Anatomy. — This college is ultimately to include all the Fine Arts, that is, in the Formative Arts: Architecture, Sculpture, Painting, Engraving, and the various forms of Industrial Art; and in the Phonetic Arts: Music, Oratory, Poetry, and Belles-Lettres Literature. At present, courses in instruction in architecture, painting, and music only have been organized. [The musical members of the Faculty are omitted in the list above given.] — The courses of study already established include systematic and progressive instruction in the theory, history, and practice of architecture and painting, and in those branches of mathematics, natural science, history, language, and philosophy which bear most intimately and directly upon the arts, and without a knowledge of which success in the higher domains of art is impossible. The professors are proficient and practical workers in their several departments, and the students have access to their studios and offices, so that they have opportunity of witnessing works of art in process of completion. The aim is to develop the individuality of the student, rather than to mould his or her talent after the same arbitrary method. The complete course in architecture as well as in painting extends over four years. The subjects taught are as follows: 1. Free-Hand Drawing from the flat, from objects and casts, from nature, from memory, and from original designs; in the choice of media, lead-pencil, pen, charcoal, crayon, India ink, and sepia, the students are left largely to their own tastes. 2. Architectural Drafting, including instruction in the use of instruments; the drawing of plans, elevations, sections, ornaments, details, and working drawings; the principles of taste in their application to architectural composition; the study of executed works and works in progress, and the sketching of completed buildings; the use of building materials; principles and processes of construction; laws and usages in drawing up contracts and specifications, in makings estimates and measurements, and in superintending the erection of buildings. Special instruction is also given in Decorative Art in its relations to archititecture, and in Landscape Gardening. 3. Oil and Water-Color Painting, including the use of colors, the principles of technical execution, and the laws of composition. 4. Linear Perspective and the Projection of Shades and Shadows. 5. Modelling. Prominence is given to this study, as a most important means of cultivating a feeling for solid form. 6. Etching, including the printing of etchings. 7. Photography, as a valuable aid to the architect, and more especially to the painter. (Students may also make a special study of photography.) 8. Æsthetics. Instruction is given by lectures in the general principle of the science of æsthetics, which gives the foundation of all the Fine Arts. The principles of Art Criticism, which apply especially to architecture and painting, are treated more at length in separate courses of lectures. 9. History of the Fine Arts. 10. Classical Mythology and Archæology. 11. Christian and Mediæval Archæology. 12. Art Literature, consisting of critical remarks, etc., upon the most important books and periodicals on the subject of art. 13. Related studies, including Mathematics, Natural Science, Languages, History, English Literature, Rhetoric, and Elocution. Essays and a thesis to be preserved in the archives of the college must be presented during the Senior year. The College of Medicine offers excellent opportunity to such students as may desire to make more extensive studies in human and comparative anatomy. [No mention is made of study from the nude in the " Manual " issued by the College of Fine Arts.] — Candidates for admission to the Course in Architecture are examined in English Grammar, Geography, American History, Arithmetic, Natural Philosophy, Algebra as far as the Calculus of Radicals, Plane Geometry, and Free-Hand Drawing, sufficient to represent the progress usually made by students in at least one year of thorough and systematic study. Candidates for admission to the Course in Painting are examined in English Grammar, Geography, American History, Arithmetic, Natural Philosophy, and Free-Hand Drawing, sufficient to represent the progress usually made in at least two years of thorough and systematic study. Special students, or those not proposing to graduate, may enter at any time and take up such branches of study as they are prepared to pursue. — Expenses: Matriculation fee, $5; tuition, $100 per year (or $33⅓ for a single term); graduation in each course, $20. — The college confers the degrees of Bachelor of Architecture and of Bachelor of Painting. Special students may receive certificates of progress and proficiency. Every candidate for graduation in architecture is required to leave in the college an original project drawing, with specifications; and an original graduating painting will be required of candidates in painting. Students who have acquired a complete education as photographic artists may receive the degree of Bachelor of Painting. Graduates who have pursued professional work for three years after graduation may receive the Master's degree upon presentation to the college of an approved original work in their respective branch, an examination in an approved course of reading in æsthetics and in the history of their respective arts, and the payment of $25. Any person, not a student of the college, who is not less than twenty-eight years of age, and can give evidence that he has fully mastered any course of study in the College of Fine Arts, can obtain the appropriate degree, on passing the requisite examination. The charge for such examination is the same as for one year's tuition, with the usual graduation fee. — An Annual Exhibition of the works produced by the students is held during the last week of each college year. — Students during the season of 1881-2 : Regular Course in Painting, 16 (3 male, 13 female); Special Course in Painting, 15 (all female); Regular and Special Course in Architecture, 1 male each. Total, 33 (5 male, 28 female). The greater portion of the former students are at present engaged in teaching in seminaries and colleges. — The College of Fine Arts has several thousand photographs, including over a thousand on glass for stereopticon use, engravings, and chromolithographs, together with a sufficient number of copies and plaster preparations and casts to answer the demands of the course of instruction. These, with the graduating paintings and drawings, a number of other pictures, and a few busts, form the nucleus of a museum. As a nucleus to a Library of the Fine Arts a number of valuable books have been gathered, and the Reading Room is supplied with some of the most important art journals. — In addition to the regular work of the College, much has been done by the Faculty to educate the general public, especially in Syracuse, in art matters. Courses of public lectures are held nearly every winter. During the summer of 1876 a Normal Art Institute was held, lasting six weeks, and attended by teachers from New York and from other States. An extensive free Loan Exhibition was held at the same time.

Toledo. O. — TOLEDO HISTORICAL AND GEOGRAPHICAL SOCIETY. — This Society makes the collection of Indian relics a specialty.

TOLEDO UNIVERSITY OF ARTS AND TRADES. — [No reply to inquiries.]

Urbana, Ill. — ILLINOIS INDUSTRIAL UNIVERSITY. — Chartered Feb., 1867. — Officers B'd of Trustees: Pres., Emory Cobb; Cor. Sec., Prof. T. J. Burrill; Rec. Sec., Prof. E. Snyder; Treas., John W. Bunn; Bus. Agent, Prof. S. W. Shattuck. Officers of Fac : Regent, Selim H. Peabody, Ph. D., LL. D.; Sec., Jas. D. Crawford, M. A. — Aims: To offer freely the most thorough instruction which its means will provide in all the branches of learning, including scientific or classical, useful in the industrial arts, or necessary to the liberal and practical education of the industrial classes. Theory is supplemented by practice, i. e., by work in the shop, the field, the garden, etc. — The University embraces four Colleges. 1. College of Agriculture. 2. College of Engineering (subdivided into the School of Mechanical Engineering, the School of Architecture, and the School of Civil and Mining Engineering). 3. College of Natural Science (School of Chemistry and School of Natural History). 4. College of Literature and Science (School of Modern and School of Ancient Languages). Besides these there are two additional Schools, that of Military Science and of Art and Design. — In the Agricultural Course, free-hand drawing is optional in the first year, architecture required in the third year; in the Mechanical Engineering Course, drawing, including projection and machine drawing, free-hand sketches of machinery, ornamentation, and lettering, is required through the whole course of four years; in Civil and Mining Engineering, projection drawing, free-hand drawing from landscapes and buildings, lettering and ornamental work, topographical drawing and mapping, and designing and drawing of engineering structures, are practised the first three years; in Chemistry, free-hand drawing is required the first year, to a limited extent, while in Natural History and in the School of Modern Languages, it is optional. In the School of Ancient Languages and in that of Military Science, no provision is made for drawing. — *The School of*

Architecture. Prof. of Arch., N. Clifford Ricker, M. Arch.; Peter Roos, Prof. of Ind. Art and Designing; Jerome Sondericker, B. S., Instructor in Right Line Drawing. The course (four years) embraces the knowledge of theory and principles, of constructive details, and of the ordinary routine work of office practice, so far as these can be taught in a technical school. The technical instruction is given chiefly by lectures, with references to text books, and is illustrated by sketches, engravings, photographs, and models; practical applications are made by students. Drawing is practised throughout the course, and, as far as possible, original work is executed. Drawing from casts and modelling in clay give facility in sketching details and correct knowledge of form. In shop practice, joints in carpentry and joinery, cabinet making, turning, metal and stone work are executed, also models at reduced scale of roof and bridge trusses, ceilings, domes, and stairs. The course includes mathematics, mechanics, physics, chemistry, geology, French, political economy, constitutional history, history of civilization, and history and æsthetics of architecture.— Number of students, season of 1881–2, 14, all males. — (An interesting account of the course of instruction in this School of Architecture, by Prof. Ricker, will be found in the last, or fifteenth, Proceedings of the American Institute of Architects.) — *School of Art and Design.* Professor Peter Roos. — This school, besides providing instruction in free-hand drawing for the students in other departments, offers to such as have a talent or taste for art the best facilities for pursuing studies in industrial designing or other branches of fine art. Students not seeking a professional training may avail themselves of the two years' course in industrial art, which will qualify any person of ordinary ability who faithfully completes it, to teach drawing and designing in public schools, or to enter professions in which artistic taste and skill are indispensable to success. The course includes drawing from copies and casts, ornamental and decorative design, color, perspective, modelling in clay and wax, drawing landscapes and animals from copy, sketching from nature in charcoal and color, artistic anatomy, and the history of art. A more advanced course is designed for those who wish to become accomplished either as designers, painters, or teachers. In order that the student may acquire thoroughness in his specialty the subject at this stage is divided into two divisions, — decorative and pictorial The teacher student must give attention to both branches, and with him theory will necessarily supersede practice. Opportunity is afforded such pupils to teach in the elementary classes. The Advanced Course in Painting takes in copying from pictures and leads up to still-life and landscape from nature, and portrait painting from life in oil and water-colors, and pictorial composition. The Advanced Course in Designing includes the study of the human figure, the application of ornamentation to various manufactures, a knowledge of the processes of manufacture, designs for church decoration, for stained-glass windows, etc. [No mention is made of study from the nude in any of the classes of the school] — Students in the School of Art, season of 1881–2, 4 (3 males, 1 female). — The tuition is free in all the University classes; matriculation fee, $10; incidental expenses, $7.50 per term. — Degrees are given by the institution, but not in the School of Art. Special students receive certificates, with statement of work done and credits attained. — *The Art Gallery* of the University, established in 1874, the gift of citizens of Champaign and Urbana, is one of the largest and finest of the West. It occupies a beautiful hall, 61 by 79 feet, and embraces 13 full-sized casts from antiques, such as the Laocoön, the Venus of Milo, etc.; 40 statues of reduced size, and a large number of busts, ancient and modern, bas-reliefs, etc., in all over 400 pieces. There are also hundreds of large autotypes, photographs, and fine engravings, and a gallery of historical portraits, mostly large French lithographs of peculiar fineness, copied from the great national portrait galleries of France.— The gallery is open to the public, free of charge, on Thursdays, from 8 A. M. to 5 P. M.; on other days a fee of 10 cents is charged; but strangers from other places are admitted without charge. A printed catalogue of the gallery was published in 1876. — The Illinois Industrial University is the State University of Illinois. It was opened in March, 1868, and in 1871 female students were admitted on the same term as males. Its property and endowment funds, not including 25,000 acres of land in Minnesota and Nebraska, are valued at about $752,000, the result of congressional land grants, appropriations by the State of Illinois, and donations, in the shape of bonds, buildings, and farms, valued at over $400,000, by Champaign County. The University is located in the township of Urbana, but its P. O. address is Champaign, Ill.

Utica, N. Y. — UTICA ART ASSOCIATION. — Incorporated Jan., 1866. — Officers: Pres, Geo. W. Adams; V. P., Robt. S. Williams; Sec., C. A. Doolittle; Treas., J. M. Crouse; Cor. Sec., Benj. D. Gilbert. — Object: The holding of exhibitions, and, eventually, the establishment of a permanent gallery of art in Utica. — Present number of members, 40. — It is the intention of the Association to hold annual exhibitions, but this has not been strictly adhered to, eight exhibitions only having been held so far. The last of these opened at the City Library Building on Jan. 16, 1882, and contained 262 works by 157 artists. The Association has been quite prosperous, and its efforts to effect sales for its contributors have resulted, since its organization, in the disposal of works of art valued at over $100,000.

Vineland, N. J. — VINELAND HISTORICAL AND ANTIQUARIAN SOCIETY. — Collection of local curiosities.

Waltham, Mass. — WALTHAM PENCIL AND BRUSH CLUB. — Priest's Block, Main St. Organized April, 1882. — Officers: Pres., Geo. E. Johnson ; Sec., Hiram P. Barnes. — Objects: Advancement of the members in art from the comparison which club membership affords; and to assist the artistic feeling in the community. — The only condition of membership is that applicants shall be possessed of the artistic impetus. Present number of active members, 25. — The Club maintains a class in water-color painting, F. Childe Hassam, instructor, and has announced an exhibition.

Washington, D. C. — CORCORAN GALLERY OF ART. — Pennsylvania Ave., cor. 17th St. — Chartered May 24, 1870; opened to the public, 1874. — Officers B'd of Trustees: Pres, Jas. C. Welling ; V. P., Chas. M. Matthews; Sec, Anthony Hyde; Curator, Wm. MacLeod ; Asst. Cur. and Lib., F. S. Barbarin. — This gallery, including ground, building, contents, and endowment fund, is the free gift of Mr. Wm. W. Corcoran to the public. In the deed to the Trustees, dated May 10, 1869, the object of the institution is stated as "the perpetual establishment and encouragement of Painting, Sculpture, and the Fine Arts generally," with the condition that "it should be open to visitors without charge two days in the week, and on other days at moderate and reasonable charges, to be applied to the current expenses." The cost of the building and ground was $250,000; the pictures and statuary contained in the museum at its opening were valued at $100,000. The institution is maintained by an endowment fund of $900,000, yielding an annual income at present of over $70,-000. — The Gallery has an excellent collection of casts from the antique, and from Renaissance and modern sculptures ; a collection of 118 bronzes by Barye, said to be the largest in existence ; an extensive collection of ceramics and art-industrial objects ancient, modern, Oriental and European ; a series of Kensington and other electrotype reproductions ; and a number of original works in bronze and in marble, among the latter Vela's celebrated statue of "The Last Days of Napoleon I.," "The Greek Slave," "Genevra," "Proserpine," by Hiram Powers ; "Penseroso," and "Endymion," by W. H. Rinehart, etc. The collection of paintings, about 200 in all, gives a tolerably good chronological view of American art within certain limits, as will be seen by the following partial list of artists represented: Gilbert Stuart, Rembrandt Peale, Thos. Sully, J. Vanderlyn, Henry Inman, Chester Harding, Saml. Waldo, C.

L. Elliott, T. P. Rossiter, Geo. A. Baker, D. Huntington, G. P. A. Healy, B. C. Porter, Thos. Le Clear, Thos. Doughty, Alvan Fisher, Thos. Cole, J. F. Kensett, S. R. Gifford, R. Gignoux, A. B. Durand, F. E. Church, W. Whittredge, A. Bierstadt, Wm. MacLeod, J. F. Cropsey, J. R. Tilton, Jas. M. Hart, Geo. Inness, John R. Key, Wm. S. Mount, E. Leutze, H P. Gray, Eastman Johnson, Louis Lang, Geo. H. Boughton, J. G. Brown, F. A. Bridgman, A. A. Brooke. Besides these works of native artists, there are European pictures by Bail, Barye, Begas, Emile Breton, Cabanel. Chialiva, Chierici, Comte, Bouder, Detaille, Blaise Desgoffe, De Brackeleer, Faed, Ed. Frère, Gérôme, Hildebrandt, Japy, Kaemmerer, Leroux, Moretti, C. L. Müller, Erskine Nicol, Portaels, Preyer, Priou, Robbe, Salmson, Ary Scheffer, Schreyer, Vely, O. Von Thoren, Ziem, etc., and a few old paintings attributed to Murillo, Van Dyck, Canaletti, Sir Peter Lely, Raphael Mengs, Jos. Vernet, and Geo. Morland. — Open daily, Sundays and public holidays excepted, from 10 A. M. to 4 P. M. from Oct. 1 to May 1, and from 9 A. M. to 4 P. M. from May 1, to Oct. 1. On Tuesdays, Thursdays, and Saturdays, admission free; other days, 25 cents. During winter, weekly Night Exhibitions are held, admission 10 cents. On Mondays, Wednesdays, and Fridays persons are allowed, under certain regulations, to draw from the casts and copy the pictures. — Catalogue, 25 cents. Photographs are also published (136 up to date, of different styles or sizes) of pictures, etc., contained in the Gallery, which are for sale at the door. — Number of visitors from Jan. 1, 1881, to July 31, 1882, 132,933 (21,783 on pay days, 111,150 on free days). — It is the intention of Mr. Corcoran to establish a *Free Art School* in connection with the Gallery.

PUBLIC BUILDINGS. — For a description of the works of art in and around the Capitol, such as Greenough's statue of Washington; the groups, reliefs, and figures by Crawford, Greenough, Persico, Capellano, Powers, etc.; the bronze doors by Randolph Rogers and Crawford; the paintings by John Trumbull, J. Vanderlyn, W. H. Powell, J. G. Chapman, R. W. Weir, in the Rotunda; the frescos by C. Brumidi; the paintings on the staircases by W. H. Powell, E. Leutze, Walker; the statues in the National Statuary Hall, including works by most of the best known American sculptors; and the numerous statues, busts, and paintings scattered through the various halls and rooms, the reader must be referred to the local guide-books. — A collection of the portraits of the various secretaries of the treasury is to be found in the corridors of the *Treasury Department.*

UNITED STATES NATIONAL MUSEUM. — Officers: Director, Spencer F. Baird, Sec. of the Smithsonian Institution; Asst.' Dir. and Curator Dept. of Arts and Industries, G. Brown Goode; Curator of Archæological Dept., Charles Rau; Lib., Frederick W. True; Registrar, Stephen C. Brown. — This is the only Museum which receives direct aid from the U. S. government. It was organized in 1846 by the act of Congress transferring to the Smithsonian Institution (the well-known scientific institution founded by a bequest to the U. S. of $500,000 by Jas. Smithson, an English scientist, who died in the year 1829) the custody of the "National Cabinet of Curiosities," at that time deposited in the Patent Office buildings. The collections were given a place in the building of the Smithsonian Institution, but are now being installed in the new structure, lately erected for the special uses of the Museum by the government at a cost of about $250,000. — The Museum has so far enjoyed an annual allowance from the U. S. of about $20,000. — Its collections, which are already of an immense extent, and are continually increasing with great rapidity, consist mainly of specimens brought home by U. S. exploring and surveying parties, supplemented by exchanges, by gifts from foreign governments and from individuals, and but rarely by purchases. They are intended to form an Anthropological Museum, organized upon the broadest and most liberal interpretation of the term "anthropology," and illustrating the characteristics of civilized as well as savage races of mankind, and their attainments in civilization and culture. The central idea will be *man*, and the manner in which he adapts the products of the earth to his needs. It follows from this that in the main the Museum is devoted to natural history and ethnology, in which latter department, so far as it relates to the native races of America, it is already richer than any other museum. It is, however, of great interest and importance also for the study of primitive art, on account of its rich collections of aboriginal antiquities and the products of Indian art of the present day, confined not only to the U. S., but taking in the whole extent of North, Central, and South America. It possesses also some specimens of art-archæological interest from other parts of the globe.— As the new fire-proof building, which is of immense dimensions, measuring 327 feet in length, and covering a net area of 102,200 square feet, has been only lately finished, everything, as a matter of course, is in a transition state for the present, and will be so for some time to come. A "Visitors' Guide to the Smithsonian Institution and National Museum," edited by W. J. Rhees, Chief Clerk of the Institution (Washington: Judd & Detweiler. 1880. Price 35 cents), will serve to give a slight idea of the collections as they were in the old building. A more extended and strictly scientific account of the archæological section is to be found in "Smithsonian Contributions to Knowledge, 287. The Archæological Collection of the United States National Museum, in charge of the Smithsonian Institution, by Charles Rau (Washington City: Published by the Smithsonian Institution, 1876.) A thorough system of descriptive labels and guide-book manuals will be provided for in the new Museum.

WASHINGTON ART CLUB. — Corcoran Building. — Organized 1876. — Officers: Pres., W. W. Corcoran; V. P., S. H. Kaufmann; Sec., J. M. March, 1522 16th St. N. W.; Treas., W. G. Newton. — Objects: Cultivation of the Fine Arts, advancement and diffusion of art knowledge, and the promotion of good-will and social enjoyment. — Present membership: 22 Active, 11 Associate, 3 Honorary members. Total, 36. — The *Art School* connected with the Club, in charge of Mr. C. E. Messer, is reported to be in a most prosperous and encouraging condition, with a very large membership.

West Point, N. Y. — UNITED STATES MILITARY ACADEMY. — Supt., Col. Wesley Merritt; Lt.-Col. Chas. W. Larned, Professor of Drawing. — The following is the complete official programme of the *Course of Instruction in Drawing*, as furnished by the authorities in charge of the Academy. Its aim does not pretend to be high art; it is simply art in harness in the shop and in the field. — First Year. (3d Class) 1. Topography and Map Drawing; 2. Construction of Problems in Descriptive Geometry, Shades and Shadows, and Perspective; 3. Reconnaissance and Field Work. Course of Instruction: Beginning with the academic year, the 3d class is instructed in the conventional signs of topography, and shortly after the inception of the work a lecture on that subject is delivered by the head of the department, or one of his assistants. After the completion of the conventional signs a lecture is delivered embracing the following subjects: Drawing instruments, their use and care: drawing papers, names, qualities, and uses; methods of preparing paper for use; general rules to be observed in rectilinear and map drawing; construction of borders; lettering, different styles, and methods of construction; scales, proportional and Vernier, scales of distance, their varieties and construction. Immediately thereafter a third lecture embracing the following subjects: Definition of topography and its objects; historical sketch of its progress and methods; explanation of the different systems and their relative merits; methods of hill shading; construction of scales of shade and their application; principles of contours and sections. Following these lectures the work of drawing scales of shade, inclination, distance, proportion, the drawing of maps from skeleton and plaster models, and the study of hill shading in ink and pencil is carried on. Before the semi-annual examination, a fourth lecture

embracing the following subjects is delivered: Methods of projection of meridian and parallels; methods of plotting from field work; plotting meridian and compass variations. Between the close of the semi-annual examination and the first of March instruction is given in colored topography, beginning with conventional tints, and including the construction of maps from skeleton data. From March 1 to about April 15, construction of problems in descriptive geometry, shades and shadows, and perspective, the problems being generally variations and combinations of those given in text books. From April 15 until close of academic year, June 1, practical topography in the field and reconnaissance. Before going into the field a lecture is delivered, embracing the following subjects: Preparation and arrangement of note book; use of prismatic compass; method of field sketching; use of odometer, predometer, pacing; hill sketching; methods of running contours; methods of U. S. Coast Survey; precautions necessary in reconnaissance and field sketching; improvised methods of work; practicability of slopes for troops. Before the close of the academic year a sixth lecture embracing the following subjects: General methods of large surveys; measurement of bases; general principles of triangulation and plotting; filling in; establishment of stations; methods of Coast Survey and Surveys west of 100th meridian Cadets are required to take careful notes of all lectures, and retain them for use and reference. — Second Year. (2d Class.) 1. Free-Hand Drawing in Black and White; 2. Theory of Color and Laying of Tints; 3. Mechanical, Architectural, and Constructive Drawing. Divided into two periods: 1. Free-Hand drawing, from Sept. 1 to Jan. 1; 2. Mechanical, architectural, and constructive drawing and color from close of semi-annual examination until June 1. Course of Instruction: Beginning with the academic year lectures are delivered on the subject of free-hand drawing and perspective; outline; light and shade; proportion; methods and materials. The class is instructed in free-hand drawing in black and white, pencil, crayon, or charcoal, beginning with simple block models after Harding's system, and increasing in complexity until a fair proficiency in the drawing of outline is attained. Shading is then studied in the simpler forms, and the models are increased in difficulty according to the proficiency of the student. The flat is very sparingly used for purposes of illustration, the models used being the "Cours de Dessin" of Ch. Bargue and J. L. Gérôme. Elementary instruction in landscape drawing follows the above. After the close of the semi-annual examination a lecture is delivered embracing the following subjects: Theory of color; modern chromatics; quality and character of pigments. Use of Water-Color: Instruction in this course begins by the laying of flat tints and grades, illustrating the laws of harmonious contrast and the formation of compound and broken colors. Succeeding these, problems in mechanical and constructive drawing are undertaken by the students; architectural plans and elevations and working drawings in military and ordnance construction from data and mechanical models. At the close of the year lectures are given on the subject of the principal orders of architecture, their origin, characteristics, and general proportion. Cadets are required to take careful notes of lectures. — The *Art Works* in possession of this department are confined to a collection of the best drawings of cadets, selected from the work of the different classes for a period of forty years or more; a number of engravings of greater or less value, and a few original water-colors by G. J. Knox, Allom (11), John Varley (6), Pyne, Prout, Richardson (2), Davidson (2), Salmon, A. Delacroix, Catherwood, Gignoux, Abert, Abery, Cooper, Bartlett, Bentley, and Copley Fielding. There is also a large collection of plaster copies of the antique, wood-cuts, lithographs, etc. — All of these, except the collection of prints, are open to the public daily during the hours prescribed by the Superintendent for visitors.

Wilkesbarre, Pa. — WYOMING HISTORICAL AND GEOLOGICAL SOCIETY. — Cabinet of Indian curiosities and other relics, and over 7,000 coins.

Worcester, Mass. — American Antiquarian Society. — Incorporated Oct. 24, 1812. — Officers: Pres, Hon. Stephen Salisbury, LL. D.; V. P's., Hon. Geo. F. Hoar, LL. D., Hon. Geo Bancroft, LL. D.; For. Cor. Sec., Hon. J. Hammond Trumbull, LL. D.; Dom. Cor. Sec., Chas. Deane, LL. D.; Rec. Sec., Col. John D. Washburn; Treas., Nathaniel Paine; Asst. Libr. in charge, Edmund M. Barton. — Objects: The advancement of the arts and sciences, and to aid in collecting and preserving such materials as might be useful in marking their progress, not only in the U. S., but elsewhere; to assist historians by the preservation of MSS., books, etc.; the collection, preservation, and elucidation of American antiquities, natural, artificial, and literary. — The American members of the Society are limited to 140; foreign members unlimited. Initiation fee of American members, $5; members residing in New England pay an annual fee of $5; life membership, $30. — The Society was practically founded by Isaiah Thomas, who provided the first building occupied by it, gave to it his library, and bequeathed funds to provide for its operations and maintenance. Since then considerable donations have been made by Hon. Stephen Salisbury and others, so that the funds held by the Society are now quite considerable. — Besides a very large library, in which there are several old MSS., richly illuminated, early Bibles, and illustrated books, etc., the Society owns a Cabinet containing Indian and other antiquities and relics, coins, medals, engravings, casts of Michelangelo's statue of Christ in Sta. Maria Sopra Minerva, and of the same sculptor's celebrated Moses, and a number of interesting portraits and busts, principally of men prominent in the history of Massachusetts. Among the portraits are several by Chester Harding, one supposed to be by Copley, another by Alexander, etc. Others are principally interesting on account of the subjects represented, including portraits of Gov. Endicott, Gov. Winthrop, Gov. Leverett, five members of the Mather family, etc. Among the busts are works by Cerrachi, Clevenger, Dexter, Kinney, Powers, and King. A partial list of these portraits and busts may be found in "An Account of the American Antiquarian Society, with a List of its Publications," prepared by Nathaniel Paine for the International Exhibition of 1876, and published by the Society. — Open week days free to all, from 9 A. M. to 12 M. and from 2 to 5 P. M., except Saturday afternoons.

Worcester County Free Institute of Industrial Science. — Incorp. May 10, 1865. — Officers: Pres, Hon. Stephen Salisbury, LL. D.; Sec., Rev. Edw. P. Hall; Treas., Philip L. Moen. Principal, Chas. O. Thompson, A. M., Ph. D., 18 Boynton St. — This Institute offers a good education, based on mathematics, the living languages, physical sciences, and drawing, and sufficient practical familiarity with some branch of applied science to secure its graduates a livelihood. It is specially designed to meet the wants of those who wish to be prepared as mechanics, civil engineers, chemists, or designers, for the duties of active life. For the acquisition of practical familiarity with different branches of applied science, the same facilities are offered as in the best schools of technology elsewhere. In mechanics, shop-practice is added to the course and incorporated in it. Thus the students who select chemistry, work in the laboratory; the civil engineers, at field work or problems in construction; those who select drawing, in the drawing-room; those who select physics, in the physical laboratory. The mechanical section practise in the workshop through the whole course (which in this department extends over three and a half years, while the other courses are absolved in three years); and as the "Washburn Machine Shop" connected with the Institute is managed as a manufacturing establishment, the products of which are sold, the student always works in the wholesome atmosphere of real business. The ease with which more than 90 per cent of the graduates have secured employment is evidence of the soundness of the principles upon which the school is organized. — *All* students are taught Free-Hand Drawing. By carefully studied exercises in outline drawing, shading and coloring, from copies, models, and casts, discipline of the sense of form and proportion is secured, and an ability to delineate objects is acquired, which is of great value in all departments of applied science. In the Mechanical Drawing room, instruction is given in the use of instruments, shading and coloring, plane and isometric projections, and the theory of shades, shadows, and perspective. All drawing is done under the eye of the instructor. Students who evince marked power in drawing are admitted to special practice in this department. A course of lessons is devised for each student in practice, preparatory to designing for textile fabrics, lithography, fresco and ornamental painting, or similar arts. Students enjoy access to collections of illustrations and examples. Professor of Drawing: Geo. E. Gladwin, 16 Harvard St. — Students, male only, must have attained the age of sixteen, and must give evidence of proficiency in the common English branches; but from 1884 some knowledge of French will be required. — No charge for tuition to residents of Worcester County; others, $150 per year. There are, however, 20 Free State Scholarships, for residents of the State of Massachusetts, and three Free Scholarships, established by the Hon. Geo. F. Hoar, for residents of certain towns. — The school was founded by Mr. John Boynton of Templeton, who gave for the purpose $100,000. The State contributed $50,000, Hon. Stephen Saulsbury over $200,000, Hon. Ichabod Washburn provided the machine shop and an endowment of $50,000, Mr. David Whitcomb over $20,000, and a number of smaller donations, in money, machines, materials, etc., have been received from various sources. — The Institute confers the degree of Bachelor of Science, the diplomas designating the department to which the graduate belonged. It also confers honorary degrees.

ARTISTS' DIRECTORY.*

THE following list contains the names of those American architects, sculptors, designers, engravers, etc., who are members of the societies, or have exhibited in the exhibitions enumerated below, and who, having been favorably passed upon by an Examining Committee or a Jury of Admission, can claim that they have been recognized by an authority supposed to be competent. The numbers inserted after the name of each artist refer to the societies and exhibitions here specified.

1. National Academy of Design. — Academicians.
2. National Academy of Design. — Associates.
3. Society of American Artists.
4. American Water-Color Society.
5. Philadelphia Society of Artists.
6. New York Etching Club.
6a. Philadelphia Society of Etchers. (Resident Members.)
7. Salmagundi Sketch Club.
8. Ladies' Art Association, New York. (Active members.)
9. American Institute of Architects. (Members " in good standing.")
10. Society of American Wood-Engravers.
11. Artists' Fund Society, New York.
12. National Academy, 57th Annual Exh., Mch. 27–May 13, 1882.
13. Society of American Artists, 5th Annual Exh., April 6–May 20, 1882.
14. American Water-Color Society, 15th Annual Exh., Jan. 30–Feb. 25, 1882.
15. New York Etching Club Exhibition, Jan. 30–Feb. 25, 1882.
16. Black and White, 4th Annual Exh., Dec. 1–Dec. 21, 1881.
17. Penns. Academy of the Fine Arts, Special Exh., Nov. 7–Dec. 26, 1881.
18. Philad. Society of Artists, 3d Annual Exh., Nov. 14–Dec. 31, 1881.
19. Philad. Society of Artists, 1st Annual W. C. Exh., April 10–May 6, 1882.
20. Boston Art Club, 25th Exhibition, Feb. 11–Mch. 11, 1882.
21. Boston Art Club, 26th Exhibition, April 28–May 27, 1882.
22. Interstate Industr. Exp., Chicago, 9th Annual Exh., Sept. 7–Oct. 22, 1881.
23. Interstate Industr. Exp., Chicago, 10th Annual Exh., Sept. 6–Oct. 21, 1882.
24. National Academy, Special Autumn Exh., Oct. 23–Nov. 18, 1882.
25. Penns. Academy of the Fine Arts, 53d Annual Exh., Oct. 23–Dec. 9, 1882.

ABBATT, Miss Agnes D., New York ; 337 Fourth Ave. 4, 12, 14, 18, 19, 22, 23, 24, 25
Abbey, Edwin A., New York ; 58½ W. 10th St. 3, 4, 6, 13, 14, 16, 23
Adams, Mrs. E. L. S., Chicago ; 119 Drexel Boul. 14, 22, 23
Adams, Willis S., Springfield, Mass. 12, 13, 20, 21
Addison, John, Chicago ; 154 La Salle St. 9
Adler D., Chicago ; Randolph and Dearborn Sts. 9

---

* Artists will confer a great favor upon the editor by keeping him advised of changes of address, for use in future editions of this Directory.

Ahrens, Ellen W., Philadelphia; 3904 Girard Ave. 25
Albee, Byron, Boston ; 6 Winter St. 21
Alexander, Mrs. E. H., New York ; 58 W. 57th St. 12
Alexander, John W., New York ; B'k Building, 4 Ave. and 14th St. 12, 13, 24, 25
Alexander, Wm. 12, 16
Alger, W. H. H., Pittsburgh, Pa. 18
Allen, J. M., New Bedford, Mass. 9
Allen, Louise, New York ; 43 W. 48th St. 24
Allen, Thos , Jr., Boston; Pelham Studios, 12, 13, 25
Anderson, A. A., New York ; 58 W. 57th St. · 4, 14, 24
Anderson, O., Venice ; Via Garibaldi, 1770, 17
Andrew, Geo. T., Boston; 5 Temple Place, 16
Andrews, W. S., Philadelphia ; 1724 N. 13th St. 9
Annen, M. 12
Anshutz, Thos. P., Philadelphia ; 1802 Mt. Vernon St. 5, 17, 18, 25
Anthony, Andrew V. S., Boston ; 211 Tremont St. 4
Archer, George, Baltimore ; Charles and Lexington Sts. 9
Archibald, Wm. S., New York; 20 W. 14th St. 14, 16, 24
Armstrong, D. Maitland, New York; 335 Fourth Ave. 3, 11, 12
Arnolt, Gust. M., New York ; Home St., Morrisania, 17
Atkinson, E. H., Baltimore ; Hotel Shirley, 12, 25
Atwood, D. T., New York ; 335 Broadway, 9
Babson, Seth, San Francisco ; 318 Pine St. 9
Bacher, Otto H., Venice ; Poste restante, 6, 13, 16, 17
Bachman, H. G., Philadelphia ; 120 N. 6th St. 25
Bacon, Henry, Paris; Rue du Faub. St. Honoré, 157, 22, 25
Bailey, R. M., Boston ; 12 West St. 21
Bailey, S. T., Brooklyn, N. Y. ; 67 Pineapple St. 16, 24
Baird, W. B., Paris; Rue Odessa, 3, 17, 25
Baker C., New York ; 242 E. 61st St. 14
Baker, Miss Ellen K., Buffalo, N. Y. ; 489 Prospect Ave. 12, 17, 22, 24, 25
Baker, J. E., New York; 4 E. 20th St. 14
Baker, L., Charlestown, Mass. 21
Baker, Lizzie E., Philadelphia ; 1811 Arch St. 25
Baker, Miss M. K., Boston ; 54 Studio Building, 16, 17, 20, 21
Baker, Miss Mary L., Noroton, Conn. 12
Baker, Wm. Bliss, New York ; 29 W. 24th St. 12, 14, 16, 17, 24
Baldwin, A. H , New York ; 337 Fourth Ave. 4, 6, 14
Baldwin, E. F., Baltimore ; Charles and Lexington Sts. 9
Bannister, Edwin M., Providence, R. I. ; 2 College St. 20
Bannister, Eleanor C., Brooklyn, N. Y. ; 416 Bergen St. 12, 24
Barber, Alice, Philadelphia ; 1618 Arch St. 16, 20, 25
Barber, J. Jay, Columbus, O. ; 47 Monroe St. · 12, 17, 23, 25
Barker, W. H., Methuen, Mass. 20
Barnes, H. Seymour, New York ; 202 Broadway, 9
Barrow, J. D., Skaneateles, N. Y. 11, 12, 17, 24, 25
Barry, A., New York ; 301 E. 34th St. 16
Barse, Geo. R., Jr., Paris ; care Chas. Becker, 28 Rue Croix des Petits Champs, 25
Barstow, Miss S. M., Brooklyn, N. Y. ; 182 Washington St. 12, 17, 19
Bartberger, C. M., Pittsburgh, Pa. ; 198 Liberty St. 9
Bartle, Geo P. 16
Bartlett, Miss Jennie E., Boston ; 17 S. Russell St. 20, 21
Bartlett, Paul W., Paris; 104 Rue Blomet, 25

Bartlett, T. H., Boston ; 394 Federal St. 21, 25
Bartol, Miss Elizabeth H., Boston; 60 Mt. Vernon St. 16, 21
Bates, Dewey, London, Eng. ; 7 Red Lion Sq. 17
Bates, Mrs. Fannie H., New York ; 24 W. 14th St. 8, 12
Bauer, Augustus, Chicago; 84 La Salle St. 9
Bauer, W. C., Elizabeth, N. J. ; 1145 Elizabeth Ave. 15, 16, 17, 18, 21, 24, 25
Baur, Theodore, New York; 335 Fourth Ave. 3, 13
Bayliss, H. S., New York; 58 W. 57th St. 12, 24
Beaman, Waldo G., Boston ; 5 Tremont St. 17, 20
Beard, Daniel, New York ; 191 Broadway, 16
Beard, J. H., New York ; 1300 Broadway, 1, 12, 17, 18, 22
Beard, Wm. H., New York; 51 W. 10th St. 1, 11, 12, 23, 24
Beaux, Cecilia, Philadelphia ; 4305 Spruce St. 25
Beck, Carrie H., Philadelphia ; 1910 Wallace St. 25
Beck, Robt. K., Philadelphia ; 1709 Chestnut St. 19
Becker, Carl J., New York ; 1193 Broadway, 24
Becket, Miss M. J. C., Boston ; Hotel Vendôme, 17, 25
Beckwith, Arthur, New York ; 1155 Broadway, 17
Beckwith, J. Carroll, New York ; 58 W. 57th St. 3, 4, 12, 13, 14, 16, 18, 19, 20, 21, 25
Beech, Thos., New York; 127 Fulton St. 12
Beecher, A. D., Chicago; 102 Washington St. 22, 23
Beers, Julia H., Metuchen, N. J. 12, 24
Bell, M. F., Fulton, Mo. ; Lock Box 19, 9
Bellows, A. F., N. Y.; 337 Fourth Ave. 1, 4, 6, 12, 14, 15, 16, 17, 18, 19, 20, 21, 22, 23
Benjamin, S. G. W., New York ; 6 E. 14th St. 7, 12, 16, 24, 25
Bennett, Ritchie, New York ; 223 W. 45th St. 24
Benson, Eugene, Italy, 2
Bentham, Geo., Cedar Forks, Mich. 23
Berry, P. V., New York; 14 Park Pl. 24
Betts, E. D., New York; 1193 Broadway, 24
Bickford, Nelson, New York ; 1298 Broadway, 12
Bicknell, A. H., Malden, Mass.; cor. Parker and Ferry Sts. 16
Bierstadt, Albert, New York ; 1271 Broadway, 1
Bigelow, D. F., Chicago; 170 State St. 22, 24
Birney, W. V., Munich ; Royal Acad. of F. A. 17
Bisbing, Harry, Europe, 17, 18
Bishop, Thos., Philadelphia ; 33 S. 19th St. 17, 19
Bispham, Henry C., Europe, 12, 17, 18, 20, 22
Bissell, Edgar J., Boston ; 5 Temple Pl. 12, 17
Blaikley, Alex., Grandview, Danbury, Conn. 25
Blake, Miss A. D., Boston ; 21 W. Cedar St. 20
Blakelock, R. A., New York ; University Building, Washington Sq. 12, 17, 24
Blashfield, E. H., New York; 58 W. 57th St. 2, 3, 12, 13, 16, 23, 24, 25
Blauvelt, Chas. F., Annapolis, Md.; U. S. Naval Acad. 1, 11
Bloodgood, M. S., New York ; 4 E. 23d St. 12, 16, 24, 25
Bloodgood, Robt. F., New York ; 58 E. 13th St. 14, 25
Bloor, A. J., New York; 335 Broadway, 9
Blum, Robt., New York ; 58 W. 57th St. 12, 13, 14, 21, 22, 23, 24
Boggs, Frank M., Dieppe, France ; Quai Duquesne, 8, 12
Bolmer, M. De Forest, New York ; 51 W. 10th St. 12, 16, 17, 18, 19, 24, 25
Bolton, Rev. Wm. Jay, England, 2
Bond, Mrs. Francis, New York ; 32 E. 14th St. 8
Bonfield, V. De V., Philadelphia ; 926 N. 15th St. 5, 18

7

Bonham, Horace, York, Pa.   18
Bonwill, Chas. E. H., New York; 7 Murray St.   16
Boott, Miss Elizabeth, Boston; 48 Boylston St.   12, 13, 14, 16, 20, 21, 25
Borris, Albert, Washington, D. C.; 1425 New York Ave.   25
Boston, Fred. J., New York; 11 E. 14th St., Room 13,   24
Bothe, Miss Ida, Boston; 13 Franklin St.   20
Botto, J. B., Louisville, Ky.; 4th and Green Sts.   12, 17, 25
Boughton, Geo. II., London; West House, Campden Hill, Kensington, 1, 4, 11, 21, 22
Boutelle, DeWitt C., Bethlehem, Pa.   2
Bowlend, G. B, Staten Island, N. Y.; Wyman Cottage,   14
Bowman, J. C., New York; 311 W. 54th St.   14, 19
Boyd, Clarence, Louisville, Ky.; Courier-Journal Building,   12, 17, 24, 25
Boyd, Thos., Philadelphia; 33 S. 19th St.   19
Boyle, John J., Philadelphia; 2217½ Chestnut St.   5, 18
Boyle, Ferd. T. L., New York; 11 E. 14th St.   2
Boynton, G. R., New York; 51 W. 10th St.   16
Brackett, Arthur L., Boston; 32 Pemberton Sq.   20, 21
Brackett, Walter M., Boston; 41 Tremont St.   20
Bradbury, Mrs. Louise A., Winchester, Mass.   8
Bradford, Wm., New York; 42 E. 14th St   2, 12
Bradlee, Nathaniel J., Boston; 18 Pemberton Sq.   9
Brainard, Elizabeth, New York; 6 W. 14th St.   17
Brandegee, R. B., Berlin, Conn.   13
Brandt, Carl L., Hastings-on-Hudson, N. Y.   1, 12, 24
Branns, Henry, Baltimore; 24 North St.   9
Breuneman, G. W., New York; 15 E. 14th St.   14, 17, 18, 25
Brenner, Carl C., Louisville, Ky.; 4th Ave. and Jefferson St.   12, 17, 24, 25
Breul, Hugo, New York; 835 Broadway,   12, 14, 21, 24, 25
Brevoort, J. R., New York; 52 E. 23d St.   1, 12, 18, 22, 23, 24
Brewster, Amanda, New York; 127 E. 10th St.   13, 16
Bricher, A. T., New York; 52 E. 23d St.   2, 4, 11, 12, 14, 17, 18, 21, 22, 24
Bridges, Miss Fidelia, New York; 102 W. 54th St.   2, 4, 19, 24
Bridgman, Chas., Brooklyn, N. Y.; Phœnix Bldg., 16 Court St.   12, 17, 18, 24, 25
Bridgman, Fred. A., Paris; Boulevard de Clichy, 75,   1, 12, 13, 17, 23, 24, 25
Briggs, W. R., Bridgeport, Conn.; 436 Main St.   9
Brigham, Chas., Boston; 19 Exchange Pl.   9
Briscoe, Frank D., Philadelphia; 806 Walnut St.   18
Brisque, Julius,   18
Bristol, John B., New York; 53 E. 23d St.   1, 11, 12, 18, 22, 23, 24
Brooke, Richd. N., Washington, D. C.; 945 Pennsylvania Ave.   12, 23
Brooks, A. F., Chicago; 70 Monroe St., Room 38,   22, 23
Brooks, E. B., New York; 1196 Broadway,   12
Brooks, E. D., New York; 1175 Broadway,   13
Brown, Geo. L., Malden, Mass.; P. O. Box 695,   12, 17, 18, 20, 23, 24
Brown, Glenn, Washington, D. C.; 607 Louisiana Ave.   9
Brown, H. Latimer, Philadelphia; Fisher's Lane, Germantown,   17
Brown, Henry K., Newburg, N. Y.   1
Brown, J. Appleton, Boston; 5 Park St.   16, 20
Brown, J. G., New York; 51 W. 10th St.   1, 4, 11, 12, 13, 18, 20, 22, 23, 24
Brown, Mary C., Newark, N. J.   15, 16
Brown, Wm. M., Brooklyn, N. Y.; 416 Degraw St.   12, 17, 18, 19, 24
Brownell, Frank P., Paris; Rue de Navarin, 14,   17
Brownscombe, Miss Jennie, Honesdale, Pa.   8, 12, 14, 16, 17, 25

Chandler, F. W., Boston; 60 Devonshire St. 9
Chandler, T. P., Philadelphia; 302 Walnut St. 9
Chapin, C. H., New York; 1300 Broadway, 24
Chapin, Miss M. L., Providence, R. I.; 36 Oliver St. 12
Chapman, Cyrus D., Irvington, N. J. 12
Chapman, Mrs. J., Boston, 20
Chapman, John Gadsby, Rome, 1
Chapman, J. Linton, New York; 52 E. 23d St. 12
Chase, Harry, New York; 58 W. 57th St. 12, 13, 15, 16, 17, 20, 21, 24, 25
Chase, Wm. M., New York; 51 W. 10th St. 3, 4, 6, 13, 18, 20, 22, 23
Chestnut, Anna, Philadelphia; 1814 Wallace St. 25
Church, Frederick E., Hudson, N. Y. 1
Church, F. S., New York; 58 E. 13th St. 3, 4, 6, 13, 14, 15, 16, 19, 22, 23
Churchill, W. W., Jr., Paris; care Perier frères et Cie, Rue de Provence, 17, 20
Clapp, Henry L., Boston; 35 W. Cottage St. 20
Clark, Geo. M., New York; 58 W. 57th St. 4, 12, 14, 17, 18, 20, 21, 22, 23, 24
Clark, Henry Paston, Boston; 68 Devonshire St. 9
Clark, Theod. M., Boston; 178 Devonshire St. 9
Clark, Walter, New York; 143 W. 55th St. 7
Claus, Wm. A. J., Boston; 227 Tremont St. 20, 21
Cleenwerks, W., San Francisco, 12
Clements, Gabrielle D., Philadelphia; 750 S. 18th St. 25
Clinton, C. W., New York; 56 Wall St. 9
Closson, Wm. B., Boston; 149 A Tremont St. 10, 20, 21
Clough, G. L., Brooklyn, N. Y.; Brooklyn Institute, 24
Clover, Rev. Dr. Lewis P., Jr., Milburn, N. J. 2
Cluss, Adolph., Washington, D. C.; 413 Second St., N. W. 9
Cobb, E. P., Chicago; 2130 Michigan Ave. 18
Cobb, Fred. W., Boston; 8 Pemberton Sq. 21
Cobb, Mrs. Geo. D., Chicago; 2130 Michigan Ave. 22, 23
Coffin, Mrs. E. L., Athens, Greene Co., N. Y. 12, 14, 17, 18, 19, 20, 22, 24, 25
Coffin, W. A., New York, N. Y.; 152 W. 57th St. 12, 13, 24, 25
Colby, Geo. E., Chicago; 288 W. Washington St. 23
Cole, J. Foxcroft, Boston; 433 Washington St. 3, 17, 18
Cole, Timothy, Bath, New Utrecht, L. I., N. Y. 10
Coleman, C. C., Italy, 2
Collin, Mrs. J. B., Rutherford Park, N. J. 8
Collins, A. 13
Collis, G. S., Riverside, Ill. 22
Colman, Samuel, Newport, R. I. 1, 4, 6, 12, 14, 15, 19, 22
Colyer, Vincent, Rowyaton, Conn. 2, 11, 24
Coman, Mrs. C. B., New York; 58 W. 57th St. 8, 12, 17, 21, 22, 23, 24
Conant, Miss Corn. W., Ecouen, France, 8, 17, 23, 24, 25
Condie, E. G., New York; 360 W. 22d St. 14, 16
Conely, W. B., New York; 822 Broadway, Room 30, 12, 24
Congdon, H. M., New York; 111 Broadway, 9
Conkey, Samuel, 16
Contoit, Louis, New York; 52 E. 23d St. 24
Cook, C. Carroll, Philadelphia; 907 Arch St. 12, 17, 25
Cookman, C. E., Columbus, O. 22
Cooper, Colin C., Jr., Philadelphia; 1514 Chestnut, 17, 25
Cooper, Edith, 16
Cooper, G. E., Utica, N. Y.; Arcade Building, 9

Cooper, Wm. H., Hammonton, Atl. Co., N. J.	5, 18, 19, 24
Copeland, Alfr. B., Paris ; Quai des Grands Augustins, 37,	17, 25
Corey, Caroline C., New York ; 581 Lexington Ave.	12
Correja, Henry, Paris ; Rue de Boulogne, 23,	17, 25
Cox, Kenyon, Jr., Paris ; care Munroe & Co., Rue Scribe, 7,	13, 17, 25
Coxe, Reginald Cleveland, Paris ; Avenue Wagram, 120,	17
Cozzens, F. S., New York ; 160 Fulton St.	14, 16
Craig, Thos. B., Philadelphia ; 1520 Chestnut St.	5, 14, 18, 19, 24
Cranch, Christopher P., Paris ; Avenue De Villiers, 83,	1, 4, 11
Cranch, John, Urbana, O.	2
Crane, R. Bruce, New York ; 58 W. 57 St.	3, 4, 12, 13, 14, 16, 17, 18, 22, 23, 24, 25
Cranford, Kenneth, Paris,	12, 18, 24
Crapsey, Chas., Cincinnati ; 46 Wiggins Building,	9
Creifelds, Richd., New York ; Bank Building, 14th St. and 4th Ave.	13
Crone, Saml. H., Munich, Royal Acad. of F. A.	17
Cropsey, Jasper F., New York ; 58 W. 57th St.	1, 4, 11, 12, 14, 19, 21, 24, 25
Cross, Amy, New York ; 58 W. 57th St.	14
Culver, Louisa B., New York ; 80 Madison Ave.	12, 16, 18, 24
Cummings, Arthur, New York ; 152 W. 57th St.	12, 20
Cummings, Chas. A., Boston ; 9 Pemberton Sq.	9
Cummings, Thos. Seir, New York,	1
Curlett, Wm., San Francisco ; 330 Pine St.	9
Currier, J Frank, Munich,	3, 13
Curtis, Miss Alice M., Boston ; 149 A Tremont St.	20
Curtis, Calvin, Stratford, Conn.	12
Curtis, Ralph W., Venice ; Palazzo Barbaro,	17, 20
Cushing, Robt., New York ; 16 W. 23 St.	12
Daggy, Aug., Philadelphia ; 708 S. Washington Sq.	19
Daggy, A. S., Philadelphia ; 913 N. 29th St.	17, 18
Daingerfield, E., New York ; 52 E. 23d St.	12, 19, 23, 24
Daley, Miss Helen A.	8
Dana, Chas E., Philadelphia ; 2013 De Lancey Pl.	5, 14, 19, 20
Dana, Wm. J., Boston ; 27 Tremont Temple,	16, 21
Dana, W. P. W., Paris ; Rue Washington, 13,	1, 12, 17, 23, 24
Danforth, C. Austin, Boston ; 48 Winter St.	20, 21
Dannat, Wm., New York ; 2 W. 14th St.	3, 13
Darby, E. C., New York ; 335 W. 18th St.	24, 25
Darby, Rev. Henry, New York ; 101 W. 41st St.	12
Darley, Felix O. C., Claymont, Del.	1, 4, 11, 16
Darling, W. M.	16
Davidson, J. O., New York ; Booth Building, 6 Ave. and 23d St.	7, 12, 16
Davis, Chas. H., Paris ; care Munroe & Co., 7 Rue Scribe,	25
Davis, F. E., Baltimore ; Charles and Fayette Sts.	9
Davis, John P., New York, 109 W. 34th St.	10, 16
Davis, John Steeple,	16
Davis, Miss S. C., Brookline, Mass. ; Box 693,	20
Day, J. R., Philadelphia ; 513 N. 44th St.	17
Day, V. E., Chicago ; 3605 Lake Ave.	23
Dayton, Jeanie, New York ; 7 W. 32d St.	12
De Blois, F. B., Boston ; 48 Winter St.	12, 20, 21
De Camp, Jos. R., Venice ; care Reitmeyer & Co.	17
Decker, J, Brooklyn, N. Y. ; 216 Graham Ave.	24
De Coursy, B. R. Bigeon, New York ; 11 E. 14th St.	24

De Crano, F. F., Philadelphia, 1520 Chestnut,   5, 12, 18, 19, 24
De Haas, M. F. H., New York ; 51 W. 10th St   1, 4, 11, 12, 14, 18, 19, 20, 21, 22, 23, 24
Deiker, J., Brooklyn, N. Y. ; 216 Graham Ave.   12
De Kay, Helena, New York; 103 E. 15th St.   13
Delachaux, Leon, Philadelphia ; 1934 Locust St.   5, 12, 14, 18, 19, 21, 24
Delins, Louis E., Jersey City, N. J. ; 792 Montgom. St.   12, 14, 16
De Luce, Percival, New York ; 58 W. 57th St.   4, 7, 11, 12, 14, 16, 17, 21, 22, 23, 24
Dennis, Jas. H., Rochester, N. Y.   16
Desvarreux-Larpenteur, Jas., Paris ; Rue Feron, 9,   17
De Thulstrup, T., New York ; care Harper & Bros.   14, 21, 22
Devereux, M. T. G., New York ; 219 W. 11th St.   24
Devereux, Mrs. Walter B., New York ; 219 W. 11th St.   17
Dewey, Chas. Melville, New York; 788 B'dway,   3, 12, 13, 14, 16, 17, 18, 19, 20, 21, 24
Dewing, Mrs. Thos. W., New York; 139 W. 55th St.   12, 13, 25
Dewing, Thos. W., New York ; 139 W. 55th St.   3, 13
Dickson, Walter, Albany, N. Y. ; 53 N. Pearl St.   9
Didden, C. A., Washington, D. C. ; 710 Thirteenth St.   9
Dielman, Fred., New York; 51 W. 10th St.   2, 3, 6, 11, 12, 13, 14, 15, 17, 18, 22, 23, 24
Dieterich, Ferd., New York ; 309 E. 25th St.   12, 16, 24
Dillon, Mrs. Julia, New York; 142 E. 18th St.   12, 14, 18, 22, 24
Dillon, Mrs. J. B., New York ; 24 W. 14th St.   8
Dixon, Paul,   16
Dixwell, Miss Anna P., Boston ; 48 Boylston St.   21, 25
Dobour, John, New York ; 37 Union Sq.   12
Dodge, John W.   2
Dodge, Mira R., Washington, D. C. ; 1336 Vermont Ave.   12, 16
Dodge, Philip H., Tom's River, N. J.   12
Dodshun, A. Van Cleef, New York; 337 Fourth Ave.   12, 14, 16, 24
Dolan, A.   20
Dolph, J. H., New York ; 58 W. 57th St.   2, 3, 12, 17, 24
Don, Laura, New York; 300 W. 42d St.   12
Donoghue, John, Chicago ; 65 Reaper Block,   22
Donaghy, John, New York ; 14 Park Pl.   24
Donoho, Gaines Ruger, Paris ; care Arthur Groves, 5 Rue Scribe,   12, 13, 17, 25
Dow, Miss Florence,   21
Dowdall, Edward, New York ; 527 Canal St.   12, 16, 17, 25
Dracopolis, N. F., Pont Aven Finistère, France,   17
Drake, W. H., New York ; 21 E. 15th St.   14
Draper, Francis, Jr., Boston ; 163 Warren Ave.   20, 21, 25
Driscoll, C. F., Omaha, Nebr.   9
Dubois, Chas. E., Paris ; Rue Des S. Péres, 54,   17, 23
Du Bois, Patterson, Philadelphia ; 204 N. 36th St.   25
Dunham, Sadie E., New York ; 29 W. 37th St.   24
Dunk, Walter M., Philadelphia ; 1338 Chestnut St. 5, 12, 14, 16, 17, 18, 19, 23, 24, 25
Dunn, Alex. G.   4
Dunsmore, John W., Boston ; 2 Music Hall Pl.   12, 17
Durand, Asher B., South Orange, N. J.   1
Durand, E. L., New York ; 788 Broadway,   24
Duveneck, Frank, Europe,   3, 6, 13
EAKINS, Thos., Philadelphia ; 1729 Mt. Vernon St.   3, 12, 13, 14, 17, 18, 19, 23, 25
Eames, S. M., Bridgeport, Conn.   12
Earle, L. C., Chicago ; 170 State St., Room 21,   14, 22, 23
Earle, Stephen C., Boston ; 9 Pemberton Sq.   9

Eaton, Chas. Harry, New York; 822 Broadway,   12, 14, 16, 19, 20, 21, 22, 23, 24, 25
Eaton, Chas. Warren, New York; 282 Sixth Ave.   12, 24
Eaton, Wyatt, New York; 80 E. Washington Sq.   3, 13, 18, 20, 23
Ebbinghausen, Lavinia, Philadelphia; 2114 Brandywine St.   25
Echtler, A., Paris.   18
Eddy, Miss Sarah J., Providence, R. I.; 4 Bell St.   17, 20, 25
Edwards, G. W., New York; 28 E. 14th St.   7, 12, 14, 16
Eggleston, Allegra, New York; 115 E. 16th St.   13
Ehninger, John W., Saratoga Springs, N. Y.   1, 12, 14, 15
Eichhorn, Aug., Orange, N. J.; Library Building,   9
Eldred, L. D., Boston; 26 Pemberton Sq.   20
Elkins, Miss Ida, Brooklyn, N. Y.; 1275 Dean St.   8
Ellis, Harvey, Rochester, N. Y.   16
Ellis, Lucy,   16
Ellis, Mary Routh, Philadelphia; 263 S. 4th St.   25
Ely, E. U., New York; Grammercy Park House,   14
Ely, H. K., New York; Grammercy Park House,   18
Emmett, Miss L. F., East Rockaway, L. I., N. Y.   14
Emmett, Miss Rosina, East Rockaway, L. I., N. Y.   3, 12, 13, 14, 17, 21, 25
English, Frank F., Philadelphia; 249 N. 6th St.   17, 25
Enneking, J. J., Boston; 149 A Tremont St.   20, 21, 23
Eno, H. C, New York; 58 E. 25th St.   6
Eppinghausen, Chas., Terre Haute, Ind.   9
Essig, Geo. E., Philadelphia; 1728 N. 10th St.   25
Este, Florence, Philadelphia,   14, 21
Evans, De Scott, Cleveland, O.   12
Evans, Joe, New York; 36 E. 31st St.   13
Evans, John W.   16
Evans, T. D., Pittsburgh, Pa.; 48 Fifth Ave.   9
Evers, John, Hempstead, L. I., N. Y.   1
Faber, Herm., Philadelphia; 524 Walnut St.   6a, 16, 17, 25
Fagan, Lawrence, New York; 1267 Broadway,   12, 17
Fagundus, N. Josephine, New York; 28 E. 78th St.   12
Fairchild, Lizzie M., Cambridge, Mass.   21
Fairman, Jas, New York; 40 E. 23d St.   17, 25
Falconer, J. M., Brooklyn, N. Y.; 110 St. Felix St.
    4, 6, 11, 12, 14, 15, 16, 17, 19, 21, 24, 25
Fanshaw, Sam'l R., New York; 835 Broadway,   2, 17
Farmer, E. H, New York; 25 W. 37th St.   16, 24
Farny, H F., Cincinnati; 62 Pike's Building,   23
Farnham, A. M., Newburg-on-Hudson, N. Y.; Box 166,   12, 25
Farrar, Henry, New York; 51 W. 10th St.   4, 6, 11, 14, 15, 19, 21, 22, 23
Farrar, T. C., London; Queen Anne House, Primrose Hill, W.   4
Fassett, Mrs. C. Adele, Chicago; 44 Central Music Hall,   22
Fay, Miss Rose, Chicago; "The Walton," Washington Park,   23
Fellow, F. Wayland, New Haven; 68 Whitney Ave.   12, 25
Fenety, Andrew C., Boston; 43 Studio Building,   16, 21
Fenn, Harry, New York; 7 W. 14th St.   4, 14, 16, 19
Ferguson, Henry A., New York; 52 E. 23d St.   2, 14, 18, 24
Fernbach, Henry, New York; 318 Broadway,   9
Ferris, Gérôme, Philadelphia; 1523 Chestnut St.   12, 14, 15, 17, 19, 24, 25
Ferris, Stephen J., Philadelphia; 1523 Chestnut St.   5, 6a, 15, 17, 19, 25
Ficken, H. E., New York; 19 W. 22d St.   9

Field, Miss Elizabeth C., New York; 24 W. 14th St.   8
Field, E. L., Chicago; 50 Dearborn St.   22, 23
Filmer, John, New York ; 318 Broadway,   16
Finck, Frederick, New York; 798 Broadway,   12, 24
Fisher, Alanson, Brooklyn, N. Y.; 126 Sixth St., E. D.   2
Fisher, Mrs. Ellen T., Brooklyn, N. Y.; 358 Adelphi St.   14, 18, 21, 24
Fiske, Chas. A., Greenwich, Conn.   12, 14, 17, 24
Fitch, John L., New York; 51 W. 10th St.   2, 11, 12, 24, 25
Fitler, Wm. C., New York ; 117 E. 14th St.   12, 14, 16, 19, 21, 24, 25
Flagg, Chas. Noel, New York ; 152 W. 57th St.   12, 13, 17, 25
Flagg, Geo. W., New York; 22 W. 10th St.   1, 24
Flagg, Jared B., New York; 152 W. 57th St.   1
Flagg, Montague, New York; 152 W. 57th St.   12
Flaherty, J. F., Philadelphia ; 907 Arch St.   18
Flannery, Lot, Washington, D. C.   12
Fletcher, Daisy, Elizabeth, N. J.; 233 W. Grand St.   17
Florance, Lucien G., New York; 1300 Broadway,   24
Fludder, Jas., Newport, R. I.   9
Ford, H. C.   22
Foster, Ben., Brooklyn, N. Y.; 309 Henry St.   13
Fowler, Frank, New York; University Building, Washington Sq.
   3, 7, 12, 13, 14, 16, 17, 18, 20, 21, 23, 25
Fowler, Mrs. M. B. Odenheimer, New York ; Univ. Bldg., Washington Sq.
   12, 16, 17, 18, 20, 23
Fowler, Trevor T.   24
Fox, John A., Boston ; 12 Post Office Sq., Room 7,   9
Francis, Florence A., New York; 40 E. 23d St.   14, 24
Frank, Eugene C., New York ; 1 Union Sq.   12, 13
Franklin, Mary, New York; 58 W. 57th St.   15, 17
Frederick, G. A., Baltimore ; 25 N. Charles St.   9
Fredericks, Alfred, New York ; 58 W. 57th St.   2, 4, 12, 14, 16, 17, 18, 20, 21
Freeman, Chas. H., Jr., Venice ; Casa Jacovitz, Riva Schiavoni,   17
Freeman, Jas. E., Italy,   1
Freer, Fred. W., New York ; University Building, Washington Sq.
   3, 12, 13, 14, 16, 17, 18, 20, 21, 22, 23, 24, 25
Freitag, Conrad, New York ; 173 South St.   24
French, Daniel, Concord, Mass.   3
French, Frank, New York ; 76 Chambers St.   16
Frommuth, Chas. H., Philadelphia ; 2102 North Front St.   17
Frost, A. B., Philadelphia ; 1330 Chestnut St.   16, 19, 25
Fuechsel, Herm., New York; 51 W. 10th St.   11, 12, 18, 24
Fuller, Geo., Boston ; 149 A Tremont St.   2, 3, 13, 20, 22, 23
Fuller, Thos., Ottawa, Can.; Department Public Works,   9
Fullerton, Emma W., Philadelphia ; 3307 Hamilton St.   17, 25
Furness, Miss Rebekah T., Philadelphia; 347 S. 18th St.   17, 23
Gallison, Henry H., Boston ; 44 Studio Building,   20, 21
Galvan, S. M., Philadelphia; 4505 Rubicam Ave., Germantown,   18
Gardin, Mrs. A. T., Chicago,   23
Garrett, Edm. H., Boston ; 28 School St.   20, 21
Gaugengigl, I. M., Boston ; 45 Studio Building,   17, 20
Gaul, Gilbert, New York ; 51 W. 10th St.   1, 12, 13, 17, 18, 22, 23, 24
Gay, Edward, New York ; Mt. Vernon,   2, 11, 12, 16, 17, 18, 24
Gay, Geo. H., Chicago ; 86 Ashland Block,   22, 23

Heinigke, Otto, Bay Ridge, L. I., N. Y. 14, 15
Hellawell, J. 16
Hennessy, W. J., London; 5 Langham Chambers, Portland Pl., W. 1, 4, 11, 12, 17
Henry, E. L., New York; 51 W. 10th St. 1, 12, 14, 16, 17, 22, 24
Hensel, Edward S, Philadelphia; 810 Walnut St. 25
Henshaw, Mrs A. N., Elizabeth, N. J.; 158 Park Pl. 12, 17, 18, 24, 25
Herrick, Miss C. K., Orange, N. J.; Brick Church, Essex Co. 8, 12, 24
Herrick, Mrs. S. B., New York; The Century, Union Sq. 12
Herzog, Herm. 12
Hess, John N. 25
Hetz, Carl, Munich, 22
Hetzel, Geo., Pittsburg, Pa. 12, 17, 18
Hewitt, W. K., Philadelphia; 715 Walnut St. 5, 17, 25
Hicks, John H., New York; 51 W. 10th St. 12, 18
Hicks, Thos., New York; 6 Astor Pl. 1, 11, 12, 15, 17
Higgins, Geo. F., Melrose Highlands, Mass. 20, 21
Hill, Edward, Boston; 12 West St. 20, 21
Hill, J. Henry, Nyack Turnpike, N. Y. 12, 15, 21
Hillern, Bertha von, Boston ; Hôtel Vendome, 17, 25
Hilliard, W. H., Paris, 12
Hind, J. F., New York ; 45 E. 35th St. 4, 14
Hinton, Mrs. Lucy Bronson, Nyack, N. Y. 8
Hirst, Claude R., New York; 32 E. 14th St. 12, 24
Hitchcock, Geo., Paris, 14
Hitchings, Henry, Boston ; High School, Montgomery St. 21
Hobbs, Geo. Thompson, Philadelphia; 520 Walnut St. 12, 17
Hodgdon, S. P., Boston ; 616 Washington St. 21
Hoeber, Arthur, Paris ; 3 bis Rue des Beaux Arts, 24, 25
Hoesslin, Geo. von, Munich; care Merck, Finck & Co. 17, 25
Hogan, Thos. 16
Holbrook, Harriett J., New York; 11 W. 12th St. 12
Holbrook, Mrs., New York ; 18 Laight St. 8
Holloway, Edw. S, Philadelphia ; 1233 S. Broad St. 17
Holly, H. Hudson, New York; 111 Broadway, 8
Holme, Lucy D., Philadelphia ; 1623 Filbert St. 17, 25
Holmes, Miss Ella A., Chicago ; 358 Warren Ave. 23
Holmes, Mrs. G. W., Philadelphia ; 1512 Chestnut St. 17, 18
Holmes, Mrs. H. V., Chicago ; 1601 Prairie Ave. 22
Holmes, Mrs. Mary, Philadelphia ; 1512 Chestnut St. 25
Holmes, W. H., Washington, D. C. 14, 23
Homer, Winslow, Europe, 1, 4, 14, 19, 21, 22
Hope, James, Watkins, N. Y. 2, 12
Hope, T. H., Philadelphia; 1815 Columbia Ave. 12
Hopkins, Geo. E., Cincinnati ; 64 Pike's Building, 15
Hoppin, Howard, Providence, R. I. 9
Hoskin, Robert, New York; care Harper & Bros. 10, 16
House, Mrs. J. Alford, Bridgeport, Conn.; 88 William St. 14, 19
Houston, Mrs. Frances C., Boston ; 12 West St., Room 23, 12, 20
Hovenden, Mrs. H. Corson, New York ; 58 W. 57th St. 12, 13, 14, 22, 23
Hovenden, Thos., New York ; 58 W. 57th St. 1, 3, 4, 12, 13, 14, 17, 20, 22, 23
Howard, S. M., Wheeling, W. Va.; 1207 Main St. 9
Howes, John Townsend, Yonkers, N. Y. 12
Howland, A. C., New York ; 52 E. 23d St. 1, 7, 11, 12, 16

Kappes, Alfred, New York; 1 Great Jones St.   4, 12, 13, 14, 18, 19, 20, 24
Keenan, Margaret C., New York ; 58½ W. 10th St.   12, 13, 23, 24
Keith, Wm., San Francisco,   12
Keller, Geo., Hartford, Conn. ; Trust Co.'s Block,   9
Kelley, J. Henderson, Philadelphia ; 21 S. 42d St.   17
Kelley, Jas. P., Philadelphia; 1123 Chestnut St.   5, 17, 25
Kendall, E. H., New York ; 71 Broadway,   9
Kendrick, Dyer T., Boston ; 56 Studio Building,   20, 25
Kennard, Beulah L.   25
Kennicott, Mrs. M. A., Chicago ; 96 State St.   12, 22, 23, 24
Key, John R., Chicago; Grand Pacific Hotel,   16
Kibbe, Josephine B., Canandaigua, N. Y.   25
King, F. S., Orange Valley, N. J.   10
King, Geo. W., Auburn, N. Y.   24
Kingsbury, Edward, Boston,   20
Kinsella, Jas., New York ; 237 E. 24th St.   12
Kirkpatrick, Frank L., Philadelphia ; 2141 Percy St.   17, 23, 25
Knapp, C. L., Danbury, Conn.   12, 18, 24
Knapp, C. W., Philadelphia ; 1510 Chestnut St.   5, 18, 19
Knapp, H. G., New York ; 61 Broadway,   9
Knight, Du Bois, Detroit, Mich.   22
Knowlton, Helen M., Boston ; 169 Tremont St.   25
Knox, Geo. W., Auburn, N. Y.   12
Koehler, Robert, Munich ; care American Consul,   17
Kollock, Mary, New York; 58 W. 57th St.   12, 16, 18, 20, 21, 24, 25
Kost, Fred. W., Clifton, S. L, N. Y.   12, 16, 24
Kotz, Daniel, Chicago ; 83 Ashland Block,   15, 22, 23
Konpal, Miss Marie, Chicago ; 70 Reaper Block,   22, 23
Kramer, Peter, Jr., Munich,   24
Kreisler, Marie, New York ; 45 W. 11th St.   12
Kruell, Gustav, East Orange, N. J.; 14 Pulaski St.   10, 16
Kurtz, W., New York ; 6 E. 23d St.   12
La Farge, John, New York ; 33 E. 17th St.   1, 3, 4, 20
Laffan, Wm M., New York; care Harper & Bros.   15
La Fontaine, R. M., New York; 114 W. 16th St.   24, 25
Laird, Alicia H., Richmond, Va.; 809 Franklin St.   25
Lambdin, Geo. C., Philadelphia ; 1520 Chestnut St.   1, 11, 12, 14, 18, 19
Lambdin, J. R., Philadelphia ; 1224 Chestnut St.   18, 25
Lampert, Emma E., New York ; 127 E. 10th St.   14, 16, 19
Lauder, Benjamin, New York ; 14 John St., Room 7,   15, 16, 21, 24
Lane, Miss Harriet C., New York; 337 Fourth Ave.   8, 12, 24
Lang, Louis, New York; 13 Waverley Pl.   1, 11, 12, 18
Langerfeldt, T. O., Boston ; 144 Tremont St.   21
Lanman, Chas., Georgetown, D. C.   2, 12, 17
Lansil, Walter F., Boston ; Milton Ave., cor. Fuller St., Dorchester,   20, 24, 25
Lautuman, K., Seneca, N. Y.   12
Lathrop, Francis, New York ; 39 W. 9th St.   3
Lauber, Joseph, New York ; 232 Fifth St.   7, 15, 16, 21, 24
Laver, Aug., San Francisco; 19 Stock Exchange,   9
Lawrie, Alex. (deceased?),   2
Lay, Oliver J., New York ; 52 E. 23d St.   2, 11, 12, 24
Lazarus, Jacob H., New York ; 1155 Broadway,   2
Leaming, Thos., Philadelphia; 126 Chestnut St.   12, 24

Leavitt, E. C., Providence, R. I.; Hoppin Homestead Building,   12, 20
Leavitt, Sheldon, New York; 42 E. 22d St.   12, 16, 17, 24
Le Brun, Napoleon, New York; 24 Park Pl.   9
Le Clear, Thos., New York; 1271 Broadway,   1, 12, 22
Lederer, Karl A., Chicago; 409 Dayton St.   22
Lederle, Jos., New York; 196 Broadway,   9
Ledochowski, X.. Chicago,   23
Le Fevre, Alice, New Rochelle, N. Y.   12
Le Fevre, Wm. J., Philadelphia; 1334 Chestnut St.   6a, 12, 15, 24, 25
Leganger, N. T., New York; 52 E. 23d St.   12, 17
Lehr, Adam, Cleveland, O.   12
Leisser, M. B., Pittsburg, Pa.   12
Lent, Frank T., New York; 52 E. 23d St.   12, 14, 17, 18, 19
Lesley, Margaret W., Philadelphia; 1008 Clinton St.   25
Leupp, M, New York; University Building, Washington Sq.   19
Levin, Katharine, Philadelphia; 558 N. 16th St.   19, 25
Levis, Sarah, Philadelphia; 228 S. 21st St.   12, 25
Lewin,   20
Lewis, Edmund D., Philadelphia; 704 Walnut St.   16, 17, 18, 19, 20, 21, 24, 25
Lewis, H., Düsseldorf,   17
Lewis, W. Whitney, Boston; 5 Pemberton Sq.   9
Lienau, Detlef, New York; 111 Broadway,   9
Lind, E. G., Atlanta, Ga.; 63 Whitehall St.   9
Linder, Henry, New York; 1 Great Jones St.   12
Lindsley, Miss L. E., New Rochelle, N. Y.   12, 24
Linford, Chas., Philadelphia; 1420 Chestnut St.   17, 25
Linsly, Wilford, New York; 51 W. 10th St.   24
Linton, Hobart, Boston; 48 Studio Building,   21
Linton, W. J., New Haven, Conn.; Post Office Box 489,   1, 4, 24
Lippincott, Wm. H., New York; 44 W. 30th St.   12, 13, 14, 17, 18, 21, 23, 24
Littell, E. T., New York; 48 Exchange Pl.   9
Lloyd, Fannie Powell, Rome, Italy,   12, 18, 24, 25
Lloyd, G. W., Detroit, Mich.; 34 Fort St., W.   9
Lloyd, G. W. E., Rome, Italy,   25
Lockhart, W. J., Rochester, N. Y. (deceased),   16
Lockman, Dewitt,   16
Loehnitz, R., Chicago; 84 La Salle St.   9
Longfellow, Ernest, Cambridge, Mass.   12, 17, 18, 20, 21, 24
Longfellow, Wm. P. P., Boston; 220 Devonshire St.   9
Loomis, Chester, Paris; care Munroe & Co., 7 Rue Scribe,   17, 20
Loop, Henry A., New York; 80 Madison Ave.   1, 11, 12, 18, 24
Loop, Mrs. H. A., New York; 80 Madison Ave.   2, 8, 12, 24
Loring, S. E., Chicago; Laflin and 15th Sts.   9
Lovewell, R., Chelsea, Mass.   15, 21
Low, Will H., New York; 152 W. 57th St.   3, 12, 13, 14, 20, 23, 24
Ludlow, A. Inez, New York; 118 E. 54th St.   12, 17, 24
Lummis, F. E., Philadelphia; 520 Walnut St.   25
Lungren, F. H., Paris,   13, 14, 16, 23
Lyman, Jos., Jr., Paris; 51 W. 10th St.   12, 14, 16, 17, 18, 20, 23, 24
MACDONALD, J., New York; 55 Broadway,   16
Macdonough, J., New York; 142 Broadway,   12
Macdowell, Elizabeth, Philadelphia; 2016 Race St.   25
Macdowell, Miss Susan H, Philadelphia; 2016 Race St.   12, 25

MacKnight, Mrs. S. R., New York; 337 Fourth Ave.   12, 16, 22
Macy, Wendell, Nantucket, Mass.   25
Macy, W. Ferdinand, Rockville, Conn.   18
Macy, W. S., New York; 52 E. 23d St.   11, 12, 13, 16, 18, 22, 23, 24
Magill, Beatrice, Swarthmore, Delaware Co., Pa.   17, 25
Magrath, Wm., London,   1, 4, 23
Mann, Miss E. P., Boston; Percy Pl, Roxbury,   21
Mansfield, J. W., New York; 61 W. 42d St.   13, 15, 17, 18, 20, 21
Marchant, Edw. W., Philadelphia; 1711 Filbert St.   2
Marr, Carl, Munich,   20
Marshall, C. E., New York; 214 E. 17th St.   13
Marshall, H. R., New York; 74 Wall St.   9
Marshall, Wm. Edgar, New York.   15
Martin, Homer D., New York; 51 W. 10th St.   1, 3, 11, 13
Martinez, F. F., New York; Bank Building, 4th Ave. and 14th St.   12, 17
Mason, Abraham J.   2
Mason, G. C., Jr., Newport, R. I.; 3 Catherine St.   9
Matlack, Eleanor, Philadelphia; 3310 Woodland Ave.   16, 19
Matteson, T. H., Sherburne, N. Y.   2
Maxson, Miss Eleanor,   12
May, E. H., Paris; 13 Rue Washington,   2, 12
Mayer, Constant, New York; 1298 Broadway,   2, 12, 17, 18, 24
Maynard, Geo. W., New York; 80 E. Washington Sq.
    2, 3, 4, 7, 12, 13, 14, 16, 18, 19, 20, 21, 22, 23, 24
Maynicke, Miss Emma, Columbia, Tenn.; Columbia Institute,   8
McArthur, John, Jr., Philadelphia; Architect's Office, Public Building,   9
McCarter, Harry B., Philadelphia; 2015 N. 11th St.   12, 17
McCloskey, Wm. J., Philadelphia; 303 N. 19th St.   17
McCord, Geo. H., New York; 52 E. 23d St.   2, 11, 12, 14, 16, 17, 18, 19, 23, 24
McCord, Herbert,   16
McCutcheon, S. G., New York; 229 E. 32d St.   4, 6, 14, 15, 16, 19, 21
McDonald, Miss M. J.   4
McDougall, J. A., New York; 52 E. 23d St.   12, 16, 18, 22
McEntee, Jervis, New York; 51 W. 10th St.   1, 12, 18, 22, 23
McEntee, Miss Lily, New York; 142 E. 18th St.   8, 14, 22, 24
McEwen, Walter,   17
McFadden, J. F., Philadelphia; 1932 Spruce St.   19, 25
McIlhenney, Chas., Philadelphia; 132 N. 40th St.   18
McIlhenney, C. Morgan, New York; Booth's Theatre Building,   12, 14, 16, 21, 24
McKean, J. T. C, St. John, N. B.; Ritchie Building,   9
McKim, C. F., New York; 57 Broadway,   9
McKinstry, Geo. A., Hudson, Columbia Co., N. Y.   12, 24, 25
McLaughlin, J. W., Cincinnati; 46 Johnson Building,   9
McLaughlin, Miss M. Louise, Cincinnati; 1 Chapel St.   13, 23
McNair, Marion, Geneseo, N. Y.   12
McNeal, Ambrose, Chicago; 2530 Michigan Ave.   22
Meakin, L. H., Cincinnati,   15
Meline, Louis D., Washington,   12
Melrose, Andrew, Guttenberg, N. J.   12
Meneghelli, Enrico, New York; 6 E. 14th St.   17, 24, 25
Mente, Chas., Munich,   14, 21
Merritt, Mrs. Anna Lea, London; The Cottage, Tite St., Chelsea Embankment,
    17, 20, 25

Metcalf, Willard L., Boston ; 57 Tremont St.   20
Middleton, Stanley, Brooklyn, N. Y.; 152 Joralemon St.   12, 24
Miller, Chas., H., New York ; 108 E. 23d St.   1, 3, 4, 6, 11, 12, 13, 22, 23, 24
Miller, D. K., Pittsburgh, Pa.; 120 Smithfield St.   9
Miller, E. F., Columbus, O.; 71 N. High St.   19
Miller, E. H., Washington,   15, 21
Miller, Francis, New York; 80 E. Washington Sq.   7, 14, 16
Millet, Frank D., New York; 578 Fifth Ave.   2, 3, 12, 13, 14, 19, 22, 23
Milliken, Geo., Philadelphia ; 3614 Walnut St.   25
Mills, Chas. S., New York ; 658 Broadway,   12, 24
Minor, Robt. C., New York; University Building, Washington Sq.
                              3, 11, 12, 14, 16, 17, 18, 19, 20, 21, 23, 24
Mitchell, J. A., New York ; 1155 Broadway,   12, 16, 17, 20, 21
Mitchell, Neil, New York; 51 W. 10th St.   12
Mitchell, Rosalie, Stoneton, Md.   25
Mitchill, B. N., New York ; 58 E. 13th St.   14, 25
Mix, E. T., Milwaukee ; Insurance Building,   9
Monks, J. A. S., Boston ; 3½ Beacon St.   21
Mooney, Edward, Upper Red Hook, N. Y.   1
Moore, Albert,   16
Moore, Chas. H., Cambridge, Mass. ; Harvard College,   14
Moore, Edwin A., New York ; 52 E. 23d St.   12, 14, 19, 24
Moore, Humphrey H., Alameda, Malaga, Spain ; Casa de Don Juan Clemens,   11
Moran, Edward, S. Brooklyn, N. Y., ; 197 Ninth St.   2, 4, 12, 14, 16, 18, 22, 23
Moran, Mrs. Edward, S. Brooklyn, N. Y. ; 197 Ninth St.   22
Moran, John, Philadelphia ; 2608 Girard Ave.   17
Moran, Leon, S. Brooklyn, N. Y.; 197 Ninth St.   12, 13, 14, 16, 17, 18, 22, 23, 24
Moran, Mrs. M. Nimmo, New York ; 166 W. 55th St.   6, 15, 22
Moran, Percy, S Brooklyn, N. Y.; 197 Ninth St.   12, 14, 16, 17, 18, 22, 23, 24
Moran, Peter, Philadelphia ; 1322 Jefferson St.   5, 6, 6a, 12, 14, 15, 18, 19, 24, 25
Moran, Thomas, New York ; 166 W. 55th St.   2, 4, 6, 12 14, 15, 16, 18, 22, 23
Morgan, Miss Annie, New York ; 58 W. 57th St.   8
Morgan, A. C., New York ; 58 E. 49th St.   7
Morgan, Wm., New York ; 58 W. 57th St.   2, 11, 12, 17, 18
Morris, A.   12
Morse, A. C., Providence, R. I. ; 5 Custom House St.   9
Morse, L. H., Quincy, Mass.   21
Mortimer, Stanley, New York ; Booth Building, 6th Ave. and 23d St.   13
Morton, Henry J.   ·   2
Moser, John, Atlanta, Ga. ; 63 Whitehall St.   9
Moser, J. H., Atlanta, Ga.   12, 14, 25
Mosler, Henry, Paris ; Rue de Navarin, 11,   12, 18
Moss, Frank, Paris ; Rue de Laval, 13,   17, 23, 24, 25
Mounier, Louis, New York ; 28 W. 14th St.   12
Mueller, R. A., Brooklyn, N. Y. ; 668 Gates Ave.   10
Muhrman, Henry, Europe,   4, 14, 19
Müller, K., New York ; 75th St., East of Ave. A.   11, 12
Munzig, Geo. C., Boston ; 48 Boylston St.   12, 20, 25
Murdoch, Miss C. R., Ecouen, Seine et Oise, France (deceased),   12, 17
Murdoch, John, Baltimore ; S. E. cor. Lexington and Charles Sts.   9
Murphy, J. Francis, New York ; 788 Broadway,
                              4, 7, 12, 13, 14, 16, 19, 20, 21, 22, 23, 24
Murray, E. H., West River, Md.   12

Myers, Annie M., Jersey City, N. J.; 266 Montgomery St.   12
NATT, Phœbe D., Philadelphia ; 20 S. 39th St.   12, 17, 19, 25
Neal, Fannie T., New York ; 326 W. 14th St.   14
Neely, J., Jr., Philadelphia ; 617 Market St.   6a
Nehlig, Victor,   1, 14, 16
Nerte, O. Von, Washington ; 1400 K St., N. W.   9
Nesmith, Howard M., Brooklyn, N. Y.; 287 Warren St.   12, 24
Newell, Miss Anna, Chicago,   22
Newell, Miss Helen, Chicago,   22
Newell, Hugh, Baltimore ; Maryland Institute,   4, 12, 14
Newman, Benj. T., New York ; 310 E. 18th St.   24
Newmarch, Strafford, Brooklyn, N. Y. ; 316 Gates Ave.   12
Nicholls, Burr H., Pont Aven, Finistère, France,   12, 17, 18, 22, 24, 25
Nickerson, E. I., Providence, R. I. ; 45 Westminster St.   9
Nicoll, J. C., New York ; 51 W. 10th St.
     2, 4, 6, 11, 12, 14, 15, 16, 17, 18, 19, 20, 21, 22, 23, 24
Niemeyer, John H., New Haven, Conn.; Yale Art School,   12, 13, 24, 25
Noble, T. S., Cincinnati ; 168½ Walnut St.   2
Northcote, James, Brooklyn, N. Y.; 295 Baltic St.   24, 25
Norton, S. J., Glen Head, Queen's Co., L. I., N. Y.   14, 19
Norton, W. E., London ; 16 Lyme St., N. W.   20
Nourse, Miss E., New York ; 74 W. 45th St.   19
Nowell, Miss Annie C., Boston ; 149 A Tremont St.   20, 21, 25
Noyes, Emily, New York ; 113 E. 14th St.   12, 24
Nutting, Benj. F., Boston ; 12 West St., Room 28,   21
Nye, Frances A., Brooklyn, N. Y.; 81 Nassau St.   24
OAKLEY, Mrs. Juliana, Europe,   8
O'Brien, L. R.   16
Ochtman, Leonard, Albany, N. Y. ; 86 State St.   12
O'Donavan, W. R., New York ; 19 W. 11th St.   2, 3, 13, 22
Oertel, Johannes E., Morgantown, N. C.   2, 12, 17, 20
Ogilvie, Clinton, New York ; 52 W. 23d St.   2, 12, 25
Oliver, Clark, Lynn, Mass.   21
Oliver, Miss S. E. C., Boston ; 26 Studio Building,   12
Osborne, Chas., New York ; 2 Neilson Pl.   7, 16
Osborne, Sid., New York ; 2 Neilson Pl.   7
Osborne, Mrs. S. M., New York ; 237 W. 34th St.   18
Otter, Thos. P., Doyleston, Bucks Co., Pa.   17
Oudinot, A. F., Boston ; 145 Tremont St.   20
Owen, Chas. R., Philadelphia ; 666 N. Broad St.   25
PAGE, William, Tottenville, S. I., N. Y.   1
Paine, B. D., Philadelphia ; 1008 S. 19th St.   17
Palmer, Miss A. C., Boston ; 149 A Tremont St.   20
Palmer, Walter L., Albany, N. Y.; 5 Fayette St.   3, 12, 13, 25
Parker, Edgar, Boston ; 433 Washington St.   20
Parker, John A., Jr., Keene Valley, N. Y.   2, 12
Parker, Stephen Hills, Paris ; Rue des S. Pères, 10,   17
Parmele, T. W., New York ; 6 E. 43d St.   14
Parmelee, P. W., Jamaica Plain, Mass.   21
Parrish, Stephen, Philadelphia ; 1334 Chestnut St.   6, 12, 15, 17, 18, 24, 25
Parsons, Miss Catherine, Fort Hamilton, N. Y.   8
Parsons, Chas., New York ; 82 Cliff St.   2, 4, 11, 14
Parton, Arthur, New York; 52 W. 10th St.   2, 11, 12, 14, 16, 18, 19, 20, 22, 23, 24

8

Parton, Ernest, London; 8 Elm Tree Road, St. John's Wood,   11, 12
Pattison, J. William, Ecouen, Seine et Oise, France,   14, 17
Payne, H. C., Chicago; 88 Ashland Block,   22
Pearce, Chas. Sprague, Paris; Rue Tourlaque, 9,   17, 23, 24, 25
Pearson, Robt., Malden, Mass.   20
Pearson, Wm., Malden, Mass.   20
Pease, E. Sherman, Salisbury, Conn.   14, 19
Peck, H. S.   16
Peck, Miss Mary F., Newtown, Fairfield Co., Conn.   14, 21, 25
Peele, John T., London, England,   2
Peet, W. C., New York; 90 Nassau St.   14
Peirce, Miss Edith Loring, Philadelphia; 1508 Chestnut St.   19, 24, 25
Peirce, H. Winthrop, Paris; care Munroe & Co., 7 Rue Scribe,   25
Pell, Miss E., New York; 52 E. 23d St.   22
Pelz, P. J., Washington; 703 Fifteenth St.   9
Penfold, F. C., Pont Aven, Finistère, France,   12, 17, 24
Pennell, Joseph, Philadelphia; 1334 Chestnut St.   6, 6a, 15, 25
Pennie, R. M., Paris,   24
Perkins, Miss F. A., New York; 209 W. 46th St.   12, 17
Perlberg, ——, New York; 43 W. 48th St.   24
Perkins, Granville, New York; 58 W. 57th St.   4, 12, 14, 19, 21
Perry, E. Wood, New York; 42 E. 14th St.   1, 4, 12, 14, 16
Perry, Ione H., New York; 256 W. 55th St.   12
Peto, John F., Philadelphia; 1020 Chestnut St.   18, 19
Pettit, F. A., New York; 160 Fulton St.   16
Pettit, Geo. W., Philadelphia; 1010 Clinton St.   17, 18, 25
Pfister, Eugene, New York; 97 E. Houston St.   13
Phelan, Chas. T., New York; 1293 Broadway,   12, 24
Phillips, Miss Emily L., Philadelphia; 1319 Walnut St.   19
Pickering, Arthur J., Chicago; 209 State St., Room 19,   23
Picknell, Wm. L., Paris; Rue du Cherche-Midi, 13,   17, 20, 22, 23
Pierce, Chas. F., Boston; 12 West St., Room 32,   20, 21
Pine, Theodore, New York; 58 W. 57th St.   12, 24
Pistor, Rudolph, New York; Bank Building, 4th Ave. and 14th St.   12, 18
Platt, C. A., New York; 90 Lexington Ave.   6, 12, 15, 16, 21, 24, 25
Platt, Geo. W., Chicago; 70 Monroe St., Room 39,   23
Platt, Miss S. J., Chicago; 170 State St.   22
Plimpton, W. E., New York; 28 E. 14th St.   12, 18, 24
Plumb, Henry G., New York; 744 Broadway,   7, 12, 14, 16, 17, 24, 25
Poindexter, W. M., Washington; 701 Fifteenth St.   9
Pollock, Miss, Baltimore; Wilson Building,   12
Poore, H. R., Philadelphia; 1334 Chestnut St.   12, 17, 18, 24, 25
Porter, Benj. C., Boston; 48 Boylston St.   1, 12, 20, 21
Porter, C. B.   12
Post, Geo. B., New York; 15 Cortlandt St.   9
Potter, W. A., New York; 121 E. 23d St.   9
Powers, Miss Caroline E., Chicago; 155 Warren Ave.   14, 19, 22, 23
Prague, J. G., New York; 47 Bible House,   9
Pranishnikoff, Ivan P.   4
Preble, G. R., New York; 16 E. 66th St.   17
Pressey, Miss Helen A.   21
Preston, Wm. G., Boston; 186 Devonshire St.   9
Preussner, Mrs. R. B., Chicago; 66 Park Ave.   22

Schuchard, F., Jr., New York ; 51 W. 10th St.   12, 18, 20, 23, 24
Schwerdt, C. F., Chicago ; 170 State St.   23
Scofield, L. T., Cleveland, O.; Case Block,   9
Scott, Mrs. E. M., New York; 142 E. 18th St.   12, 14, 16, 18, 22, 23, 24
Scott, Julian, Plainfield, N. J.   2, 11, 12, 14, 24
Scott, W. S , Philadelphia; 1520 Chestnut St.   18
Scott, Wm. Wallace, New York ; Cooper Union,   4
Scully, Mrs. M. M., Pittsburgh, Pa.; Lang Ave , East End,   17, 25
Sears, C. Payne, New York ; 66 Broadway,   25
Sears, W. T., Boston; 9 Pemberton Sq.   9
Seiss, C. Few, Philadelphia ; 1338 Spring Garden St.   19
Selinger, John, Providence, R. I.; 27 Butler Exchange,   13, 20, 21
Sellstedt, L. G., Buffalo, N. Y.   1, 12
Senat, Prosper L., Philadelphia; 1520 Chestnut St.   5, 12, 14, 18, 19, 23
Seymour, M., New York; Booth's Theatre Building,   19, 23
Shapleigh, Frank H., Boston ; 79 Studio Building,   20
Share, H. P., New York ; University Building, Washington Sq.   7, 16
Sharp, Miss Anna, Bryn Mawr, Pa.; care J. W. Townsend,   25
Shattuck, Aaron D., New York; 51 W. 10th St.   1, 12
Shaughnessy, S. J., New York ; 1227 Broadway,   24, 25
Shaw, Annie C., Chicago ; 2825 Prairie Ave.   13, 15, 20, 21, 22, 23, 25
Shaw, C. A., Madison, Wis.   15, 21
Shaw, George R., Boston ; 17 Congress St.   9
Shaw, Martha J., New York; 1155 Broadway,   12, 24, 25
Shearer, C. H., Philadelphia; 824 Arch St.   17, 18
Sheldon, Ella A., Philadelphia ; 1904 N. 12th St.   25
Shelton, Geo. F., New York ; Univ. Bldg, Washington Sq. 4, 12, 14, 16, 17, 18, 24, 25
Shelton, W. H., New York ; 1 Union Sq.   7, 12, 14, 16, 18, 25
Shepherd, Mrs. Jessie Curtis, New York; 337 E. 58th St.   8
Sheppard, Warren, Brooklyn, N. Y.; 281 Ninth St.   17, 24
Sheppard, W. L., Richmond, Va.   16
Shields, John D., Newark, N. J.; 70 Congress St.   24
Shields, Thos. W., New York ; Univ. Bldg., Washgt. Sq. 12, 13, 14, 16, 17, 18, 23, 35
Shirlaw, Walter, New York; Univ. Bldg., Washgt. Sq.   3, 4, 6, 22
Shoemaker, W. L., Philadelphia ; 818 Oxford St.   17
Shumway, Henry C., New York ; 43 E. 21st St.   1
Shurtleff, R. M , New York; 58 W. 57th St. 2, 3, 4, 12, 13, 14, 16, 19, 20, 21, 22, 23, 24
Shute, A. B., Boston ; 28 School St., Room 66,   20
Silliman, Benj., Jr., New York ; 140 Nassau St.   9
Silva, Francis A., New York; 11 E. 14th St.   4, 11, 12, 14, 18, 19
Simm, Fanny P., Philadelphia ; Day's Lane and Cottage Ave., Germantown,   25
Simon, Hermon, Philadelphia ; 520 Walnut St.   16, 18, 25
Simpson, Jas., Philadelphia ; 1029 Arch St.   6a, 15
Siter, E. C., Philadelphia ; 2033 Locust St.   17
Skinner, Edw. F., Chicago,   12
Sloan, Junius R., Chicago; 816 W. Adams St.   23
Smart, T. L., New York ; 96 Fulton St.   16
Smedley, W. T., New York ; Bank Building, 4th Ave. and 14th St.   13, 14, 16, 24
Smiley, M. F., Scarsdale, Westchester Co., N. Y.   12, 24
Smillie, Geo. H., New York ; 337 Fourth Ave.

       1, 4, 6, 12, 13, 14, 15, 16, 18, 20, 21, 22, 23, 24
Smillie, James, Poughkeepsie, N. Y.; 1 Eastman Terrace,   1
Smillie, James D., New York; 337 Fourth Ave.   1, 4, 6, 14, 15, 21, 22, 23

Smillie, Mrs. N. S. Jacobs, N. Y.; 337 Fourth Ave.   4, 12, 13, 14, 16, 18, 20, 21, 22, 23
Smith, Allen J.   2
Smith, Calvin Rae, New York; 58 W. 57th St.   7, 12, 16, 18, 24
Smith, F. Hopkinson, New York; 150 E. 34th St.   4, 14, 16, 18, 19, 21, 22, 23
Smith, Gean, Chicago; 170 State St., Room 30,   22, 23
Smith, Henry P., New York; 862 Broadway,   4, 12, 14, 18, 19, 23, 24
Smith, Jennie L., Bridgeport, Conn.   14
Smith, Mortimer L., Detroit, Mich.   12
Smith, Russell, Weldon, Montgomery Co., Pa.   17, 25
Smith, Sidney L., New York; 80 E. Washington Sq.   13
Smith, Thos. L., New York; 337 Fourth Ave.   2, 12, 20, 24
Smith, W. C., Nashville, Tenn. ; 68½ Church St.   9
Smith, Xanthus, Weldon, Montgomery Co., Pa.   25
Smithmeyer, J. L., Washington, D. C., 703 Fifteenth St.   9
Smithwick, J. G., New York ; care Harper & Bros.   10, 16
Snell, George, Boston ; 15 Studio Building,   4
Snyder, W. H., Brooklyn, N. Y.; 228 Madison St.   12, 17, 24, 25
Sonntag, Wm. L., New York ; 120 E. 22d St.   1, 4, 11, 12, 14, 17, 24
Southard, R. P., Charleston, S. C.; 9 Broad St.   9
Southwick, Jeanie Lea, Worcester, Mass.; 6 Home St.   14, 19
Spang, W., Philadelphia; 1020 Chestnut St.   17, 25
Spencer, Mrs. Lily M., Newark, N. J.   8
Spencer, Miss Mary, Cincinnati ; 184 W. 4th St.   20
Spooner, Chas. H., Philadelphia ; 1520 Chestnut St.   5, 18, 19
Spread, Henry F., Chicago; 210 La Salle St., Room 25,   12, 22, 23
Spring, Edward A., Perth Amboy, N. J.   13
Stark, Otto, New York ; 1295 Broadway,   14, 24
Starkweather, N. G., New York ; 822 Broadway,   9
Stearns, Junius B., Brooklyn, N. Y.; 389 Fulton St.   1, 12
Steers, Miss Anna, New York ; 12 E. 47th St.   8
Stephen, J., New York ; 9 W. 14th St.   12
Stephens, Geo. F., Philadelphia ; 1136 Girard St.   25
Sterling, Annie E., Bridgeport, Conn. ; 736 Main St.   12, 19, 25
Sterling, Julian H., Bridgeport, Conn.; 297 Washington Ave.   12, 17, 25
Sterner, Albert E., Chicago; 88 Ashland Block,   23
Stetson, Chas. Walter, Providence, R. I.; 35 N. Main St.   20, 25
Stevens, E. W., Philadelphia ; 1305 Butler St.   12
Stewart, Edw. B., Lynn, Mass.   20
St. Gaudens, Aug., New York; 148 W. 36th St.   3, 13, 22, 23
St. Gaudens, Louis, New York; 80 E. Washington Sq.   13
St. John, Mrs. S. H., Paris ; care Munroe & Co., Rue Scribe, 7,   17
Stiefel, J. Harry, Munich,   17, 20
Stiepevich, V. G., New York ; 1193 Broadway,   12, 17
Stiles, Mark, New York ; 51 W. 10th St.   12
Stillman, Wm. J., Florence, Italy,   2
Stimson, Eleanor, New York ; 14 W. 48th St.   24
Stimson, J. Ward, New York ; 11 E. 14th St.   12, 13, 24
Stites, J. R., New York ; 30 E. 14th St.   12, 16, 25
Stone, Alfred, Providence, R. I.; 65 Westminster St.   9
Stone, Miss Ellen, New York; 25 E. 45th St.   24
Stone, John, Embreeville, Chester Co., Pa.   17
Stone, James M., Boston ; 57 Tremont St.   3, 20, 25
Stone, Miss Mary L., New York ; Audubon Park,   8, 12, 14, 17, 18, 19

Volkmar, Chas., New York ; Tremont,   7, 12, 15, 16, 24
Vollmer, Ad . New York ; 23d St. and 8th Ave.   12, 25
Vollmering, Jos., New York ; 58 E. 13th St.   2
WAAS, M. A., Philadelphia ; 521 N. 11th St.   17, 25
Wade, E. Virginia, Philadelphia ; 1930 Race St.   25
Wadsworth, Miss A. E., Boston ; 3 Studio Building,   12
Wagner, Fred., Norristown, Pa. ; 255 Main St.   18, 25
Wagner. Jacob, Boston ; 7 Hamilton Pl.   20
Wagner, M. L., Norwich, N. Y.   25
Wales, Miss S. M. L., Boston,   21
Walker, Chas. A , Boston ; 42 Court St.   16, 21
Walker, Horatio, Rochester, N. Y.; 48 Elwood Building,   14
Walker, Mrs. Wm. B., Brooklyn, N. Y. ; 1217 N. 42d St.   25
Wall, N. W., Trinidad, Col.   9
Wallace, J. L., Philadelphia ; 1314 Savery St.   17
Wallace, Mary Wyman, Brooklyn, N. Y. ; 1328 Bergen St.   19, 25
Wallace, W. H.   16
Waller, Frank, New York ; 337 Fourth Ave.   12, 14, 16, 17, 18, 22, 23, 24, 25
Wallis, Mrs. M. E., New York ; 116 E. 25th St.   12, 24
Wallis, R. W., Chicago ; 119 E. Monroe St.   22
Walter, T. U., Philadelphia ; 720 N. Broad St.   9
Walters, M. Josephine, Hohokus, N. J.   12, 14
Walton, Wm., New York ; 47 Lafayette Pl.   12, 19, 24, 25
Ward, Chas. C., St. George, N. B.   4, 14
Ward, Edgar M., New York ; 119 W. 52d St.   2, 12, 14, 19, 22, 23, 24
Ward, J. Q. A., New York ; 9 W. 49th St.   1
Ware, Miss Agnes, Providence, R. I. ; 329 Broad St.   20
Ware, W. R., New York ; 9 W. 35th St.   9
Warner, Olin L., New York ; 80 E. Washington Sq.   3, 13, 21
Wasson, Geo. S., Boston ; 433 Washington St.   17, 20, 25
Waterhouse. M. S., New York ; 1271 Broadway,   12, 24
Waterman, E. J.   20
Waterman, Marcus, Boston ; 616 Washington St.   2, 4, 17, 20
Watts, Alex., Chicago ; 13 S. Clark St.   22
Waugh, Fred J., Philadelphia ; 4100 Pine St.   17
Waugh, Miss Ida, Philadelphia ; 4100 Pine St.   5, 17
Waugh, S. B., Philadelphia ; 816 Chestnut St.   17, 24, 25
Way, A. J. H., Baltimore ; 99 N. Charles St.   12, 17, 18, 24, 25
Way, Geo. B., Baltimore ; 99 N. Charles St.   17
Webber, C. T., Cincinnati ; 231 W. 4th St.   20, 23
Webber, Wesley. Boston ; 1 Pemberton Sq.   20
Weber, Carl, Philadelphia ; 238 N. 13th St.   5, 12, 18, 19, 25
Weber. C. Philipp, Philadelphia ; 1334 Chestnut St.   5, 17, 25
Weber, F., New York ; 139 E. 8th St.   13, 16, 24, 25
Weber. Otis S., Boston ; 12 West St.   20
Weber, Paul, Munich ; 48 Schwanthaler St.   17, 25
Webster, Miss Addie L.   21
Weeks, F. L., Paris ; care Munroe & Co., Rue Scribe, 7,   17, 25
Weir, J. Alden, New York ; 80 E. Washington Sq.   3, 6, 12, 13, 14, 20, 22, 23
Weir, John F., New Haven, Conn. ; 158 Trumbull St.   1, 11, 12
Weir, Robert Walter, New York ; 24 E. 10th St.   1, 4
Weissbein, Louis, Boston ; 3 State St.   9
Welch, Thaddeus, Sing-Sing, N. Y.   14, 20, 21

ART TEACHERS' DIRECTORY.*

Adams, Chas. L., Mass. Inst. of Tech., Boston, Mass.; 1 Summer Ct., Dorchester.
Adams, Willis S., Springfield Art Association, Springfield, Mass.
Alexander, J. W., Princeton Sketch Club, New York; Bank Bldg., 4th Ave. and 14th St.
Angerer, Victor, Franklin Inst., Philadelphia ; 2831 Girard Ave.
Anshutz, Thos., Pennsylvania Academy, Philadelphia; 1802 Mt. Vernon St.
Babcock, Rev. Chas., Cornell University, Ithaca, N. Y.
Babcock, J. C., G. S. Mech. and Tradesmen, New York ; 2121 Third Ave.
Bailey, Miss M. A., State Normal Art School, Boston, Mass.; 57 Tremont St.
Baldwin, Bert L., Ohio Mechanics' Institute, Cincinnati, Ohio.
Barth, Carl, Franklin Institute, Philadelphia; 1216 Mt. Vernon St.
Bartlett, Geo H., State Normal Art School, Boston, Mass.; 12 Pemberton Sq.
Bartlett, T. H., Boston School of Sculpture, Boston, Mass. ; 394 Federal St.
Barton, Miss Minnie, Salem Art Club, Salem, Mass.
Baur, Theod., Cooper Union, New York ; 160 W. 24th St.
Beard, Frank, Syracuse University, Syracuse, N. Y. ; West Adams St.
Bielby, Mrs. C. F. A., Decorative Art Society, Buffalo, N. Y.
Bigelow, D. F., Chicago Academy of Fine Arts, Chicago, Ill. ; 170 State St.
Blauvett, Chas. F., United States Naval Academy, Annapolis, Md.
Boyle, F. T. L., Brooklyn Institute, Brooklyn, N. Y.; 11 E. 14th St., New York.
Brackett, W. F., State Normal Art School, Boston, Mass.
Braman, Benj., Cooper Union, New York ; 117 E. 30th St.
Brewster, Miss A., Society of Decorative Art, New York ; 127 E. 10th St.
Broome, Isaac, Ladies' Art Decorative Society, Dayton, Ohio.
Brush, G. D., Cooper Union, New York ; 109 W. 34th St.
Buckingham, Jno., Tech. Schools of Metr. Museum, New York; 162 Second Ave.
Buell, Edgar M., B. Ar., Syracuse University, Syracuse, N. Y. ; 63 E. Castle St.
Burrison, H. K., Mass. Institute of Technology, Boston, Mass. ; 20 Beacon St.
Burrows, W. S., Ohio Mechanics' Institute, Cincinnati, Ohio.
Carpenter, N. H., Chicago Academy of Fine Arts, Chicago, Ill.
Carter, C. M., State Normal Art School, Boston, Mass.; 616 Washington St.
Carter, Miss E., Rhode Island School of Design, Providence, R. I.
Carter, Miss Grace, Decorative Art Society, Baltimore, Md.
Carter, Mrs. Susan N., Cooper Union, New York ; 74 Irving Pl.
Champney, J. W , National Academy of Design, New York ; 337 Fourth Ave.
Chase, Wm. M., Art Students' League, New York ; 51 W. 10th St.
Chesnutwood, Miss, Decorative Art Society, Buffalo, N. Y.
Chichester, Edw. L., Decorative Art Society, Buffalo, N. Y.
Churchill, A. D., School of Mines, Columbia Coll., N. Y. ; E. 49th St., c. Madison Ave.
Clark, Theo. M., Mass. Institute of Technology, Boston, Mass.; 78 Devonshire St.
Cleaves, Edw. Chase, Cornell University, Ithaca, N. Y.
Clevenger, Dr. S. V., Chicago Academy of Fine Arts, Chicago, Ill.

* The names here given are those of the teachers and lecturers connected with the Art Schools, etc., enumerated in this Directory. The addresses, wherever specified, refer to studios or private residences, so far as known. Corrections are solicited.

Comfort, Geo. F., A. M., Syracuse University, Syracuse, N. Y.; 383 East Ave.
Cookman, Chas. E., Columbus Art School, Columbus, Ohio.
Crampton, J., G. S. Mechanics and Tradesmen, New York; 329 W. 92d St.
Croasdale, Miss Eliz., School of Design for Women, Philadelphia.
Crowninshield, Fred., Museum of Fine Arts, Boston, Mass.; 156 Beacon St.
Davis, Miss Hannah E., Art Association, Quincy, Ill.
Davis, John P., Cooper Union, New York; 109 W. 34th St.
Dean, Francis W., Harvard University, Cambridge, Mass.; 40 Matthews Hall.
Denison, Chas. S., M. S., C. E , University of Mich., Ann Arbor; 40 S. Ingalls St.
Dennis, J. H., Art Club, Rochester, N. Y.
De Steigner, Miss Ida, University of Denver, Denver, Col.
Dewing, T. W., Art Students' League, New York; 139 W. 55th St.
Dickson, Miss M. E., University of Denver, Denver, Col.
Diehl, Cour., Missouri State University, Columbia, Mo.
Dielman, Fred., Art Students' League, New York; 51 W. 10th St.
Dimmock, M., Richmond Art Association, Richmond, Va.
Dole, Mrs. F. L., Decorative Art Society, Buffalo, N. Y.
Donlevy, Miss Alice, Ladies' Art Association, New York; 24 W. 14th St.
D'Ooge, Rev. Martin L., Ph. D., Univ. of Mich., Ann Arbor, Mich. ; Washtenaw Ave.
Eakins, Thos., Penns. Academy, Philadelphia; 1729 Mt. Vernon St.
Edgar, Miss Fannie, Columbus Art School, Columbus, O.
Eglau, Max, Cooper Union, New York; 767 Broadway.
Eifler, F., New York Turnverein, New York.
Elder, J., Richmond Art Association, Richmond, Va.
Ellis, Mrs. M. C. B., Cooper Union, New York.
Eustis, Henry L., Harvard University, Cambridge, Mass.; 29 Kirkland St.
Faber, Herm., School of Design for Women, Philadelphia; 524 Walnut St.
Farrar, Miss Frances, Milwaukee College, Milwaukee, Wis.
Fearing, Clarence W., Massachusetts Institute of Technology, Boston, Mass.
Ferris, Stephen J., School of Design for Women, Philadelphia; 1523 Chestnut St.
Fettweis, C. L., Ohio Mechanics' Institute, Cincinnati, O.; 159 Plum St.
Fichte, C. O., G. S. Mechanics and Tradesmen, New York; 896 Broadway.
Field, Miss E. C., Ladies' Art Association, New York; 24 W. 14th St.
Foster, John P. C., M. D., Yale College, New Haven, Conn.; 109 College St.
Franklin, Wm. W., Ohio Mechanics' Institute, Cincinnati, O.
Friede, Gustav, Richmond Art Association, Richmond, Va.; 731 E. Main St.
Fry, John H., St. Louis School of Fine Arts, St. Louis, Mo.
Fuchs, Otto, State Normal Art School, Boston, Mass.; 150 K St.
Fullerton, Emma W., School of Design for Women, Philadelphia.
Gifford, R. Swain, Cooper Union, New York; 152 W. 57th St.
Gilles, Ernest, Technical Schools of Metropolitan Museum, N. Y.; 308 E. 51st St.
Gladwin, Geo. C., Worcester Free Institute, Worcester, Mass.; 16 Harvard St.
Godart, Jules, Society of Decorative Art, San Francisco, Cal.
Goodnough, W. S., Columbus Art School, Columbus, O.; 161 Hamilton Ave.
Goodyear, Wm. H., Cooper Union, New York; 52 E. 49th St.
Gookins, J. F., Chicago Acad. of Design, Chicago, Ill.; Am. Exp. Bldg., Room 10.
Granbery, Miss Virg., Packer Colleg. Inst., Brooklyn, N. Y.; 140 E. 47th St., N. Y.
Grant, Miss Fanny, Society of Decorative Art, San Francisco, Cal.
Greely, M. Elizabeth, Adelphi Academy, Brooklyn, N. Y.; 39 Schermerhorn St.
Gribbon, John D., Technical Schools of Metrop. Museum, N. Y.; 312 E. 37th St.
Grundmann, Otto, Museum of Fine Arts, Boston, Mass.; 149 A Tremont St.
Gutherz, Carl, St. Louis School of Fine Arts, St. Louis, Mo.
Hamerel, Mme., Decorative Art Society, Buffalo, N. Y.

Harney, Paul E., St. Louis School of Fine Arts, St. Louis, Mo.
Hartley, J. S., Art Students' League, New York; 205 W. 56th St.
Hassam, F. Childe, Pencil and Brush Club, Waltham, Mass.; 28 School St., Boston.
Hastings, Miss M. A., Packer Collegiate Institute, Brooklyn, N. Y.
Heich, John B., Ohio Mechanics' Institute, Cincinnati, O.
Henderson, Annie W., School of Design for Women, Pittsburgh, Pa.
Hertzberg, Prof. C., Coll. and Polyt. Institute, Brooklyn, N. Y.; 140 Duffield St.
Hochstein, A., Ladies' Art Association, New York; 58 Seventh St., Hoboken, N. J.
Holcombe, Mrs. L. W., Chicago Academy of Design, Chicago, Ill.
Holloway, Chas. S., St. Louis School of Fine Arts, St. Louis, Mo.
Honey, Fred. R., Yale College, New Haven, Conn.; 14 Lincoln St.
Hopkins, Geo. Edward, Univ. of Cinc., Cincinnati, O.; 64 Pike's Building.
Hoppin, Rev. Jas. M., D. D., Yale College, New Haven, Conn.; 47 Hillhouse Ave.
Hoyt, Miss R. L., State Normal Art School, Boston, Mass.
Humphreys, Wm. H., University of Cincinnati, Cincinnati, O.; 168½ Walnut St.
Huygue, Mary J., Ladies' Art Association, New York.
Ingalsbe, Miss, Society of Decorative Art, San Francisco, Cal.
Ives, Halsey C., St. Louis School of Fine Arts, St. Louis, Mo.
Jahn. Albrecht, School of Design for Women, Philadelphia.
Jamison, Agnes D., School of Design for Women, Pittsburgh, Pa.
Jayne, Horace F., School of Industrial Art, Philadelphia.
Jorgensen, Chris., California School of Design, San Francisco, Cal.
Kaiser, Albert J., Ohio Mechanics' Institute, Cincinnati, O.
Kastner, Chas., Massachusetts Institute of Technology, Boston, Mass.
Keen, W. W., M. D., Pennsylvania Academy, Philadelphia; 1729 Chestnut St.
Keller, Martha Jane, University of Cincinnati, Cincinnati, O.
Kellogg, Miss A. D., Chicago Academy of Fine Arts, Chicago, Ill.
King, Miss M. L., Salem Art Club, Salem, Mass
Knight, Sophie J., Ladies' Art Association, New York.
Kretschmar, Howard, St. Louis School of Fine Arts, St. Louis, Mo.
Laird, Miss Alicia, Richmond Art Association, Richmond, Va.
Lambdin, Geo. C., School of Design for Women, Philadelphia; 1520 Chestnut St.
Lander, Miss Louisa, Salem Art Club, Salem, Mass.
Lane, Miss H. C., Ladies' Art Association, New York.
. Larned, Lt. Col. Chas. W., United States Military Academy, West Point, N. Y.
Law, Miss Frances Tate, School of Art Needle-Work, Philadelphia.
Leland, Chas. G., Ladies' Decorative Art Club, Philadelphia.
Letang, Eugene, Mass. Institute of Technology, Boston, Mass.; 2 Van Renss. Pl.
Lietze, Ernest, Ohio Mechanics' Institute, Cincinnati, O.
Lindsley, Harr. W., Ph. B., Yale College, New Haven, Conn.; Cutler Building.
Long, Miss Mary, Art Association, Quincy, Ill.
Longfellow, Wm. P. P., Mass. Inst. of Techn., Boston, Mass.; 220 Devonshire St.
M'Allister, Mary, School of Design for Women, Philadelphia.
Marquand, Allan, College of New Jersey, Princeton, N. J.
Mason, W. A., Columbus Art School, Columbus, O.
Mather, Richard H., D. D., Amherst College, Amherst, Mass.
Maurer, Edm., Cooper Union, New York; 75 W. 3d St.
Maurer, Emil, Cooper Union, New York; 75 W. 3d St.
Maynard, Geo. W., Cooper Union, New York; 80 E. Washington Sq.
McComas, W. R., Ohio Mechanics' Institute, Cincinnati, O.
McDougall, J. A., Jr., Cooper Union, New York; 52 E. 23d St.
Mead, Miss M. V., Society of Decorative Art, New York.
Merrill, Miss L. E., Salem Art Club, Salem, Mass.

Messer, E. C., Washington Art Club, Washington, D. C.
Metzner, H., New York Turnverein, New York; 212 E. 83d St.
Miller, Edw. C., Cooper Union, New York.
Miller, L. W., School of Industrial Art, Philadelphia.
Mills, J. Harrison, Academy of Fine Arts, Denver, Col.; 104 Tabor Opera House.
Molinary, A., Southern Art Union, New Orleans, La.
Monckton, J., General Society of Mechanics and Tradesmen, New York.
Moore, Chas. H., Harvard University, Cambridge, Mass.; 19 Follen St.
Moran, Peter, School of Design for Women, Philadelphia;· 1322 Jefferson St.
Morgan, Miss Annie, Ladies' Art Association, New York; 58 W. 57th St.
Morris, Miss M. J., Richmond Art Association, Richmond, Va.; 206 W. Grace St.
Munsell, A. H., State Normal Art School, Boston, Mass.; 45 Quincy St.
Niemeyer, J. H., Yale College, New Haven, Conn.; 8 Art School.
Newell, Hugh, Maryland Institute School of Art, Baltimore, Md.
Noble, Thos. L., University of Cincinnati, Cincinnati, O.; 168½ Walnut St.
Norton, Chas., Eliot, Harvard University, Cambridge, Mass.; Kirkland St.
Norton, Miss Dora M., Columbus Art School, Columbus, O.
Osborne, Chas. F., Cornell University, Ithaca, N. Y.; 42 Eddy St.
Ostrander, W., Techn. Schools of Metr. Mus., New York.; 47 Christopher St.
Page, Charles, School of Design for Women, Philadelphia; 1329½ N. 8th St.
Palladino, B., Technical Schools of Metropolitan Museum., New York.
Paul, Miss E. D., Ladies' Decorative Art Club, Philadelphia.
Pennypacker, Sara C., School of Design for Women, Philadelphia.
Perelli, A., Southern Art Union, New Orleans, La.
Perry, Geo. L., Massachusetts Institute of Technology, Boston, Mass.
Pitman, Benn, University of Cincinnati, Cincinnati, O.
Piton, Camille, Ladies' Art Association, New York,
Platt, Miss Mary M., Packer Collegiate Institute, Brooklyn, N. Y.
Porter, W. A., Spring Garden Institute, Philadelphia.
Powers, Miss C. E., Cooper Union, New York.
Price, Wm. L., Franklin Institute, Philadelphia; 731 Walnut St.
Purdy, W. S., Gen'l Soc. of Mechanics and Tradesmen, New York; 149 Broadway.
Pyne, C. C., Technical School of Metr. Museum, New York; 1267 Broadway.
Randolf, C. H., General Society of Mechanics and Tradesmen, New York.
Ranger, Ward V., Syracuse University, Syracuse, N. Y.
Rebisso, Louis Thos., University of Cincinnati, Cincinnati, O.; 18 Hunt St.
Ricker, N. Clifford, M. Arch, Ill. Industrial University; Champaign, Ill.
Robertson, J. Roy, Ladies' Art Association, New York; 109 W. 34th St.
Robitscher, Mrs. B. B., Ladies' Art Association, New York; 166 E. 72d St.
Roos, Peter, Ill. Industrial University, Champaign, Ill.
Rose, E., Rhode Island School of Design, Providence, R. I.; 32 Hammond St.
Rossignoli, Nic., Cooper Union, New York.
Rupert, A. J. Chicago Academy of Fine Arts, Chicago, Ill.; 60 Lakeside Building.
Sartain, Wm., Art Students' League, New York; 152 W. 57th St.
Saxton, J. A., Cooper Union, New York.
Scott, I. E., Chicago Society of Decorative Art, Chicago, Ill.
Scott, W. W., Cooper Union, New York.
Shaughnessy, Stephen J., St. John's College, Fordham, N. Y.
Shave, Miss R. M., Ingham University, Le Roy, N. Y.
Sheppard, W. L., Richmond Art Association, Richmond, Va.
Singer, R., New York Turnverein. New York.
Smith, Arthur L., St. Louis School of Fine Arts, St. Louis, Mo.
Smith, C. R., National Academy of Design, New York; 58 W. 57th St.

Smith, Jos., Technical Schools of Metropolitan Museum, New York.
Smith, Miss S. E., Salem Art Club, Salem, Mass.
Smith, Mrs., Society of Decorative Art, Boston, Mass.
Sondericker, Jerome, B. S., Ill. Industrial University, Champaign, Ill.
Spread, H. F., Chicago Academy of Fine Arts, Chicago, Ill.; 210 La Salle St.
Stanwood, Jas. B., Ohio Mechanics' Institute, Cincinnati, O.
Staunton, P. P., Ingham University, Le Roy, N. Y.
Stone, Miss Lucy, General Society of Mechanics and Tradesmen, New York.
Stratton, H. F., School of Industrial Art, Philadelphia.
Tadd, J. Liberty, Ladies' Decorative Art Club, Philadelphia; 1334 Chestnut St.
Taylor, Miss Ida, Art Club, Rochester, N. Y.
Thorne, Wm. H., Franklin Institute, Philadelphia.
Turner, C. Y., Art Students' League, New York; 11 E. 14th St.
Turney, Olive, School of Design for Women, Pittsburgh, Pa.
Uhle, H., Ladies' Decorative Art Club, Philadelphia; 207 Levant St.
Vanderpoel, J. H., Chicago Academy of Fine Arts, Chicago, Ill.
Van De Warker, E. Ely, M. D., Syracuse Univ., Syracuse, N.Y.; 45 Montgomery St.
Van Ingen, Henry, Vassar College, Poughkeepsie, N. Y.
Van Kuyck, H., General Society of Mechanics and Tradesmen, New York.
Volk, S. A. Douglas, Cooper Union, New York; 109 W. 34th St.
Volkmar, Chas., Society of Decorative Art, New York; Tremont, New York City.
Wade, Miss C. D., Chicago Academy of Fine Arts, Chicago, Ill.
Wadman, Geo., Ohio Mechanics' Institute, Cincinnati, Ohio.
Walker, Horatio, Art Club, Rochester, N. Y.; 48 Elwood Building.
Wallace, John, Pennsylvania Academy, Philadelphia.
Ware, Wm. R., School of Mines, Columbia College, New York; 9 W. 35th St.
Weir, J. Alden, Cooper Union, New York; 80 East Washington Sq.
Weir, John F., Yale College, New Haven, Conn.; 58 Trumbull St.
Wells, Newton P., M. P., Syracuse University, Syracuse, N. Y.; 5 Harlow Block.
Whitaker, G. W., R. I. School of Design, Providence, R. I.; 65 Westminster St.
Whittaker, John B., Adelphi Academy, Brooklyn, N. Y.; 745 Lafayette Ave.
Whittemore-Gregg, Rebecca R., University of Cincinnati, Cincinnati, Ohio.
Wiles, Irving R., Ingham University, Le Roy, N. Y.; 51 W. 10th St., N. Y.
Wiles, L. M., Ingham University, LeRoy, N. Y.; 52 E. 23d St., N. Y.
Williams, Geo. P., School of Design for Women, Philadelphia; 524 Walnut St.
Williams, Virgil, California School of Design, San Francisco, Cal.
Willson, Fred. N., C. E., College of New Jersey, Princeton, N. J.
Wilmarth, Lem E., National Academy of Design, New York; 51 W. 10th St.
Wilson, Nettie, University of Cincinnati, Cincinnati, Ohio.
Winant, Miss Henrietta, Southern Art Union, New Orleans, La.
Winter, Peter, Winter Art Association, Brooklyn, N. Y.; 87 Hanson Pl.
Wood, Miss A. A., Cooper Union, New York.
Wood, John Z., Art Club, Rochester, N. Y.
Woodward, E., Rhode Island School of Design, Providence, R. I.
Woodward W., Rhode Island School of Design, Providence, R. I.; 208 Pine St.

NECROLOGY.*

BOUVY, FIRMIN, genre painter, born in Belgium, died at his residence, 1423 Stockton St., San Francisco, Cal., Oct. 17, 1881, at the age of about fifty-eight years. He came to San Francisco about five years before his death, after he had travelled extensively in Europe and the East. His favorite subjects were monks. A somewhat more extended notice of the deceased may be found in the San Francisco "Chronicle" of Oct. 18, 1881.

BRYANT, HENRY, portrait and landscape painter, born at Manchester Green, in 1812; died at East Hartford, Conn., on Wednesday, Dec. 7, 1881. He began his career as an engraver, but turned his attention to oil painting about 1832, and was elected an Associate of the National Academy in 1837.

CASS, GEO. N., landscape painter, born at Canaan, N. H.; died at Arlington Heights, near Boston, Mass., March 17, 1882, aged fifty, after a lingering illness. He was a pupil of Geo. Inness. At the sale of the late Alvin Adams's collection, which took place about the time of the artist's death, four of his pictures, all of them landscapes with cattle, were sold at prices ranging from $100 to $250. The influence of his teacher was traceable in all of Mr. Cass's work, although he did not succeed in reaching the strength of his prototype.

DARRAH, MRS. SOPHIA TOWNE, landscape painter, died at Manchester, Mass., Dec. 24, 1881, after she had been practically an invalid for nearly thirty years. She was the daughter of the late John Towne, of Philadelphia, and early gave promise of artistic talent, devoting herself at first to music. Soon after her marriage with Mr. Robert K. Darrah, of Boston, in 1845, she began to direct her attention more exclusively to painting, and in 1849 became a pupil of Paul Weber, whose style she closely followed during the first period of her artistic career. Later she experienced the influence of the French school, and of its follower, Wm. M. Hunt; and resolutely set to work to overcome the peculiarities of style acquired by earlier training. This effort of the reason made itself unpleasantly felt in some of her work, by forced lowness of tone, and an equally forced breadth in handling. Gradually, however, she assimilated the methods which she had at first only imitated, and among her later studies were some of truly excellent quality. A memorial exhibition of her works was held at the Boston Museum of Fine Arts, from Feb. 22 to March 8, 1882. The special catalogue published for the occasion enumerates 60 oils, 202 water-colors, and 8 charcoals. In accordance with the terms of the will of the deceased, 420 of her oil and water-color paintings were sold at auction for the benefit of the Mass. Society for the Prevention of Cruelty to Animals, realizing about $11,000. The sale took place in Boston, at the gallery of Messrs. Williams & Everett, from March 1 to 4, 1882.

FRAZAR, MISS CARIE, sculptress, died at the home of her father in Watertown, near Boston, Mass., on Monday, Oct. 10, 1881. She graduated from the High School of her native town in 1871, at the head of her class, the graduation theme being "The Right of Woman to Full Education," and acquired the classical knowledge necessary to enable her to enter Amherst College, had that institution been

* The Necrology of American Art is taken up here at the point where it was discontinued in the last number of the "American Art Review."

open to women. After leaving school, she devoted her time to art, studying anatomy, even to dissection, and spending many months in a stone-cutter's shop. She
exhibited portraits in relief and intaglio at three successive exhibitions of the
Boston Art Club, a bust of a child at the Museum of Fine Arts, Boston, in 1880, and
a portrait in intaglio at the National Academy of Design, New York, in 1881.

GIGNOUX, FRANÇOIS REGIS, N. A., landscape painter, born at Lyons, France, in
1816; died at Paris, France, on Monday, Aug. 14, 1882. Intending to become an historical painter, he studied at the Ecôle des Beaux-Arts, Paris, and under Delaroche
and Vernet, but by the advice of the former, gave his attention to landscape. Mr.
Gignoux came to America in 1840, and was elected a National Academician in 1851.
He was also the first president of the Brooklyn Art Association, organized in June,
1864. Until his return to France in 1870, he was so thoroughly identified with
American art, that one of his paintings, "Mount Washington," was exhibited in the
American Department of the World's Fair of 1867, at Paris. Many of his works
represented winter scenes ("Niagara in Winter," etc.).

GILMAN, ARTHUR a well-known architect of New York, died in July, 1882,
after a long and painful illness. The following facts are taken from a more extended
account of his professional activity, in the "American Architect" of July 22. Mr.
Gilman, originally intended for the ministry, was educated at the Dummer Academy
and at Trinity College, Hartford, but soon gave his attention to architecture. In
1844, in an article published in the "North American Review," he attacked the
Greek classicism then in vogue here, and predicted the victory of the Gothic movement. The article attracted much attention, and Mr. Gilman was invited to deliver
a course of lectures in Boston, at the conclusion of which he went to Europe to
study. Some years later he was consulted on the subject of the Back Bay improvements in Boston, and to his instrumentality is due the adoption of the scheme
which has made this part of Boston one of the most beautiful urban regions of the
world. Among his works, executed in conjunction with Mr. Bryant, his then part-
ner, may be named the City Hall, the First Church on Arlington St., and the Brewer-
Beebe houses on Beacon St., all in Boston. In 1865 he removed to New York, and
there devised, with Mr. Kendall, the façade of the Equitable Life Assurance Com-
pany's building on Broadway. Mr. Gilman was a member of the American Institute
of Architects.

GLESSING, THOMAS BALTHAZAR. scenic artist, died at the Hotel Albany,
Boston, on Saturday, Sept. 30, 1882. Mr. Glessing was born in London, of a German father and English mother, on Nov. 26, 1817, and came to America in 1841.
Being encouraged by his brother-in-law, the late Wm. E. Burton, the famous com-
edian, he followed the stage with success for some years. A taste for painting
finally led him to make scene painting his profession. In this capacity he was employed in many of the larger theatres of the country, including the Globe of Boston,
and Booth's Theatre in New York. During the last eight years of his life he was
the artist of the Museum Theatre, at Boston. Mr. Glessing painted also in oil.

GOULD, THOMAS RIDGWAY, sculptor, born Nov. 6, 1818, at Boston; died Nov. 26,
1881, at Florence, Italy. He was essentially self-taught in art, and was compelled to
follow mercantile pursuits until 1861. In that year, although the breaking out of the
war of secession had cost him his fortune, he gave himself up entirely to sculpture,
and after seven years of hard struggling went to Florence, where he made his home,
visiting his native country only occasionally. The following are among the best
known of his works: "Bust of Emerson," in the Library of Harvard College; two
colossal busts, "Christ," and "Satan," executed about 1861, which first drew public
attention to him; "Governor Andrew," bust, in marble, said to be the only bust of
the great war governor modelled from life; "Junius Brutus Booth," bust, in Booth's
Theatre, New York; "Michelangelo," bust, owned by Mr. Edwin Booth; "The

West Wind," statue in marble, owned by Mr. Demas Barnes, Brooklyn, N. Y., and frequently repeated; "The Ghost in Hamlet," alto-relievo in marble; "Timon," statue in illustration of Shakespeare's play; "Cleopatra," sitting statue belonging to Mr. Isaac Fenno, Boston Highlands; "Ariel"; "Steam," and "Electricity," two heads in relief, Herald Building, Boston; "John Hancock," statue in the Town Hall at Lexington; "Governor Andrew," statue, Hingham, Mass.; "Kamehameha I., King of the Hawaian Islands," colossal bronze statue, executed twice, as the first was lost at sea. Mr. Gould also wielded the pen, and wrote, among other things, a book on Junius Brutus Booth, the actor. The body was embalmed and brought to Boston. An account of the funeral services held over the remains, and several tributes to the memory of the deceased, will be found in the Boston "Advertiser" of Feb. 13, 1882.

HAGEN, JOHN C., portrait painter, died in December, 1881, in his seventy-fifth year. He was among the founders of one of the early "Sketch Clubs" of New York, and was called by his friends the Poet Artist, as he was the author of a volume of poems entitled "Footprints of Truth, or Voice of Humanity," and occasionally wrote ballads for the club alluded to. Among his portraits was one of Thomas Paine. A specimen of his work may be seen at the rooms of the New York Historical Society, a portrait of Gen. Joseph Reed, copied from the original by Charles Wilson Peale.

HAHS, PHILIP B., genre painter, died Aug. 28, 1882, at Philadelphia, in the thirtieth year of his age, after an illness of five months. He studied at the Pennsylvania Academy, and was in 1880 volunteer assistant to Prof. Eakins. The humorous delineations of negro life which within the last two or three years he sent to the Academy Exhibitions in New York and in Philadelphia, and to the exhibitions of the Philadelphia Society of Artists, of which body he was a member, had rapidly made him quite popular. One of his earlier and best productions, "Lullaby," exhibited at the Second Annual Exhibition of the Phil. Society of Artists, in Nov., 1880, is owned by Mr. Thomas B. Clarke, of New York. A sketch of this picture is given in the catalogue of the exhibition alluded to.

HOLLINGSWORTH, GEORGE, born in Milton, near Boston, Oct. 17, 1813; died of heart disease at his home on Blue Hill Ave., in his native place, March 20, 1882. He was a son of the late Mark Hollingsworth, of the original firm of Tileston & Hollingsworth, the well-known paper manufacturers, and it is stated that he was the only member of the family who did not take to his father's trade. Exhibiting considerable artistic talent, young Hollingsworth was sent to Europe, where he spent eighteen months in study and travel. After his return in 1837, he opened a studio in Boston, and applied himself diligently to the practice of his art. Some of the portraits produced by him in those days have been pronounced equal to the best. He worked slowly and very conscientiously, never seeking to flatter or please, but aiming only at truth. It was owing mainly to the enthusiasm and the exertions of Mr. Hollingsworth, that the "Artists' Association of Boston" was formed some forty odd years ago, with Washington Allston, for whom the deceased had great admiration and reverence, as president. The Association established itself in Harding's Building, in School St., and counted among its members artists like Harding, Alexander, etc. It was principally due, also, to the activity of Mr. Hollingsworth, that the Association started a Life School, the first of its kind established in Boston, and probably in all New England. In 1850 he was chosen master of the Lowell Institute Drawing School, which he managed until its discontinuation in 1878, consequent upon the breaking up of its old quarters under the Marlboro' Hotel. From this time forward his activity was principally that of an educator, and he gradually withdrew from the regular practice of his profession, so that the present generation knows nothing of his merits as an artist. The system of teaching adopted in this school from the very beginning, based entirely upon drawing from objects, and absolutely discarding the use of flat copies, was at that time considered such a radical departure from established usage, that it drew down upon the head of its principal the violent ridicule of the press and of the defenders of the old system. But the school persevered; its success was soon phenomenal, and its fame spread far and wide. Mr. Hollingsworth left an account of the school, which has never as yet been printed, and which, through the kindness of a relative of the deceased, is herewith given to the public entire : — " A DESCRIPTION OF THE LOWELL INSTITUTE DRAWING SCHOOL. BY ITS MASTER. — During the year 1850, the Lowell Institute, wishing to establish a School for Drawing, placed it under the direction of Mr. George Hollingsworth, in a room large enough to contain about 70 desks and easels. Near the middle thereof Mr. H. piled three large cubes or boxes, different in size, and placed at varied angles one upon another. Round these the pupils sat or stood in two or three rows, those behind on a higher plane, so every one, having a different view of the same objects, could not copy from his neighbor, yet was aided and stimulated by seeing the work around him. Each box being the simplest and easiest object that could be furnished for study, yet the three as a whole proved very difficult, inasmuch as the combination of lines in all required perfect accuracy in each, or the fault would be apparent; thus teaching at the outset the beauty and necessity of truth, and inevitably leading to the law of perspective and its study. This law was now explained and illustrated upon a picture plane of wire cloth (never, I think, before used for this purpose *), through which similar boxes could be seen and so drawn thereon ; the vanishing lines, continued to a point, proved and illustrated every rule as stated. Meanwhile the boxes, properly lit, furnished to many the first great lesson of light and shade. These were studied till understood, and every point to which each surface or plane tended properly located, — a great lesson, the foundation of all true art. The second step was to a white globe suspended before a burner. The varied tints it reflected were carefully studied from different positions and against different backgrounds, till the law of light and shade, as seen on a rounded surface, was thoroughly comprehended and represented on a flat surface. Thus something beyond mere imitation was learned. This study was further continued in the more complicated forms of a vase, whose circles and curves were drawn from several points of view, as also the lights and shadows seen in its gently varied shape. By these three steps the pupil was remarkably fitted for the next, the study of the human form, as seen in the cast of Houdon's anatomical figure, and after this, that of the Venus de Medici. Thus in these four lessons, beginning with the simplest form and continued to the most complicated, were studied the great representative lines; the shapes and shadows contained in them were all recognized and represented, and the laws revealed in them understood and applied to all things. This done in one room, in one circle, and under every eye, was in itself the best instruction, giving the class an opportunity of observing every method, from the worst to the best, no special manner being taught, as Mr. H. was particularly careful to develop individuality rather than a style or school. These few objects alone were furnished as the severest possible, and those from which any change or departure would be most readily perceived, as it is his creed ' that the expression of the simple truth shows highest skill,' and that a departure therefrom, allowed or tolerated in a pupil, leads to carelessness and inaccuracy of eye or hand, or, what is worse, lying in art, substituting the conceits, the whims, or the stupidity of the artist for the infinite and harmonious loveliness of nature. In addition, a few years later, in a smaller room adjoining, a Life School was set up and maintained to which not only the more advanced pupils

---

* Mr. Hollingsworth was in error here. Picture planes of gauze, for the purpose of drawing upon them objects seen through them, were known already to Leone Battista Alberti. See this artist's " Treatise on Painting," Book II., written in the 15th century. — EDITOR.

were admitted, but also artists and others from outside. Thus oftentimes the best artists of Boston worked side by side with and so taught the poorest. All this free, and limited only by the size of the room and by the time allowed, a two hours' session for each sex twice a week during the six colder months of the year. Painting and modelling were done and encouraged, and every method allowed by which the pupil could best express 'the truth, the whole truth, and nothing but the truth.' This school, established by the Trustee of the Lowell Institute, the Hon. John A. Lowell, has continued from 1850 until the present year (1878). Since the first year, Mr. Wm. T. Carlton has been associated with Mr. Hollingsworth." — The school exercised a marked influence upon the development of art in Boston and throughout New England. Of the more than five thousand pupils which are said to have profited by its instruction during the twenty-eight years of its existence, quite a number have become well known in the world of art. Among these may be named Henry Bacon, J. Wells Champney, W. Mark Fisher, Thos. Gould, Frank Millet, Martin Millmore, Wm. E. Norton, F. P. Vinton, Moses Wight, etc. — As a man, Mr. Hollingsworth was beloved by all who knew him. "His recognition of the poor," says an obituary notice in the Boston "Evening Traveller," of April 28, 1882, "was touching and beautiful. At times he would take the children of public institutions *en masse* to his picturesque and delightful old place, where he would, by the river he loved so well, in generous feastings, give them a foretaste of the beauty and the kindliness he taught, and which his genius enabled him so gracefully to bring together." — This rather lengthy notice will not be thought out of place in a book which is principally devoted to a record of the present condition of art education in the U. S. In the movement which has led to the establishment of the many schools here enumerated, Mr. Hollingsworth was a pioneer. Unfortunately, pioneers are apt to be forgotten, and it is but just, therefore, that a monument should be erected to him in a place where it is most likely to meet the eyes of those best fitted to judge of the value of his labors.

KING, JOHN CROOKSHANKS, sculptor and cameo cutter, born Oct. 16, 1806, at Kilwinning, Ayrshire, Scotland; died in the Massachusetts General Hospital, Boston, Mass., April 21, 1882. He early desired to become an artist, but adverse circumstances compelled him to follow his father's trade, which was that of a machinist. In 1829 he went to New Orleans, and thence to Cincinnati, where he stayed with interruptions until 1836, made the acquaintance of Hiram Powers, and began to model, one of his first attempts being a bust of his wife. In New Orleans, to which city he returned about 1837 to stay until 1840, he modelled a number of busts, among them those of Rev. Theod. Clapp, Jas. H. Caldwell, and Pierre Soule, and exercised the art of cameo cutting. To Boston Mr. King came in 1840, and it was here that he executed the works by which he became known, — busts in marble of Daniel Webster, John Quincy Adams, Dr. Samuel Woodward, and others. For quite a number of years Mr. King was unable to work, owing to the infirmities of age. A short autobiographical account, up to January, 1853, may be found in "Familiar Sketches of Sculpture and Sculptors," Boston, Crosby, Nichols & Co., 1854.

LOCKHART, WM. J., painter in oil and water-colors, illustrator and designer, born March 2, 1846, at Verona, N. Y.; died of consumption, after an illness of some months, on Nov. 23, 1881, at his residence, 12 Howell St., Rochester, N. Y. He studied at the Academy of Design in New York, entering the Life Class at the age of twenty. At the Black and White Exhibition held in New York in 1880, he had a drawing entitled "Trophies," and in that of 1881 another, "Musings," which he sent just before his death. Several of his works were also shown at the last exhibition of the Rochester Art Club, April, 1882, of which association the deceased was one of the founders.

MACKAY, WILLIAM HENRY, wood engraver, died of consumption at East Boston, Mass., in August, 1882, at the age of eighteen years. Although so young, Mr. Mackay was an artist of great promise. In the first "Scribner Prize Competition" in 1880, after a practice of only two years, he took the first prize for his engraving of Jas. M. Hart's " From shifting shade to sunshine pass." (See " Scribner's Monthly " for April, 1881.) In the second competition he again took the first prize " for best work by former competitors," his subject this time being a nearly full-length portrait of a lady, after a photograph from life. (See " Century Magazine " for June, 1882.) He was a pupil of Mr. Victor L. Chandler, of Boston.

MURDOCH, MISS CLARA RACYLIA, landscape and animal painter, died at Auburn, N. Y., on Nov. 15, 1881. She was the daughter of Lyman Murdoch, and was born at Venice Centre, Cayuga Co., N Y., to which place the body was taken for interment. Miss Murdoch was a born artist, but she refined her native talent by assiduous application. She was at one time a pupil of J. H. Oertel, and had already attained success in her profession when she went abroad in 1876 for further study.. The first picture, " La Barrière," which she sent to the Paris Salon of 1881 from Ecouen, where she had made her home, was hung on the line, and elicited favorable comments from the French press. Her health failing rapidly, probably from overwork, she returned to America in September, 1881, in the hope of regaining strength; but the voyage, which was rather rough, completely prostrated her. After she had remained at her home a few weeks, she went to Auburn to visit her friend, Dr. Amanda Sanford, and to receive medical treatment; but an attack of paralysis ended her life. Two of her paintings, " La Barrière," alluded to above, and " May in an Old Land," both of them landscapes with figures and sheep, were in the exhibition held at the Pennsylvania Academy, Philadelphia, in November, 1881, and were subsequently shown at the Fifty-Seventh Exhibition of the National Academy. They showed that America has lost in Miss Murdoch perhaps the most promising of her women painters. Good in drawing, refined in color, carefully studied, and delicately yet firmly executed, these works showed none of the eccentric striving after an outwardly assumed air of freedom which mars so many of the works of the female painters of the day. The French critic spoke the truth, who characterized the qualities of " La Barrière " as " delicacy of sentiment and sincerity."

QUIDOR, JOHN, figure painter, born on a farm near Gloucester, N. J., died in Jersey City, Dec. 13, 1881, at the age of eighty-one years. Quidor was almost forgotten at the time of his death, although he was formerly well known in the art circles of New York. Col. T. B. Thorpe, in his " Reminiscences of Charles L. Elliott," says that Quidor was " the only avowed figure painter then [about 1828] in New York, and possibly, except Washington Allston, the only one in the country." This, however, is not correct, as Col. Trumbull and S. F. B. Morse were at that time both in New York. In the fierce war which was waged against Mr. Inman and the newly born National Academy, it was asserted that " as a general painter, as an original genius, Mr. Quidor is vastly superior to Mr. Inman. We challenge Mr. Inman or any one of the National Academicians to produce specimens equal to several of his works as displayed on banners and fire-engine backs." Quidor and Inman were both pupils of Jarvis, the well-known portrait painter, and Quidor became the teacher of Charles Loring Elliott. An amusing and interesting account of his studio and mode of living at that time is given in the pamphlet by Col. Thorpe, before alluded to, who also studied with him. Quidor painted a number of immense canvases, chiefly scriptural and historical subjects, and in September, 1847, opened a special exhibition in New York, " with the avowed intention," says T. S. Cummings, in his " Annals of the N. A. D.," p. 202, " of making his fortune," an object which, unfortunately, he did not accomplish. The best-known of his works is " The Dance on the Battery," exhibited at the National Academy something like fifteen years ago.

Rotch, Benjamin S., born March 4, 1817; died Saturday, Aug. 19, 1882, at Milton, near Boston, Mass. He was of Quaker stock, graduated at Harvard in 1838, and in early life was engaged in manufacturing in New Bedford. "In 1846 he married the eldest daughter of the Hon. Abbott Lawrence," says an appreciative obituary notice in the Boston " Advertiser," of Aug. 31, "and accompanied the latter to England when he was appointed our minister at the Court of St. James. It was during this and subsequent visits to Europe that he had the opportunity to improve and cultivate that interest in the fine arts which rendered his influence in artistic matters most valuable in this community. Gifted with a refined taste and sensitive feeling for form and color, his careful study of foreign collections, supplemented by practical work, made him a competent and fastidious critic, as well as a painter whose landscapes have shown to advantage in our local exhibitions." Mr. Rotch was one of the Trustees of the Boston Museum of Fine Arts, and a member of the Committee on the Museum.

Sims, James P., one of the best and most favorably known architects of the United States, according to the "American Architect " of June 3, 1882, died in Philadelphia in May, 1882, in his thirty-third year. After graduation from the University of Pennsylvania, Mr. Sims received his technical training under his brother, the late Henry Sims, which he supplemented by a period of study and travel in Europe. Among the buildings executed by him are the Holy Trinity Memorial Chapel, and Christ Church Chapel, in Philadelphia, Christ Church at Germantown, Philadelphia, and the new Episcopal Church at Morristown. Mr. Sims died very suddenly, probably of apoplexy, while sitting in his office. He was a member of the American Institute of Architects.

Staigg, Richard Morrell, N. A., born in Leeds, England, Sept. 7, 1817; died at Newport, R. I., at two o'clock on the morning of Oct. 11, 1881. His father, a Scotchman, by trade a stone-mason and builder, early recognizing his talent, placed him in an architect's office, and allowed him to study drawing in the evening at the Leeds Mechanics' Institute. In 1831, Richard came to America with his father, and found employment with a sign painter in New York. At Newport, R. I., to which the family soon removed, he worked as an ornamental painter, and had the advice of Miss Jane Stuart, the daughter of Gilbert Stuart, in his attempts at portraiture. From the year 1838 he found considerable employment as a miniature painter, and in this specialty he continued until about twenty years ago, when he began to paint in oil, partly owing to the condition of his eyes. Mr. Staigg devoted his time principally to portraiture, counting among his sitters such men as Webster, Everett, Prescott, etc., although among his works there are also a number of genre pictures. He worked in Newport, Boston (where he enjoyed the friendship and instruction of Allston, whose miniature he painted), New York, Baltimore, and Washington, and paid several visits to Europe. Mr. Staigg was elected a National Academician in 1861, and married in 1872. A memorial exhibition of his work was held at the rooms of the Art Club, Boston, from Dec. 5 to Dec. 17, 1881. The catalogue, which contains also a biographical sketch (from which the above details are taken), and a photograph from life of the deceased, enumerates 141 works, 25 being miniatures, 103 oils, and 13 water-colors and drawings. Mr. Staigg was at his best in his miniatures, which are indeed excellent. In his relations as a man he was highly esteemed.

STATISTICAL TABLE OF EXHIBITIONS

Held in the United States from January, 1881, to October, 1882.

This table contains only the more important exhibitions of which the statistics could be obtained. The value of works sold is computed in most cases at catalogue prices.

Year	Opening and Closing Days	City	Exhibition	No. of Works Exhibited.	No. of Artists Exhibiting.	No. of Works Sold.	Value of Works Sold.
1881	Jan. 24 / Feb. 23	New York	American Water-Color Society, 14th	803	966	290	$28,068 00
"	" 29 / " 19	Boston	Art Club, 23d	289	181	—	20,098 30
"	" 29 / " 8	New York	Artists' Fund, 21st	113	65	113	10,420 00
"	Feb. 1 / " 28	"	Exhibition of New York Paintings, 4th	85	?	39	4,483 00
"	March 3 / " 28	Springfield, Mass.	Art Club, 3d	74	35	74	3,200 00
"	" 7 / March 19	Brooklyn	Art Association, 42d	607	?	42	42,838 00
"	" 22 / May 14	New York	Academy, 56th	752	438	120	2,000 00
"	" 28 / April 29	"	Society of American Artists, 4th	147	80	?	5,958 00
"	April 4 / May 29	Philadelphia	Penns. Academy, 52d	585	298	41	288 00
"	" 11 / " 16	Boston	Museum of Fine Arts, American Etchings.	548	106	47	2,500 00
"	" 22 / " 21	"	Art Club, 24th	475	229	50	2,275 00
"	Sept. 6 / Oct. 8	Cincinnati	Industrial Exposition, 9th	418	253	8	3,510 00
"	" 6 / " 15	Milwaukee	Industrial Exposition, 1st	452*	197	33	30,075 00
"	" 7 / " 22	Chicago	Interstate Industrial Exposition, 9th	382	181	65	650 00
"	" 13 / Nov. 12	Boston	Mass. Charitable Mechanics' Assoc, 14th	462*	278	4	
"	Oct. 11 / " 27	Philadelphia	Mus. of Fine Arts, Am. Wood-Engravings	399	62	26	9,858 00
"	Nov. 7 / Dec. 26	"	Penns. Academy, Aut. Exhibition	428	272	60	15,010 00
"	" 14 / " 31	"	Philadelphia Society of Artists, 3d	408	191	?	
"	" 15 / " 20	Providence	Art Club	157	66	?	5,900 00
"	Dec. 1 / " 21	New York	Salmagundi Club, 4th B. & W.	505	225	—	5,900 00
"	" 7 / " 17	Brooklyn	Art Association, 43d	299	80	25	3,590 00

1882			Place	Exhibition				Receipts
Jan.	9	Jan. 17	New York	Artists' Fund, 22d	106	63	106	15,851 00
Jan.	16	Feb. 25	Utica	Art Association, 8th	262	157	?	27,000 00
"	30	" 25	New York	American Water-Color Society, 15th	650	243	231	3,000 00
"	30	" 28	New York	New York Etching Club	284	73	312†	10,140 00
Feb.	1	March 11	Springfield, Mass.	Exhibition of New York Paintings, 5th	92	57	31	3,335 00
"	11	" 16	Boston	Art Club, 25th	220	164	29	5,099 00
"	17	" 29	New Orleans	Art Union	206	95	41	5,099 00
"	23	" 10	New York	Rejected Water-Colors	305	141	29	1,440 00
"	25		Chicago	Art League, 2d	91	14	28	650 00
March	9		Brooklyn	Art Club, 3d	62	26	62	3,413 00
"	14	May 25	New York	Art Association, 44th	746	233	81	4,806 00
April	27	May 13	Philadelphia	Academy, 57th	838	495	123	40,800 00
"	3	June 1	New York	Pennsylvania Academy, Belgian Exhibition	295	186	34	32,632 00
"	6	May 20	Philadelphia	Society of American Artists, 5th	192	126	?	4,000 00
"	10	" 6	Providence	Phil. Society of Artists, 1st Water-Color	354	131	35	3,250 00
"	17	April 13	Rochester	Art Club, 3d	195	105	15	915 00
"	19	May 21	Boston	Art Club, 3d	174	53	?	
"	28	" 27	Portland, Me.	Art Club, 26th	284	173	29	1,438 75
June	1	Aug. 15	Denver, Col.	Society of Art, 1st	226	143	4	?
Aug.	5	Sept. 30	Louisville	National Manuf'ring and Mining Exhibition	402	188		
Sept.	5	Oct. 21	Milwaukee	Industrial Exposition	333	196	?	5,000 00
"	6	" 21	Cincinnati	Industrial Exposition, 2d	358‡	161	22	?
"	6	Nov. ?	Boston	N. E. Manufac'rers and Mechanics' Institute	465	262	?	19,296 60
Oct.	18	" 23	Chicago	Interstate Industrial Exposition, 10th	680	352	54	
"	23	Dec. 9	New York	Academy, Special Autumn Exhibition, 10th	329	199		
"	23		Philadelphia	Pennsylvania Academy, 53d	529	316		
					475	267		

* Paintings and statuary only. There were also large collections of engravings, etc.
† Includes duplicates.
‡ Paintings only. Of drawings, engravings, etchings, etc., there were 625.

COMING EXHIBITIONS.

SPECIAL SKETCH EXHIBITION OF THE PHILADELPHIA SOCIETY OF ARTISTS. — Opens Nov. 4, 1882, at the galleries of the Society, 1725 Chestnut St. Sketches by members only admitted.

EXHIBITION OF ARTISTS' SKETCHES AND STUDIES. — Opens about Nov. 8, 1882, at the American Art Gallery, Kurtz Bldg., Madison Sq., New York.

FIFTH ANNUAL BLACK AND WHITE EXHIBITION (Salmagundi Club). — Opens Dec. 2, 1882, at the National Academy of Design, New York.

ANNUAL EXHIBITION OF THE BROOKLYN ART ASSOCIATION. — Opens Dec. 4, 1882, in the galleries of the Association, Montgomery, near Clinton St., Brooklyn, N. Y.

EXHIBITION OF THE PAINT AND CLAY CLUB. — Opens Dec. 13, 1882, at the rooms of the Club, 419 Washington St., Boston. Works by members only admitted.

FIRST EXHIBITION OF THE PHILADELPHIA SOCIETY OF ETCHERS. — Opens Dec. 27, 1882, at the Penn. Academy of Fine Arts. No works received after Dec. 21. For particulars and blanks apply to J. Neely, Jr., Sec., 1334 Chestnut St., Philadelphia.

FOURTH ANNUAL EXHIBITION OF THE PHILADELPHIA SOCIETY OF ARTISTS. — Opens Dec. 30, 1882, at the galleries of the Society, 1725 Chestnut St. No works received later than Dec. 14. For particulars and blanks apply to Newbold H. Trotter, Sec., 1520 Chestnut St., Philadelphia.

TWENTY-SEVENTH EXHIBITION OF THE BOSTON ART CLUB. — Will be held during the winter, at the gallery of the Club, Dartmouth and Newbury Sts. Date not yet fixed. For particulars apply to Wm. F. Matchett, Sec., 68 Devonshire St., Boston.

TWENTY-THIRD ARTISTS' FUND EXHIBITION. — Opens Jan. 31, 1883, at Kirby's Gallery, 845 and 847 Broadway, New York. Sale at same place, Feb. 6 and 7. Contributions received from members of the association only.

SIXTEENTH ANNUAL EXHIBITION OF THE AMERICAN WATER-COLOR SOCIETY. — Opens Jan. 29, 1883, at the National Academy of Design, New York. No works received after Jan. 14. For particulars and blanks apply to Henry Farrer, 51 W. 10th St., New York.

EXHIBITION OF THE NEW YORK ETCHING CLUB. — Opens Jan. 29, 1883, at the National Academy of Design, New York. For particulars and blanks, apply to J. C. Nicoll, Sec., 51 W. 10th St., New York.

EXHIBITION OF WORKS BY BOSTON ARTISTS. — Will be held in February, 1883, at the American Art Gallery, Kurtz Building, Madison Sq., New York.

SECOND WATER-COLOR EXHIBITION OF THE PHILA. SOCIETY OF ARTISTS. — Will be held in February, 1883, at the galleries of the Society, 1725 Chestnut St. For particulars and blanks apply to Newbold H. Trotter, Sec., 1520 Chestnut St., Philadelphia.

METROPOLITAN EXHIBITION OF AMERICAN PAINTINGS. — Will be held in March, 1883, at the American Art Gallery, Kurtz Building, Madison Sq., New York. For particulars apply at the Gallery.

SIXTH EXHIBITION OF THE SOCIETY OF AMERICAN ARTISTS. — Will be held in April, 1883, at the American Art Gallery, Kurtz Building, Madison Sq., New York. The Society invites those whom it desires to submit works for acceptance.

THE EXHIBITIONS OF WORKS OF LIVING AMERICAN ARTISTS at the Museum of Fine Arts, Boston, will be resumed in the spring of 1883. Date, etc., will be announced in due time. For particulars apply to Chas. G. Loring, Curator, at the Museum.

THE FIFTY-FOURTH ANNUAL EXHIBITION OF THE PENNS. ACADEMY OF THE FINE ARTS, to be held in the autumn of 1883, will receive additional interest from the " Temple Competition in Historical Painting " connected with it. The competition is open to citizens of the U. S. only, irrespective of place of residence. The works submitted must be in oil, must not exceed 8 x 10 feet, and the subject must be taken from the latter half of the 18th century, and must have some connection with the War of Independence. Artists desiring to compete must notify the Secretary of the Academy by Jan. 1, 1883. The prizes to be awarded will be : 1. $3,000 in money, the picture for which it is given to become the property of the Academy. 2. A gold medal. 3. A silver medal. 4. A bronze medal. For these prizes the Academy is indebted to the liberality of Mr. Joseph E. Temple. Circulars giving full particulars may be had on application to Geo. Corliss, Sec. Penn. Academy of Fine Arts, Philadelphia.

No details can as yet be given in regard to the other exhibitions of the year 1883. But as the dates of opening, etc., will be nearly the same as in the preceding year, intending exhibitors will find a tolerably reliable guide in the " Statistical Table of Exhibitions " on the preceding pages. The names and addresses of the secretaries of the various exhibiting bodies, to whom application must be made for the necessary blanks, etc., can be learned by referring to the list of " Local Institutions," pp. 4–94 of this Directory.

—

BOOKS ON ART *

AND RELATED SUBJECTS, PUBLISHED IN THE UNITED STATES FROM OCTOBER, 1881, TO OCTOBER, 1882.

Address on some growing evils of the day, especially demoralizing literature and art, from the representatives of the Religious Society of Friends for Penn., N. J., and Del. Second month, 10, 1882. Philadelphia : Friends' Book Store, 304 Arch St. 1882. 16 pp. 16mo.

AMORT, MARTHA BABCOCK. — The domestic and artistic life of John Singleton Copley, R. A. ; with notices of his works and reminiscences of his son, Lord Lyndhurst, Lord High Chancellor of Great Britain, by his grand-daughter. Boston : Houghton, Mifflin & Co. 1882. 12 + 478. Portrait. 8°. $3.

BALLARD, ROBT. — The solution of the pyramid problem ; or, pyramid discoveries, with a new theory as to their ancient use. New York : J. Wiley & Sons. 1882. 2 + 109 pp. Ill. $1.50.

BARTHOLOMEW, W. N. — Handbook No. 2 to Bartholomew's "National system of industrial drawing." New ed. New York and Chicago : Potter, Ainsworth & Co. 1882. 3 + 303 pp. Ill. Square 12°. 80 cents.

* This list contains only the original works, and the actual reprints of foreign books, issued by American publishers. Imported publications with American imprints on the title-page have not been included.

BARTLETT, TRUMAN H. — The art life of William Rimmer, sculptor, painter, and physician. Boston: Jas. R. Osgood & Co. Ill. 4°. $10.

BASCOM, J. — Æsthetics; or the science of beauty. New York: G. P. Putnam's Sons. 1881. 12°. $1.50.

BEARD, J. C. — Painting on china; what to paint and how to paint it: a hand-book of practical instruction in overglaze painting for amateurs in the decoration of hard porcelain. New York: Dick & Fitzgerald [1882]. 95 pp. Square 12°. $1.

BENJAMIN, S. G. W. — Our American artists. 2d series. Boston: D. Lothrop & Co. 1881. 68 pp. Ill. Square 8vo. $1 50.

COE, B. H. — Progressive lessons in drawing, with familiar instructions designed for schools : first studies in drawing, containing elementary exercises, drawings from objects, animals, and rustic figures, complete in 54 studies. New ed. New York: J. Wiley & Sons. 1882. 9 pp. 54 plates. Square 16mo. 60 cents.

CONWAY, MONCURE DANIEL. — Travels in South Kensington ; with notes on decorative art and architecture in England. New York: Harper. 1882. 5 + 234 pp. Ill. $2.50.

CURTIS, CHAS. B., M. A. — A descriptive and historical catalogue of the works of Don Diego Velazquez de Silva and Bartoleme Esteban Murillo. Ill. with etchings. New York: J. W. Bouton. 8°.

DEWING, MRS. T. W. — Beauty in the household. New York: Harper. 1882. 18 + 183 pp. Ill. $1.

DI CESNOLA, L. P., editor. — The Metropolitan Museum of Art; ill. by G. Gibson. New York: Appleton. 1882. 32 pp. 50 cents.

EMERSON, W. A. — Hand-book of wood-engraving. New ed. Boston : Lee & Shepard. 1881. 95 pp. Ill. 18°. $1.

EIDLITZ, LEOPOLD. — The nature and function of art, more especially of architecture. New York: A. C. Armstrong & Son. 1881. 22 + 493 pp. 8°. $4.

FULLER, ALBERT W. — Artistic homes in city and country. Boston: J. R. Osgood & Co. 1882. 44 plates. Oblong fol. $3.50.

GORRINGE, H. H. — Egyptian obelisks. New York: The author. [G. P. Putnam's Sons.] 1882. 187 pp. Ill. and plates. 4°. $15.

HAMERTON, PHILIP GILBERT. — The graphic arts: treatise on the varieties of drawing, painting, and engraving in comparison with each other and with nature. Boston : Roberts Bros. 1882. 20 + 508 pp. 12mo. $2.

HATTON, T. — Hints for sketching in water-color from nature. New York: G. P. Putnam's Sons. 1882. Square 16°. (Art hand-books.) 50 cents.

HERRICK, H. W. — Water-color painting: description of materials with directions for their use in elementary practice. Sketching from nature in water-colors. Illustrated with diagrams printed in colors. New York : F. W. Devoe & Co. 1882.

Hints for painters, decorators and paper-hangers : prepared with special reference to the wants of amateurs, by an old hand. New York: Industrial Publication Co. 1882. (Work manuals, No. 3.) 25 cents.

KELLOGG, LAVINIA STEELE. — How to paint in water-colors. New York: E. L. Kellogg & Co. 1882. 2 + 38 pp. Square 16°. 40 cents.

KEMBLE, MARION. — Introductory lessons in drawing and painting : self-instructive. Boston: S. W. Tilton & Co. 1882. 62 pp. Ill. 8vo. 50 cents.

KOEHLER, S. R. — Art education and art patronage in the United States. [Reprinted from the Penn Monthly for May and June, 1882.] Philadelphia. 1882. 26 pp. 8°.

KURTZ, CHAS. M. — Illustrated art notes upon the fifty-seventh annual exhibition of the National Academy of Design ; 135 ill., with brief personal notices of the artists whose works are reproduced. Second year. New York: Cassell, Petter, Galpin & Co. 1882. 100 pp. 8vo. 35 cents.

LELAND, CHAS. G. — Art work manuals. [Twelve on different subjects, such as ceramic painting, tapestry painting, etc.] Ill. New York: Art Interchange Publ. Co. 35 cents each ; $3 for the set of 12.

LOOMIS, LAFAYETTE C. — The index guide to travel and art-study in Europe : compendium of geographical, historical, and artistic information for the use of Americans ; alphabetically arranged ; with plans and catalogues of the chief art galleries, tables of routes, maps, and 160 ill. New York: C. Scribner's Sons. 1882. 22 + 631 pp. 16mo. $3.50.

MERRILL, SELAH. [Archæologist of the American Palestine Exploration Society.] — East of the Jordan : a record of travel and observation in the countries of Moab, Gilead and Bashan, during the years 1875–1877 ; with introd. by Roswell D. Hitchcock. New York: C. Scribner's Sons. 1881. 16 + 549 pp. Ill. and map. 8°. $4.

MOORE, C. H. — Fac-similes of examples in delineation, selected from the masters for the use of students in drawing. Cambridge, Mass. : Moses King. 1882. Portfolio, incl. text and 16 quarto plates. $5.

MORRIS, W. — Hopes and fears for art. Boston : Roberts Bros. 1882. 6 + 217 pp. 16°. $1.25.

Papers of the Archæological Institute of America. Classical series. I. — Report on the investigations at Assos, 1881, by Joseph Thacher Clarke. With an appendix, containing inscriptions from Assos and Lesbos, and papers by W. C. Lawton and J. S. Diller. Boston : A. Williams & Co. 1882. 8 + 215 pp. Ill.

Poets and Etchers. Twenty full-page etchings by Jas. D. Smillie, Samuel Coleman, A. F. Bellows, Henry Farrer, and R. Swain Gifford, illustrating poems by Longfellow, Whittier, Bryant, Lowell, Emerson, Aldrich, etc. Boston : J. R. Osgood & Co. 1881. 4°. $10.

REILY, REV. W. M. — The artist and his mission. Philadelphia : J. E. Potter & Co. 1881. 12°. $1.50.

ROSSITER, E. K., and WRIGHT, F. A. — Modern house painting. New York : W. T. Comstock. 1882. 56 pp. 20 colored plates. Oblong 8vo. $5.

RUNTZ-REES, JANET E. — Home decoration : art needle-work and embroidery ; painting on silk, satin, and velvet ; panel painting and wood-carving, with numerous designs, mainly by G. Gibson. New York: Appleton, 1881. (Appleton's Home Books.) 120 pp. 12°. 60 cents.

RUSKIN, J. — Modern painters. New York : J. Wiley & Sons. 1882. 5 vols. 12°. $5. [Contains ill. in the text, but not the plates of the original edition.]

RUSKIN, J. — The seven lamps of architecture. New York: J. Wiley & Sons. 1880. $1. [Without plates, but including the woodcuts.]

RUSKIN, J. — The stones of Venice. New York: J. Wiley & Sons. 1881. 3 vols. $3. [Without plates, but including the wood-cuts.]

RUSKIN, J. — Sesame and lilies : three lectures. New York : J. Wiley & Sons. 1882. 42 + 3 + 170 pp. 12°. $1.

Selected proofs from the first and second portfolios of illustrations from Scribner's " Monthly " and " St. Nicholas." New York : Century Co. 1881. 10 pp. 57 plates. Fol. $5.

SHEDD, MRS. JULIA A. — Famous painters and paintings. 3d ed., rev. and enl. Boston : J. R. Osgood & Co. 1881. Ill. 12°. $3.

SHEDD, MRS. JULIA A. — Famous Sculptors and Sculpture. Ill. with heliotypes. Boston : J. R. Osgood & Co. 1881. 6 + 319 pp. 12°. $3.

STRAHAN, E. — Etudes in modern French art ; ill. with 10 plates, India proofs, and numerous fac-similes of original drawings. New York : R. Worthington. 1882. 12 + 122 pp. Fol. $10.

TUTHILL, W. B. — Interiors and interior details ; 52 4° plates, with an introduction, description of plates, and notes on wood finish. New York : W. T. Comstock. 1882. $7.50.

TUTHILL, W. B. — Practical lessons in architectural drawing. New York : W. T.
Comstock. 1881. 19 pp. 33 plates, 33 ill. Obl. 8vo. $2.50.

WARREN, H. — Artistic treatise on the human figure : containing hints on proportion, color and composition. 4th ed. New York : G. P. Putnam's Sons. 1881. 82 pp.
Ill. Square 16mo. (Putnam's art hand-books, ed. by Susan N. Carter.) 50 cents.

WEIGALL, C. H. — The art of figure drawing : containing practical instructions
for a course of study in this branch of art ; with 17 ill. by the author. From 21st
London ed. New York : G. P. Putnam's Sons. 1881. 53 pp. Square 16mo. (Putnam's art hand-books, ed. by Susan N. Carter.) 50 cents.

WHEELER, W. A. and C. G. — Familiar allusions : hand-book of miscellaneous
information, including the names of celebrated statues, paintings, palaces, country
seats, ruins, churches, ships, streets, clubs, natural curiosities, and the like. Boston :
J. R. Osgood & Co. 1882. 6 + 584 pp. 12°. $3.

ART JOURNALS

PUBLISHED IN THE UNITED STATES.

THE AMERICAN ARCHITECT AND BUILDING NEWS. — Illustrated. Monthly.
Boston : Jas. R. Osgood & Co., 211 Tremont St. $7.50 a year ; $6 when paid in
advance ; single numbers 15 cents.

AMERICAN ETCHINGS. — Semi-monthly. One etching and text in each number. New York : Art Interchange Pub. Co., 140 Nassau St. $10 a year ; single
numbers 50 cents.

THE ART AMATEUR. — Illustrated. Monthly. New York : Montague Marks,
23 Union Square. $4 a year, incl. postage ; single copies 35 cents

THE ART INTERCHANGE. — Illustrated. Fortnightly. New York : Art Interchange Pub. Co., 140 Nassau St. $2 a year ; single copies 10 cents.

THE ART JOURNAL. — Illustrated. Monthly. New York : Patterson & Neilson,
12 Dey St. $9 p. a. ; sold by subscription only. (A London publication, issued in the
United States with additional American matter.)

THE DECORATOR AND FURNISHER. — Illustrated. Monthly. Edited by A. Curtis
Bond. New York : E. W. Bullinger, 75 Fulton St. $4 p. a. ; single numbers 35
cents.

THE MAGAZINE OF ART. — Illustrated. Monthly. New York : Cassell, Petter,
Galpin & Co., 739 and 741 B'way. $3.50 p. a. ; single numbers 35 cents. (A Lon-
don publication, issued in the United States with additional American matter.)

THE LAW OF COPYRIGHT IN THE UNITED STATES.*

FROM THE REVISED STATUTES OF THE UNITED STATES,
IN FORCE DEC. 1, 1873, AS AMENDED BY ACT
APPROVED JUNE 18, 1874.

SECTION 4948. All records and other things relating to copyrights and required by law to be preserved shall be under the control of the Librarian of Congress, and kept and preserved in the Library of Congress; and the Librarian of Congress shall have the immediate care and supervision thereof, and, under the supervision of the Joint Committee of Congress on the Library, shall perform all acts and duties required by law touching copyrights.

SEC. 4949. The seal provided for the office of the Librarian of Congress shall be the seal thereof, and by it all records and papers issued from the office, and to be used in evidence, shall be authenticated.

SEC. 4950. The Librarian of Congress shall give a bond, with sureties, to the Treasurer of the United States, in the sum of five thousand dollars, with the condition that he will render to the proper officers of the treasury a true account of all moneys received by virtue of his office.

SEC. 4951. The Librarian of Congress shall make an annual report to Congress of the number and description of copyright publications for which entries have been made during the year.

SEC. 4952. Any citizen of the United States, or resident therein, who shall be the author, inventor, designer, or proprietor of any book, map, chart, dramatic or musical composition, engraving, cut, print, photograph or negative thereof, or of a painting, drawing, chromo, statue, statuary, and of models or designs intended to be perfected as works of the fine arts, and the executors, administrators, or assigns of any such person, shall, upon complying with the provisions of this chapter, have the sole liberty of printing, reprinting, publishing, completing, copying, executing, finishing, and vending the same; and, in the case of a dramatic composition, of publicly performing or representing it, or causing it to be performed or represented by others. And authors may reserve the right to dramatize or translate their own works.

SEC. 4953. Copyrights shall be granted for the term of twenty-eight years from the time of recording the title thereof, in the manner hereinafter directed.

SEC. 4954. The author, inventor, or designer, if he be still living and a citizen of the United States or resident therein, or his widow or children if he be dead, shall have the same exclusive right continued for the further term of fourteen years, upon recording the title of the work or description of the article so secured a second time,

---

* Reprinted from the circular officially issued by the U. S. government, and to be had on application to Mr. A. R. Spofford, Librarian of Congress, Washington, D C.

and complying with all other regulations in regard to original copyrights, within six months before the expiration of the first term. And such person shall, within two months from the date of said renewal, cause a copy of the record thereof to be published in one or more newspapers, printed in the United States, for the space of four weeks.

SEC. 4955. Copyrights shall be assignable in law by any instrument of writing, and such assignment shall be recorded in the office of the Librarian of Congress within sixty days after its execution ; in default of which it shall be void as against any subsequent purchaser or mortgagee for a valuable consideration, without notice.

SEC. 4956. No person shall be entitled to a copyright unless he shall, before publication, deliver at the office of the Librarian of Congress, or deposit in the mail addressed to the Librarian of Congress, at Washington, District of Columbia, a printed copy of the title of the book or other article, or a description of the painting, drawing, chromo, statue, statuary, or model or design for a work of the fine arts, for which he desires a copyright ; nor unless he shall also, within ten days from the publication thereof, deliver at the office of the Librarian of Congress, or deposit in the mail addressed to the Librarian of Congress, at Washington, District of Columbia, two copies of such copyright book or other article, or, in case of a painting, drawing, statue, statuary, model or design for a work of the fine arts, a photograph of the same.

SEC. 4957. The Librarian of Congress shall record the name of such copyright book, or other article, forthwith in a book to be kept for that purpose, in the words following : " Library of Congress, to wit : Be it remembered that on the —— day of ——, ——, A. B., of ——, hath deposited in this office the title of a book, (map, chart, or otherwise, as the case may be, or description of the article,) the title or description of which is in the following words, to wit : (here insert the title or description,) the right whereof he claims as author, (originator, or proprietor, as the case may be,) in conformity with the laws of the United States respecting copyrights. C. D., Librarian of Congress." And he shall give a copy of the title or description, under the seal of the Librarian of Congress, to the proprietor whenever he shall require it.

SEC. 4958. The Librarian of Congress shall receive from the persons to whom the services designated are rendered the following fees: 1. For recording the title or description of any copyright book or other article, fifty cents. 2. For every copy under seal of such record actually given to the person claiming the copyright, or his assigns, fifty cents. 3. For recording and certifying any instrument of writing for the assignment of a copyright, one dollar. 4. For every copy of an assignment, one dollar. All fees so received shall be paid into the treasury of the United States.

SEC. 4959. The proprietor of every copyright book or other article shall deliver at the office of the Librarian of Congress, or deposit in the mail addressed to the Librarian of Congress, at Washington, District of Columbia, within ten days after its publication, two complete printed copies thereof of the best edition issued, or description or photograph of such article as hereinbefore required, and a copy of every subsequent edition wherein any substantial changes shall be made.

SEC. 4960. For every failure on the part of the proprietor of any copyright to deliver, or deposit in the mail, either of the published copies, or description, or photograph, required by Sections 4956 and 4959, the proprietor of the copyright shall be liable to a penalty of twenty-five dollars to be recovered by the Librarian of Congress, in the name of the United States, in an action in the nature of an action of debt, in any district court of the United States within the jurisdiction of which the delinquent may reside or be found.

· SEC. 4961. The postmaster to whom such copyright book, title, or other article is delivered, shall, if requested, give a receipt therefor ; and when so delivered he shall mail it to its destination.

SEC. 4962. No person shall maintain an action for the infringement of his copyright unless he shall give notice thereof by inserting in the several copies of every edition published, on the title-page or the page immediately following, if it be a book ; or if a map, chart, musical composition, print, cut, engraving, photograph, painting, drawing, chromo, statue, statuary, or model or design intended to be perfected and completed as a work of the fine arts, by inscribing upon some visible portion thereof, or of the substance on which the same shall be mounted, the following words, viz.: " Entered according to act of Congress, in the year ——, by A. B., in the office of the Librarian of Congress, at Washington " ; or, at his option, the word "Copyright," together with the year the copyright was entered, and the name of the party by whom it was taken out, thus : " Copyright 18 —, by A. B."

SEC. 4963. Every person who shall insert or impress such notice, or words of the same purport, in or upon any book, map, chart, musical composition, print, cut, engraving, or photograph, [or other article for which he has not obtained a copyright, shall be liable to a penalty of one hundred dollars, recoverable one half for the person who shall sue for such penalty, and one half to the use of the United States.

SEC. 4964. Every person who, after the recording of the title of any book as provided by this chapter, shall within the term limited, and without the consent of the proprietor of the copyright first obtained in writing, signed in presence of two or more witnesses, print, publish, or import, or, knowing the same to be so printed, published, or imported, shall sell or expose to sale any copy of such book, shall forfeit every copy thereof to such proprietor, and shall also forfeit and pay such damages as may be recovered in a civil action by such proprietor in any court of competent jurisdiction.

SEC. 4965. If any person, after the recording of the title of any map, chart, musical composition, print, cut, engraving, photograph, or chromo, or of the description of any painting, drawing, statue, statuary, or model or design intended to be perfected and executed as a work of the fine arts, as provided by this chapter, shall within the term limited, and without the consent of the proprietor of the copyright first obtained in writing, signed in presence of two or more witnesses, engrave, etch, work, copy, print, publish, or import, either in whole or in part, or by varying the main design with intent to evade the law, or, knowing the same to be so printed, published, or imported, shall sell or expose to sale any copy of such map or other article, as aforesaid, he shall forfeit to the proprietor all the plates on which the same shall be copied, and every sheet thereof, either copied or printed, and shall further forfeit one dollar for every sheet of the same found in his possession, either printing, printed, copied, published, imported, or exposed for sale ; and in case of a painting, statue, or statuary, he shall forfeit ten dollars for every copy of the same in his possession, or by him sold or exposed for sale ; one half thereof to the proprietor and the other half to the use of the United States.

SEC. 4966. Any person publicly performing or representing any dramatic composition for which a copyright has been obtained, without the consent of the proprietor thereof, or his heirs or assigns, shall be liable for damages therefor ; such damages in all cases to be assessed at such sum, not less than one hundred dollars for the first, and fifty dollars for every subsequent performance, as to the court shall appear to be just.

SEC. 4967. Every person who shall print or publish any manuscript whatever without the consent of the author or proprietor first obtained (if such author or proprietor is a citizen of the United States, or resident therein), shall be liable to the author or proprietor for all damages occasioned by such injury.

SEC. 4968. No action shall be maintained in any case of forfeiture or penalty

10

under the copyright laws, unless the same is commenced within two years after the cause of action has arisen.

SEC. 4969. In all actions arising under the laws respecting copyrights the defendant may plead the general issue, and give the special matter in evidence.

SEC. 4970. The circuit courts, and district courts having the jurisdiction of circuit courts, shall have power, upon bill in equity, filed by any party aggrieved, to grant injunctions to prevent the violation of any right secured by the laws respecting copyrights, according to the course and principles of courts of equity, on such terms as the court may deem reasonable.

SEC. 4971. Nothing in this chapter shall be construed to prohibit the printing, publishing, importation, or sale of any book, map, chart, dramatic or musical composition, print, cut, engraving, or photograph, written, composed, or made by any person not a citizen of the United States nor resident therein.

SEC. —. [Approved June 18, 1874, to take effect Aug. 1, 1874.] That in the construction of this act, the words "engraving," "cut," and "print," shall be applied only to pictorial illustrations or works connected with the fine arts, and no prints or labels designed to be used for any other articles of manufacture shall be entered under the copyright law, but may be registered in the Patent Office. And the Commissioner of Patents is hereby charged with the supervision and control of the entry or registry of such prints or labels, in conformity with the regulations provided by law as to copyright of prints, except that there shall be paid for recording the title of any print or label, not a trade-mark, six dollars, which shall cover the expense of furnishing a copy of the record, under the seal of the Commissioner of Patents, to the party entering the same.

P. J. ULRICH,

IMPORTER OF

ARTISTS' MATERIALS,

Cor. 12th St. and 4th Ave.,

NEW YORK.

German Artists' Canvas

AND

BRUSHES OF SUPERIOR QUALITY.

Dr. Fr. Schoenfeld's Oil and Water Colors.
Winsor & Newton's Oil and Water Colors.
Materials for China Painting.
Fancy Articles for Decoration.

SOLE AGENT FOR

HARDY-ALANS FRENCH OIL COLORS.

Orders from the country will find prompt attention. Send for price list.

HIGH-CLASS

Engravings and Etchings,

OLD AND MODERN.

Frederick Keppel, of London and 23 East 16th St. (Union Square), New York, invites attention to his large stock of the best Engravings and Etchings, at moderate prices.

Correspondence is invited, and Engravings will be sent on approval to any address.

ART STUDENTS' LEAGUE,

38 West Fourteenth Street, New York,

BETWEEN 5TH AND 6TH AVENUES.

SEASON OF 1882-1883.

INSTRUCTORS:

| T. W. DEWING. | WM. M. CHASE. | C. Y. TURNER. |
| WILLIAM SARTAIN. | J. S. HARTLEY. | FREDERICK DIELMAN. |

LIFE CLASSES: DRAWING, PAINTING OR MODELLING.

FOR GENTLEMEN. | FOR LADIES.

Four hours daily, beginning at 8 A. M. | Four hours daily, beginning at 12.30 P. M.
Three hours daily, beginning at 7 P. M.

PAINTING CLASSES FROM DRAPED MODEL OR STILL LIFE, AND CLASS IN DRAWING FROM THE HEAD.

FOR LADIES AND GENTLEMEN.

Six hours daily, beginning at 9 A. M. and 1 P. M.

DRAWING FROM THE ANTIQUE.

FOR LADIES AND GENTLEMEN.

Daily from 9 A. M. to 4 P. M., and 7 to 10 P. M.

SKETCH CLASS: One hour daily, beginning at 4.15 P. M.

COMPOSITION CLASS: Every Saturday at 8 P. M.

LECTURES ON PERSPECTIVE: First and Third Mondays of Each Month.

LECTURES ON ARTISTIC ANATOMY: Once a Week in each Life Class.

Circulars sent on application.